INFERNO

INFERNO

The True Story of a B-17 Gunner's Heroism and the Bloodiest

Military Campaign in Aviation History

JOE PAPPALARDO

ST. MARTIN'S GRIFFIN

NEW YORK

Published in the United States by St. Martin's Griffin, an imprint of
St. Martin's Publishing Group

www.stmartins.com

Designed by Omar Chapa

The Library of Congress has cataloged the hardcover edition as follows:

Names: Pappalardo, Joe, author.
Title: Inferno : the true story of a B-17 gunner's heroism and the bloodiest
    military campaign in aviation history / Joe Pappalardo.
Other titles: True story of a B-17 gunner's heroism and the bloodiest military
    campaign in aviation history
Description: First edition. | New York, NY : St. Martin's Press, 2020. |
    Includes bibliographical references and index.
Identifiers: LCCN 2020028402 | ISBN 9781250264237 (hardcover) |
    ISBN 9781250264244 (ebook)
Subjects: LCSH: Smith, Maynard H. | United States. Army Air Forces. Bombardment
    Group, 306th—Aerial gunners—Biography. | United States. Army Air Forces.
    Air Force, 8th—Biography. | World War, 1939–1945—Regimental histories—
    United States. | World War, 1939–1945—Aerial operations, American. | World
    War, 1939–1945—Campaigns—Western Front. | Medal of Honor—Biography.
Classification: LCC D790.253 306th .P37 2020 | DDC 940.54/4973092 [B]—dc23
LC record available at https://lccn.loc.gov/2020028402

ISBN 978-1-250-26425-1 (trade paperback)

Our books may be purchased in bulk for promotional, educational, or busi-
ness use. Please contact your local bookseller or the Macmillan Corporate and
Premium Sales Department at 1-800-221-7945, extension 5442, or by email at
MacmillanSpecialMarkets@macmillan.com.

First St. Martin's Griffin Edition: 2022

10 9 8 7 6 5 4 3 2 1

CONTENTS

In the space between the heavens
And the corner of some foreign field,
I had a dream.

—PINK FLOYD,

"THE GUNNER'S DREAM"

War is just one living and dying mass of confusion and delusion and stupidity and brilliance and ineptitude and hysteria and heroism anyway.

—GEN. CURTIS LEMAY,

AIRPOWER INNOVATOR

Sometimes there's a man — I won't say a hero, 'cause what's a hero?
But sometimes, there's a man.

—THE STRANGER, FROM *THE BIG LEBOWSKI*,

WRITTEN BY JOEL AND ETHAN COEN

INTRODUCTION

Ghost in the Memorabilia

July 12, 2019.

There are three steamer trunks in the spare bedroom of Maynard Smith Jr.'s home in Seminole, Florida. Inside the boxes are the artifacts from the lifetime of his father, a World War II veteran, B-17 gunner, and the first enlisted Army airman ever to receive the Congressional Medal of Honor.

Maynard Harrison Smith Sr. lived with his son and daughter-in-law in Florida during his final years, and these trunks contain the keepsakes that he left behind when he died in 1984. No one's opened them in decades.

At age seventy-two, Smith Jr. remains a large man. These days he is attached to an oxygen line, and trails a slender, green umbilical hose when he moves around the house. He's a Vietnam veteran; his father used his connections in Washington, D.C., to bump his son to the front of the two-year Coast Guard recruitment list, saving him from being drafted into the Army. Smith Jr. ended up in combat anyway, serving as a 5-inch gunner on the 254-foot cutter *Winona*.

Coast Guard cutters provided fire support for men on shore and escorted swift boats; Smith Jr. volunteered to ride on those small craft on several missions, one of which ended with a dash back to the ship with his finger plugging a gunny sergeant's bullet hole. The younger Smith also ran the nightly, onboard poker game and as such was flush with money. He's proud of his service, but certainly didn't want to go: "I said to myself, I can't run off to Canada, not with the father I got."

The father and son lived together, ran a publishing business, and shot pool at halls across the country. Over their lifetimes they backed each other up in bar fights and attended presidential inaugurations. And they hunted and fished.

"I was talking with my dad one time in a field, and this pheasant came up flying along the wood line," Smith Jr. recalls. "He followed it and popped it off. He said that he learned how to follow birds and stuff like that because of his training on the .50 caliber. You know? You have to lead the plane."

Only a faint echo of the elder Maynard Smith can still be felt in the home, a pleasant, roomy one-story house with a screened-in pool just outside of Tampa. There are photos of Smith Sr. and a few items on display that carry his stamp, like the model of a wooden boat in the living room bearing one of his nicknames, "Snuffy."

But open a steamer trunk and Smith Sr. himself erupts from within, announcing his arrival with a flurry of yellowed newspaper clippings, faded photos, military documents, Christmas cards, and programs from various military appreciation events and reunions. His son pulls out these memories by the handful.

Here's a photo of Smith Sr. shaking hands with President John Kennedy, who towers over him. Here's a news clipping featuring Smith at the elbow of the governor of Michigan in 1945. Here are his honorable discharge papers from the Army Air Forces; he's a private, having been demoted after receiving the Medal of Honor. Here's a program from a Medal of Honor Society event in Hawaii in the early 1980s, with a woman's name and hotel room number scrawled on one page. Here's a postcard to his mother written from aerial gunnery school in Texas, early in his wartime military career, and underneath it a cryptic photo from an oasis in North Africa, with a handwritten notation saying MY QUARTERS with an arrow pointing to a hilltop building on the horizon.

Maynard Smith Jr. pulls more of his father's memories from the steamer trunks, spreading the fragments across the surface of the bed. The ghostly form of a man emerges: a proud veteran, an acknowledged hero, a newspaper publisher. Closer examination reveals greatest hits of the more intimate kind: a love letter from a wartime girlfriend, a photo of him on a cruise in 1977 wearing an absurd hat with one arm flung over the shoulder of a comely older woman (not Junior's mother, he's not surprised to see), and a black-and-white photo of Smith in 1945 leaning in close to use a young woman's collarbone to sign an autograph.

"Dad," his son says drily, "had the reputation of being well endowed."

Some members of Maynard Smith Sr.'s immediate family, including a son and daughter from previous marriages, stopped speaking to him. One of his three sons died of an overdose before his father passed, the other became lost in drug abuse and died just five years after his father. Maynard Sr.'s other daughter enjoyed her paternal relationship, but she and her mother had the stronger bond and lived together in Hawaii and Florida after the couple divorced. But Maynard Smith and his namesake stayed close until the end.

In late April 1984, the elder Maynard Smith staggered into the kitchen, gasping words but garbling them badly. "Oak, oak, oak," he finally managed. Treated for a stroke, doctors discovered his heart was also failing. After a grueling month in the hospital, he was gone.

"He was not the type of man who would listen to doctors," says Debby Wolfsmith, Maynard Smith Jr.'s wife. "He wasn't going to stop putting salt on his watermelon. He wasn't good at keeping up with medications, either."

Looking over the contents of the three steamer trunks, it's clear that Maynard Smith Sr. curated this collection of memorabilia, intentionally or not, to be the idealized version of his life. The news clippings paint the portrait of a dedicated son, a war hero, and a successful publisher with the ear of important people.

The positive media coverage is extensive, but Smith left the negative press out of his personal archives. There are articles describing lawsuits against him, tangles with the Food and Drug Administration over a male enhancement cream, and an arrest for filing a false police report for his role in a very public hoax in 1952. There are a variety of columnists, local and national, taking potshots at his character.

The most famous detractor is Andy Rooney, who calls Smith Sr. "a fuck up" in his World War II memoirs, *My War*. The television columnist, with *Stars and Stripes* during World War II, is the most responsible for both creating and denigrating Smith's public image. The two short, opinionated men enjoyed bucking authority—maybe they had too much in common to get along.

Others offer mixed reactions to his name, even thirty-five years after his death. A public affairs employee at the Medal of Honor Society remembers Smith as "a crackpot" and "someone who wasn't shy about putting people in their place." Caroline Sheen, the veteran photo and art editor of *Air & Space Smithsonian* magazine, immediately dubs him "the most despised man to get the Medal of Honor." His brother-in-law, George Rayner, recalls him as "a wheeler dealer" and adds, not unkindly, that "he was crazy." His daughter Christine speaks of his keen intelligence but notes of his love life that "he didn't leave many unbroken hearts behind him."

Maynard Smith Jr. sums it up by saying, "He was a rebel, I guess you'd say."

Maynard Smith's personality produced lots of nicknames. The one that endures is "Snuffy Smith," after a short, irascible cartoon character. In a strange sort of immortality, this moniker is enshrined in the modern Air Force lexicon. It's not used as often these days but the 2019 online Urban Dictionary includes this entry:

AIRMAN SNUFFY: Hypothetical alias of an enlisted person in the U.S. Air Force who can't seem to do anything right. Used frequently in Air Force officer training texts and case studies, Airman Snuffy is analogous to the U.S. Marine Corps' Gomer Pyle.

War dehumanizes people, and not always in the expected ways. In World War II, the U.S. military and news media partnered to manufacture heroes that could be used and discarded like any other piece of general issue equipment. Smith's unlikely experience is a prime example of this public relations machine in action, and its unintended consequences. Smith encountered harrowing violence, the expected root of wartime psychological trauma, but he also suffered the stranger fate of being reduced to a public caricature.

So this is not a book about the War Department's hero, "Snuffy Smith." This is a book about Maynard Harrison Smith Sr. and his wild ride through cataclysmic history.

To understand the man in any kind of context requires opening the aperture to capture more than just his role in the European air war, although that proves to be the defining event of his life. His background is necessary to understand his reaction to war, just as the trajectory of his postwar path measures just how deeply the war impacted his life.

Surrounding Smith's narrative are those in the 8th Air Force who fought the savage and often senseless air campaign over Europe. Comparing his wartime experience to theirs (particularly Smith's friend, Marcel St. Louis) is mandatory when trying to find Smith's rightful place in history. There is also something to be said for comparing Smith's often selfish behavior against the negligent and murderous decisions of the 8th Air Force in 1942 and 1943. His sins pale when next to some of the poor command choices that unnecessarily killed tens of thousands of Allied airmen.

This tale can only be appreciated when a reader can abandon the kind of intonations found in Tom Brokaw's 1998 book *The Greatest Generation*. In it, he describes World War II veterans as "mature beyond their years, tempered by what they had been through, disciplined by their military training and sacrifices. . . . They stayed true to their values of personal responsibility, duty, honor, and faith."

It makes sense to view some World War II veterans in this glowing light, but doing so certainly doesn't illuminate the experience of Maynard Smith Sr.

Recognizing that life is more cynical than Brokaw's veneration allows doesn't diminish the bravery of Smith or anyone else; if anything it's more impressive to regard them as the imperfect human beings that they were. And it's hard to find someone as flawed, action-oriented, consistent, and shrewd as Maynard Smith Sr. He is, friend and foe universally agree, "a character." After that, opinions differ.

Settling like dust in an empty guest room, the ghost stops stirring and waits to hear his life reconstructed. He doesn't want a defense or care about a verdict, but he does demand as true a rendering as possible. It starts on the courthouse steps in a small town in Michigan.

PART 1

HOKIE GOES TO WAR

CHAPTER 1

PECK'S BAD BOY

August 30, 1942. Maynard Harrison Smith walks, scowling, from the front door of the Tuscola County Courthouse. There are about thirty young men gathered on the steps of the two-story art deco building in Caro, Michigan, but Smith can tell at a glance that they're not like him.

The men on the steps are five to ten years younger than the thirty-one-year-old, born May 19, 1911, and this makes him wince. Smith does not want to take orders from anyone, and particularly dreads being bossed around by young officers. And age is but one difference between him and the other draftees and volunteers. Smith is also the only one in handcuffs.

They're all bustling and positioning for an impending photo—an image to commemorate the latest crop of prospective Army inductees from the thumb of Michigan. In a county of just over 3,000 people, more than 750 youths have already passed the Army General Classification Test. After this photo op, this bunch will leave to take that same assessment to determine which role they will play in the global drama known as World War II.

This very courthouse used to be his safe haven. His father, Henry H. Smith, once served as a district court judge here. Before he donned the robe, the elder Smith worked as an accountant for Henry Ford, a job that saw the family prosper even during the Great Depression.

"It wasn't a millionaire kind of a thing, but they were fairly wealthy considering what other people were making, so he was a fairly privileged kid," recalls Maynard Smith's son and namesake. "He had what he wanted. I mean, he never felt like he was wealthy, but he never wanted for anything, either."

Later, when the media comes calling, Smith's neighbors will remember exploits that they say indicate a certain grace under pressure. Some, like next-door neighbor Asher Cummings, compare him to Tom Sawyer. She recalls him as part of a squad of children on a daring daylight raid to steal watermelons. The keen-eyed and irate farmer began shooting shotgun blasts into the air over the young thieves' heads. Cummings—who had a couple daughters involved in the raiding party—remembers the children dashing back home, scared and empty-handed. All but one. "Here comes Maynard, his towhead bobbing as he ran," she will recall to a newspaper reporter for the *Tuscola County Advertiser*. "And he had his watermelon. He was the only kid who came out of that patch with one."

The quintessential Hokie Smith story features the youngster at around age ten riding a pony through downtown Caro. He guides the animal through the front doors of Carl Palmer's drug store and clods inside. Later embellishments will have the child order an ice cream cone and then saunter casually back into the street, "as if it was something he did everyday" as the reporter in the *Tuscola County Advertiser* puts it.

Smith is an only child and gets a lot of parental attention. Some will call him spoiled. "If he wanted a motorcycle, he got a motorcycle," his son says. "If he wanted a car, he got a car."

The precocious boy grows into a juvenile with a lack of respect for authority. "He told me he used to chase cops down the street and down the sidewalk with his motorcycle," his son remembers. "The cop would be walking the beat, and he'd be chasing him with his motorcycle. He said it was crazy." The police, understandably upset, would try to reign in the teenage Smith: "Two or three of them would get together, put up a roadblock, and arrest him. They'd bring him in front of the judge, and his judge would be his old man."

The antics attract nicknames. The most pervasive is Hokie, maybe not surprising given the way the eponymous dance craze sweeps the nation. But it's also a disparaging derivative of his father's nickname, Hoke. Like his nickname, Maynard Smith's identity in Michigan is defined by the stature and influence of his father, and this will never change no matter how famous he becomes.

The Smiths have a home on State Street in Caro, where Maynard is born, and another in Peck, a village close to the Lake Huron waterfront that's an hour or so drive to the east. This generates his other nickname, "Peck's Bad Boy."

From his spot on the courthouse steps he can see the place where he once parked a car festooned with dripping viscera. Newspaper columnist Jim Sparling, also on the courthouse steps, will one day chronicle his juvenile delinquent highlights (and the detail about Smith's courthouse handcuffs) as a columnist for the *Tuscola County Advertiser*. Smith had been speeding around the county backroads when he encountered Ben Cody and his wife riding in a horse and buggy. He cut the wheel, missing the buggy but striking the horse dead-on. A 1943 *Detroit Times* article of the incident will include Smith's description of Cody, who "just sat there dazed holding the ends of the lines and clucking as though the horse was still there."

Smith hightailed it from the scene, the horse's intestines still draped across the fender. He instinctively headed for the courthouse and the safety of his father's shadow. Pedestrians and courthouse workers stared in horror at the gore-strewn vehicle. As always, his father's influence helped prevent arrest or charges, according to Smith's own public admissions.

The family dotes on their only child—"in her eyes, he could do no wrong," says Smith's daughter, Christine Pincince, of her grandmother—but they also try to tame him with a stint in military school. They send him to Howe Military Academy in Indiana, formerly a training ground for priests but now an all-male haven of discipline and mannered behavior. Smith hates it. He completes the twelfth grade in 1929 and never goes back to school.

Smith will self-educate his entire life, becoming a voracious reader. He develops an intellectual superiority that has nothing to do with higher education. To him, some people are enlightened and the rest are not worth his time. "He didn't walk with other people's drumbeat," his son recalls. "You know what I mean?"

However, Smith always makes time for females. He's lean and can pass for handsome, but his five-foot-five frame doesn't immediately qualify him as a heartthrob.[1] He makes up for it with confidence and a big personality. Hokie bills himself as an adventurous sort, in a land where thrills are hard to come by.

These charms woo a teenage girl named Arlene McCreedy. Smith marries her in July 1929. They have a daughter, Barbara Lou, in 1930. There's no part of young Maynard Smith that is ready for a stable life with a wife and baby. They divorce on October 22, 1932. He will never know his daughter.

---

1   Smith is usually referred to as being five feet, four inches. However, his military honorable discharge records state his height as five feet, five inches, so that is the figure used in this book.

Smith is twenty-three years old when the financial crisis sweeps Michigan in 1933. It all comes to a head on February 14 when Governor William Comstock declares a general banking holiday across the state. The reason: Henry Ford is going to pull his deposits from the dying banks of Detroit. This means little to Maynard Smith, except that it opens up a job opportunity.

The court is overwhelmed by the ensuing crisis, which is spreading across the whole nation, and Judge Smith taps his son to help appoint receivers and push paperwork. This experience gives Smith a marketable knowledge and a passing understanding of tax law; armed with this, he leaves for Detroit to work as an income tax field agent for the IRS.

Things change drastically in March 1934 when his father and mother go to Daytona Beach. The couple will meet Michigan state senator H. P. Orr and state banking commissioner Rudolph Reichert for a Florida vacation, including ringside seats at a boxing match. The pair of Michigan politicians are driving from Washington, D.C. on an improbable road trip, and arrive to the bout after the Smiths. They head inside to find H. H. Smith collapsed in his ringside seat. He's been felled by a sudden, fatal heart attack.

The entire community in Michigan is stunned and the news runs on page one of all the local newspapers. It's a heavy blow to the family, especially his boy. As an old man, Maynard Smith will keep a photo of the judge in his steamer trunk, engraved with a hand-written epitaph: "MY DAD—A REAL GENTLEMAN—TRUE PATRIOT—WONDERFUL FATHER."

He and his mother are now in charge of a sizeable inheritance. Smith, never a big fan of tax work, decides that it's time to try retirement. Smith spends his time reading books on psychology, engineering, and physics. He then holds forth on these topics to his friends and acquaintances. He doesn't feel any impetus to work. A reporter from *The New Yorker* will discuss this with him in 1943 and sum up Smith's attitude this way: "He makes no apology for his extended lounge; he just says that he liked to live in Michigan in the summer and in Florida for the winter, and so did his mother, and since they could afford to, why not?"

When he falls in love again, it's with the cream of central Michigan. This time the object of his affection is Helen Gunsell, the third daughter of William and Margaret Gunsell, a prominent Caro business family. A graduate of Caro High School in 1939, she's known for her abilities as a dancer and pianist. The bad boy and the well-to-do town stage starlet marry and their son, William H. Smith, is born in Detroit on September 14, 1941.

Smith's living in Detroit when the Japanese bomb Pearl Harbor. He registers for the draft but makes no move to volunteer. "I am not pugilistically inclined," he explains. He does work a job supporting the effort, assembling engines for Navy PT boats at the Packard Motor in Detroit. Smith also out of necessity becomes an assistant receiver for the Michigan State Banking Commission, another dry job for an increasingly frustrated man.

His second marriage also fizzles and Helen retreats back to Caro with the baby. Her family has enough money and it looks like she is going to remarry, so Smith angrily figures his financial responsibility is finished.

The law sees it differently. The judge, from the same chair where his father used to sit, reads the charges of failure to provide child support. Smith is facing pillars of the Caro community and he doesn't have a loving judge to back him up. The court gives Smith the choice: pay up and serve in the military or pay up and go to prison. It's no choice at all.

So on August 30 a shackled Smith joins the rest of the Army aspirants on the courthouse steps. The photo is taken, handshakes are offered to those unfettered. The sheriff unchains Smith just before he climbs aboard the bus that will take him and the others to Fort Custer. Smith looks out the window as the bus pulls away, taking in the receding courthouse, the familiar roads, the homes whose owners he knows by name.

Smith leans across the bus aisle to Jim Sparling. "I'll never come back here," he says bitterly. "Unless they line up on the streets to cheer."

FLEXIBLE GUNNERY

October 10, 1942. Maynard Harrison Smith is riding in the back of a pickup truck, cradling a shotgun. A handful of fellow trainees are seated in the back, gripping a railing as the pickup bumbles around a mile-long oval track through the mesquite. They're all wearing the uniform of the Army Air Forces, sweating under the South Texas sun.

"Lots of oranges," he writes his mother. "Weather like Florida."

The truck slows at a station and Smith stands, shotgun now at the ready on his shoulder. Without warning, a skeet trap flings a clay disc into the air. Smith leads the target a little and blasts it from the sky. Then he sits down as another B-17 gunner-in-training stands to take a shot. Learning the art of deflection needs to become second nature for bomber gunners, and he's finding that he's an apt pupil when it comes to firearms.

These are the early days of gunnery training at the Harlingen Aerial Gunnery School (HAGS), established in late 1941 in Cameron County, near the Mexican border. The Army airfield sits nearly four miles from the city, northeast on Rio Hondo Road. But the really loud action is here, twenty-two miles away from the base, where the gunnery ranges are safely cocooned inside thirty thousand acres of empty scrub.

The crafty mayor of Harlingen, Hugh Ramsey, lobbied for a military base here in the arid desert, but the Army balked because the terrain wasn't diverse enough for infantry training. But it's flat, empty, and dry—ideal conditions for a school to teach aerial gunnery. The lack of rain means an average of three hundred days of good flying weather, and the base's airfield buzzes with small training aircraft.

The age difference here is worse than Smith could have imagined. The average bomber crewman is twenty-two, and those in the gunner positions are often younger than that. (The officers in the cockpit tend to skew the average up a few years.) So Maynard Smith is among teenagers who routinely call twenty-five-year-olds "the old man" of their crews. That makes Smith more than just an outlier; at thirty-one he's nearly a freak.

Smith finds a bit of home in fellow trainee Marcel St. Louis. He meets the dark-haired twenty-five-year-old, who also hails from Detroit, when the pair are fresh into preliminary Army Air Forces training at Sheppard Field in Texas. The Canadian-born transplant wears his hair slicked back and has tight, thin lips. When he smiles, those lips part into an open-mouth, goofy grin.[2]

Smith later says that it's his idea to have the pair become bomber gunners. He drags St. Louis to the major in charge of selection at Sheppard and the two make a personal plea to sign up for aerial gunnery school. Those who make it through gun training earn promotions, and as a thirty-one-year-old, Smith wants to make rank as quickly as possible. "He said he went to gunnery school because when you came out, you were automatically a sergeant," Smith's son says. "He said, 'I wanted the extra pay.'"

St. Louis and Smith are sent to Harlingen, just as they requested.

---

2   Genealogical research done by the family is invaluable to re-creating his life. Their publicly posted results include photos of young St. Louis in his AAF uniform.

Smith takes credit for successfully lobbying for the assignment. "I'm a promoter, always have been," Smith later says of this unorthodox and entirely unmilitary politicking. "What could they do to me? I was already a private. You can't get any lower than that."

The Army Air Forces desperately needs crews to meet the war's demand, but they understand that this new form of warfare will make steep demands of the men. The selection process is initially designed to weed out those who can't hack it.

There are height limitations: a minimum of five feet and a maximum of five feet, eight inches. For weight, the cutoffs are less than 100 pounds or more than 180. Maynard Smith stands at five foot five, according to his military records. He's got a thin frame, but he tops out at 130 pounds.

Some of the considerations smack of quackery. Examiners take measurements of the men's faces and compare them to composites of twenty successful airmen. They're working on the theory that indicators in those features reveal the men's mental toughness. After a while the Army Air Forces realizes that there's no correlation.

Smith's lack of education isn't standing in the way. After January 1942 the AAF dropped its requirement of at least two years of college education, relying solely on a three-hour written test to screen cadets. So Smith's first hurdle is the reception center assessment test, the dreaded Army General Classification Test (AGCT). It's meant to measure a recruit's intelligence as well as his ability to learn.

The paper and pencil test is brainy: a vocabulary assessment mostly meant to identify actual or functional illiterates, a math test with increasingly tough computations, and a slate of questions probing the recruit's ability to visualize spatial relations. The test also attempts to measure how quickly someone can learn by charting "(1) native capacity, (2) schooling and educational opportunities, (3) socio-economic status, and (4) cultural background."

Dr. Walter Bingham, at the time the chief psychologist of the Classification and Replacement Branch of the Adjutant General's Office, resists complaints that good airmen are being screened out. "It does not measure merely inherent mental capacity," he says. "Performance in such a test reflects very definitely the educational opportunities the individual has had and the way in which these opportunities have been grasped and utilized. Educational opportunities do not mean schools merely. Learning goes on about the home, on the playground, at work, when one reads a newspaper, listens to a radio, or sees a movie. There is nothing in the title of the Army test that says anything about native intelligence."

Then comes the mechanical aptitude test, which isn't a hand-eye coordination thing, but another list of questions. This time the topics are simple engineering concepts, the kind of skills that can help a crewman operate the bomber's equipment under extreme duress. Smith's lifetime of fast rides and leisure reading on technical topics helps. He meets the standards for gunnery training, which are scores of 75 on the AGCT and 80 on the MA.

Smith's biggest challenge may be the interview. These one-on-one sit-downs are notorious for trivialities: lacking obvious motivation, revealing a checkered background, or even showing nervousness during this short conversation can mean disqualification. Focusing on real-world skills is useful. Maynard Smith did have a wartime job as an assembler at Packard in Detroit, experience that comes in handy when he's asked about his labor history. Machine maintenance and familiarity with tools are essential to being a gunner, as it turns out.

Any hint of perceived femininity is deemed a red flag. General Lewis Hershey, the director of the American draft system, complains that qualified men are being rejected even though they are "no queerer than the rest of us." Smith has enough small-man machismo to not worry about this.

The Army Air Forces evaluator determines that Smith has the scores, temperament, masculinity, and skills to be a B-17 gunner. This is an achievement. Only about half of the AAF enlisted personnel pass muster as members of an aircrew. Around 10 percent of the test takers qualify to be pilots; another 5 percent become bombardiers and another 5 navigators. The rest become radio operators, mechanics, or gunners.

Gunnery school seems like a good idea at the time. But now these Michigan natives are in the Rio Grande Valley, one step closer to a battlefield the likes of which no one has ever seen. The lessons being learned in Europe, Africa, and the Pacific are trickling back to the training base, and the details they hear are terrifying. The gunners figure out quickly that they will be fighting for their lives within a scant few months.

The words of Chief of the Army Air Forces Henry "Hap" Arnold, delivered in August 1941 when the first gunnery bases are established, are dutifully reported to the new arrivals. The speech is included in the pamphlet called *A Camera Trip through "HAGS"* produced by the Gunnery School. It's meant to inspire, but the words are also deeply worrisome.

"In the bombers it's the combat crew that counts. The navigator gets them to the target; it's the bombardier who drops the bombs and determines the hits or misses made. It's the gunner who sits in the turret all cramped and tense with his eyes peeled in all directions watching for the enemy diving out of the sun," Arnold says. "For a time only the pilot wore wings. Then wings were authorized for bombardiers and navigators. Now wings, aircrew wings, are authorized for the other men of that combat team. Now the gunner has something to wear on his chest to proclaim he's a first-rate fighting man."

The Harlingen Army Airfield is a kiln; a few miles from the shores of the Gulf of Mexico the sea breeze vanishes and only the heat remains. The men bake in classrooms, scorch under the sun

during PT, and sweat the sheets in the barracks. Rattlesnakes and scor-
pions abound. And this place is not like the Army basic training that
Smith encountered at Sheppard Field—instead of becoming a generic
soldier, everything he's doing here has a specific, deadly purpose.

The man known throughout Michigan for his problems with authority never loses his attitude, but also becomes an inspired listener.
Smith doesn't like the pace of training, the early hours, the hard
work, and the substandard facilities. He will later look back on Harlingen "with distaste" but also makes it a point to praise the lessons
he learns during training. In public as well as private conversations,
he will credit them for saving his life.

He believes he's smart enough to learn quickly, unlike some.
"Although the course is very intensive and technical, it is also very
interesting," he writes his mother in a handwritten letter dated October 12, 1942. "It's lots of fun, especially if it's somewhat easier for
one to grasp, but you've really got to be on the beam around here or
you'll get left."

The reason for the brainy qualification tests becomes clear as
training starts. There's a lot of time in classrooms. The men watch as
instructors fill chalkboards with ballistic calculations and primers
on the art of deflection. Tiny airplanes on sticks teach how to use
the relative wing length to estimate range. Models dangle from ceil-
ings, small enough to approximate distance, to help them recognize
aircraft. Smith proves good at aircraft recognition, and tends to win
the contests set up to liven up the education.

Smith and his classmates are here to become weapons specialists,
working .50-cal machine guns. But they don't start with the big guns.
They chew apart airplane-shaped paper targets with BB-spewing
machine guns. The first live weapon Smith gets his hands on is a
familiar .22 rifle. Over time the calibers increase until the men end
up at the turret range, where he's awed by the sight of dozens of .50

cals blazing at once. The students then climb into turrets mounted on trucks and ride the ranges, firing live rounds. Trainees are locked in rooms and plopped on ranges with malfunctioning weapons and compelled to diagnose and repair them on the spot. These drills are eventually repeated with blindfolds.

When military training becomes this specialized, the goal is not to wash out trainees but to help them succeed. There are no guarantees, however. The failure rate averages about 10 percent at all gunnery schools throughout the war years, but in 1942 Harlingen has the highest washout rate, at 16 percent. (Other bases are as low as 5 percent.)

The men are here to learn what is known as "flexible gunnery." It's one thing to hit a stationary target while standing still, and yet another challenge to hit something moving through the air while standing still. But the dynamics of shooting a mobile target from a moving platform are daunting, especially given the speed of the bombers and fighters.

One study done at the time by a colonel flying on the front lines named Claude Putnam, whom Smith is fated to fly with over Europe, calculates that at least four gunners are required to fire on an enemy airplane in order to have a 50 percent chance of stopping the attack. That doesn't mean shooting it down—that means getting shots close enough for the spooked fighter pilot to turn away.

The military has broken down the complexity of deflection shooting at enemy fighters into a step-by-step formula. First, recognize the enemy. Estimate the range, using the wingspan in the gun sight. Then hold the barrel steady for a second to estimate the enemy's speed. With this information, make a snap calculation to calculate the lead, and then fire a controlled burst.

This must all be done within seconds. The only way a gunner has a chance of hitting a fighter is if the process becomes automatic, instinctive. And the only way to gain this ability is through experience.

"There's one other very important exam, itself a shooting test at a target being towed by a plane while I'm riding in another plane," Smith tells his mother in October. "This is one of the really important ones, but the written tests must be passed first."

Smith's first flight will be in an AT-6 Texan, the era's ubiquitous single-engine trainer. He greets the pilot and climbs into the rear of the aircraft.[3] The swivel seat back there, facing the rear, is slewed to a .30-cal machine gun loaded with plastic bullets. Smith runs down the checklist to ensure the weapon is ready, receives the nod from an observing instructor, and then the AT-6 zips down the runway and lurches into the air.

From here Smith sees the breadth of the landscape and is reminded how far he is from home and how *unlike* Florida this place actually is. The flat, brown desert runs straight into the ocean, no wetlands or tropical greenery to be seen, just the unrelenting sea of scrub brush. The airplane is heading toward empty land where there are none to be bothered by their gunnery except jackrabbits and the occasional wild horse.

The AT-6 rendezvous with others, but not all of them are stocked with armed students. There are base personnel flying some of the Texans, and these peel off and begin to unreel fabric sleeves. Unfurled, these look like three wind socks fluttering 750 feet behind the airplanes. These are tow targets for the trainees, who take turns peppering targets as the AT-6 pulls up alongside. Any plastic bullet that strikes the target leaves a colored mark that evaluators will use to score the students, and this stimulates Smith's innate competitiveness.

---

3   In time, a majority of AT-6 pilots will be WASPs (Women Airforce Service Pilots), but they won't arrive until 1943.

The gunners are brought into the air over and over, eventually boarding a twin-engine bomber to practice on turret guns, whaling away at mesh targets pulled by B-26 medium bombers. Targets mounted on boats and rafts stand in for ground targets, which the gunners strafe gleefully. These are bombers, not gunships, but the gunners learn the air-to-ground shooting anyway.

After five weeks at Harlingen, Maynard Smith and Marcel St. Louis graduate from gunnery school and receive their wings on November 9, 1942. The pair of sergeants is only one step closer to Europe. They know how to shoot, but the Army Air Forces needs them to get acquainted with the B-17, and that means heading out west.

There's one thing Smith takes with him from Texas: the nickname "Snuffy." The name is not necessarily a compliment. In 1942 Hollywood brought a comic-strip character named Snuffy Smith to the big screen. The plot of the film, which is objectively bad even by the standards of the time, echoes Maynard Smith's circumstances as well as stature. Snuffy is a bootlegger who gets into a jam with revenuers, and eventually joins the military to escape his legal troubles. The character's humor comes from his lack of couth as well as his lack of height.

Smith has always had nicknames, but this one seems to be sticking. But did he like to be called Snuffy? "No," says his son. "He loved it." The name will do more than follow him through training and to England. It will take on a life of its own.

STRAIGHT AND LEVEL

November 23, 1942. Colonel Curtis LeMay watches from the top turret of the lead airplane of the 305th Bomb Group (BG), eyes keenly tracking the formation of planes behind him. He's found this position in the airplane—standing with his head in the clear, plastic bubble bulging from atop the fuselage—is the best for observation.

LeMay is hoping to survive to see tomorrow, his thirty-sixth birthday.

This mission is employing a brand-new tactic that he hopes will protect the bombers behind him and, more importantly, deliver high explosive bombs on their target with revolutionary precision. On top of the attempt at rewriting the military strategy of World War II, it's also a personal milestone for LeMay. "I'd never been over a target before," he says in a memoir. "And I was trying a thing like this."

The war has been raging for two years, but these are still the early days for the American involvement in the air battle over Europe. It's a slow ramp-up as the 8th Air Force lobbies Washington, D.C., for more bombers, which are being diverted to the Pacific and African theaters. The first American missions over Europe attack targets in the Netherlands and start, with great intention, on July 4. The B-17 Flying Fortresses and B-24 Liberators have only begun the bombing campaign over France in August.

Today, fifty B-17s from four bomber groups are attacking German targets on the coast of occupied France. At a minimum of ten men per airplane, there are at least five hundred airmen heading into harm's way. Routine but impactful problems arise across the entire mission—engines sputter out, oxygen systems malfunction, hydraulics of the gun turrets fail—and more than half the B-17s return for England before they get close to France.

Only four bombers in LeMay's command of twenty return to England with mechanical troubles. The aborted airplanes leave gaps in the formation. LeMay choreographs the 305th, spitting out curt orders over the radio to keep the planes flying close together: "Number six, get yourself further to port. Number eleven raise yourself above number fourteen."

There are now 160 men for him to shepherd to today's target, the submarine pens at Saint-Nazaire. The Germans have set up elaborate naval stations on the edge of the Atlantic, where U-boats embark to bring terror to Allied shipping lanes. The scoreboard is hidden from the public, but the Axis is winning the Battle of the Atlantic. Maybe bombers can help secure the shipping that's propping up England by shattering these Nazi submarine bases.

LeMay is a fast-rising star within the Army Air Forces. He's an experienced navigator, one with flight time in the B-17 that began well before the war started. This includes a prewar flyover of a U.S. battleship to demonstrate the bomber's ability to intercept ships, even though the Navy gave several phony coordinates to ruin the demonstration.

LeMay is already known as a tough taskmaster but also a wartime innovator; he and Brigadier General Laurence Kuter, the commanding general of the 1st Bomb Wing, developed the formations used by the entire 8th Air Force. The British string their bombers in long lines, but the pair of aviators envision the bombers protecting each other by flying in close proximity.

LeMay's version of a formation is built on groups of three airplanes, forming wedges at slightly staggered altitudes. This guarantees that overlapping fields of .50-cal bullets will greet enemy warplanes that get within six hundred yards of the formation. Attacking one bomber means exposure to the gun sights of multiple others.

Box formations have a few disadvantages as well. They are hard to organize and laborious to maintain, as LeMay is finding as he works the radio. Tight formations invite midair collisions, which kill airmen with alarming frequency in Europe.

B-17s are billed as airplanes that don't need fighter escorts. And since in 1942 no fighter escorts have the range of a Flying Fortress, missions over France largely unfold without any protection. British

Spitfires can hardly cover more than a few miles across the Channel. No escorts will be around where it matters—over the targets.

The combat box, then, is the supposed solution to fend off enemy fighters. Now the U.S. Army Air Forces needs to figure out how to actually land bombs on their targets. LeMay's experiment today aims to crack this problem, with hundreds of his men's lives at risk.

LeMay is a driven man who believes in intense training, and he shares this ethos with his men. He has earned their nickname for him, "Old Iron Ass." He entered ROTC training at Ohio State University, and the U.S. Army Air Corps accepted him in 1928. LeMay's bullish desire to succeed comes from a childhood spent on the road with his drifter parents. "If you grow up amid the confused ignominy of the very poor and insecure, and if you are sufficiently tough in spite of this, poverty can prosper you," he writes of his upbringing.

On top of the demands he characteristically places on himself, LeMay feels extra pressure from on high—there are some high-ranking superiors who are anxious for him to prove that American bombers can take the fight to the Germans in occupied turf, and into their homeland. These include aviation icons like Henry "Hap" Arnold, the world-famous Lieutenant Colonel Jimmy Doolittle, and the 8th Air Force commander, General Ira Eaker, to whom LeMay reports directly.

These men have a very specific vision of how airpower should be used that they developed in the mid-1930s. The idea is for heavy bombers to make well-aimed strikes on industrial targets, efficiently sapping the Germans' ability to wage war.

This is not at all how bombers are currently being used. The British have turned to imprecise incendiary attacks on cities, figuring that they can burn the population into submission. The talk around London, coming from Sir Arthur "Bomber" Harris's office, is that the American bombers will fly with the Brits at night and help them burn German cities to ashes.

The American bomber cabal is desperate to keep this from happening and to maintain control over the Army Air Forces units heading into combat. That makes the idea that bombers are capable themselves of keeping fighters at bay a fundamental of U.S diplomacy, not just military strategy. So add FDR to those who want to see results from LeMay.

The cabal created the B-17 specifically for daytime bombing. It doesn't carry as much ordnance as British bombers, but these aircraft aren't supposed to need as much because they have the latest, greatest bombsight in the world—the Norden. Developed in secrecy that rivals the Manhattan Project, this targeting device is meant to change everything. But bombardiers can't use it at night, which explains the American requirement for daytime raids.

American heavy bomber crews have something to prove in the skies over Europe, but it's not going well. By November 1942 the losses are already staggering. The average lifespan of a bomber crewmember is fewer than five missions. For this sacrifice, fewer than 25 percent of U.S. bombs are dropping within one thousand feet of their targets. No one wants to blame the Norden bombsight for these dismal numbers—that disappointing assessment will come later—so there must be a tactical way to improve the crews' accuracy.

LeMay has an answer, but he has to sell it to the rightfully skeptical men under his command.

The bomber crews have been through recent tactical experimentation already, and the results were dismal. Earlier this month, the Army Air Forces planned a trio of missions that took new low-level approaches, hoping to surprise the Germans by popping up right before they reach the targets. The *Memphis Belle* (41-24485), on her third mission (far from her crew's future fame), nearly gets shot down during one of these "hedge-hopping" experiments. "You know, we would skim the surface until we got to the target, stay below the attention of German fighters and radar, pop up to a couple of thousand feet, drop our bombs and get out," the *Belle*'s pilot, Lieutenant Robert Morgan, tells the *Chicago Tribune*.

It doesn't work as planned. "We got hammered," Morgan says. "Our squadron got shot up badly, just ripped to pieces on that one." Four B-17s are shot down, with forty-three crew listed as missing in action. Sixteen B-17s are damaged, three airmen onboard killed and sixteen wounded. The *Belle* tangled with a Focke-Wulf 190 that put a 20mm cannon shell into an engine, forcing the B-17 to land at a coastal air base instead of their home base at Bassingbourn. There, the crew counted sixty-two distinct holes in the plane.

Morgan's verdict on the hedge-hopping: "It didn't fool anybody." That was the last time the 8th Air Force leadership tried such low-level tactics in France, but it is far from the final untested tactic to debut during an actual mission.

This is the air war over Europe in late 1942—disorganized, experimental, and dangerous. The outcome must get better if the 8th Air Force is to retain control of their aircraft from the British, not to mention help break the Nazi hold on Europe. "The 8th Air Force was throwing men and equipment at the problem but they were not getting the results they wanted," LeMay says in his memoirs. "They weren't hitting the target."

Attacking industrial centers means facing concentrations of antiaircraft cannons. Pilots are taught to make wild evasive maneuvers on the approach to targets in order to throw off the antiaircraft crews' boresight and radar firing calculations.

But on the morning of November 23, LeMay orders his men under his command to do something simple and terrifying: fly straight through the antiaircraft fire without maneuvering.

It's hard to overstate how radical this plan is compared to the status quo. It runs against everything the British have advised the

Americans to do. LeMay's predecessor told him, and every bomb crew agreed, that "if you fly level for more than ten seconds, you'll be shot down by flak."

But LeMay dissects this conventional wisdom and comes up with a different plan. He uses data from the first missions and the rates of fire of the German cannons to calculate that only one B-17 was hit for every 372 flak shells. "In the end, there was only one answer to be found. It was apparent that we would have to go straight in on the target," he later writes. "You couldn't swing evasively all over the sky without throwing your bombs all over the lot, too."

LeMay realizes that flak is as effective as a terror weapon as it is an actual killer. Crews are typically tossed around as the B-17 swerves its way toward a target, the pilots caring more about confusing the flak gunners than setting up an accurate bomb drop. LeMay knows that he has to psychologically counterprogram the crews. He's seen the studies that indicate that maneuvering comforts aviators better than the feeling of "sitting and taking it."

Although it may feel good, maneuvering ruins accuracy. Action reports at the time show 39.7 percent of bombing errors could be attributed to nerves and evasive action. This is likely to be understated: after the war, 61.4 percent of off-target American bomb drops are attributed to avoiding flak.

When he unveils the November 23 flight plan to the crews during the pre-mission briefing that morning, the men immediately see the difference compared to their earlier missions. The flight route, stretched across a map in yarn, has few bends or turns. LeMay tells them that the 305th is to make "the longest, straightest bomb run which had ever been made by B-17s over the continent of Europe."

Even worse, the target is Saint-Nazaire, which has earned the nickname "Flak City" for the concentration and accuracy of its antiaircraft weapons. The port facilities there are primary targets for British and American bombers. And the Germans know it, too.

An airman stands and tells LeMay, bluntly, that the mission sounds like suicide. LeMay calmly explains his math, and adds that it's more dangerous over time to hit missed targets again than it is to strike them solidly the first time. LeMay then tells them that he'll be flying in the formation's lead bomber. It doesn't end the misgivings, but the room does quiet down.

If it's suicide, LeMay will be right there with them.

Now, from his position in the turret, LeMay can see dark blots fill the air. Each pops into existence with a red-orange flash. The grim but somehow beautiful display is courtesy of the German naval antiaircraft guns that guard Saint-Nazaire. At 20,000 feet, fewer anti-aircraft artillery guns can reach the bombers, but the 88mms and 105mms are enough. Each dark bloom that LeMay sees in the sky is actually the center of an expanding sphere of whirling metal. And the ugly puffs keep appearing, a swarm of detonating shells that follow the warplanes as they close in on the German facilities.

Now that the violence has started, LeMay finds he's too busy to worry about dying. But he's not too busy to fret over a humiliating failure—after all, he's trying to reinvent heavy bomber warfare on his first combat mission. "I was too concerned with the revolutionary rabbit I was trying to pull out of a hat," he later writes.

He guides the 305th straight through, as per plan. B-17s suffer flak hits, no more than usual, but none are shot down. Flak shrapnel clatters off the metal fuselages, producing unnerving noises. It's better to hear this than to feel the shudder of a shell exploding close enough to pierce the airplane. If there's a direct hit at the wrong spot, the whole bomber could go up in an instant. And no one onboard would feel a thing, if they're lucky.

There's too much time to consider such violent ends. Instead of the normal ten seconds of being what they feel are sitting ducks, crews on this mission endure seven minutes of steady flight toward their targets. The lead bombardier in LeMay's airplane is the first drop, signaling with a flare that the others do the same. Two 2,000-pound bombs per airplane rain down on the docks and marshaling yards, peppering the German facilities with high explosives.

LeMay will later report that the rail yard targets near the sub pens are struck with twice as many bombs as the prior groups who flew over Saint-Nazaire. It's the kind of progress that Eaker and Arnold are waiting to hear about.

But the Germans also have a nasty surprise to unveil on this mission. LeMay is not the only innovator in the air that day.

SHOOTING OUT THE HERD

November 23, 1942. *Hauptmann* Egon Mayer watches from behind wide goggles as the American B-17s cruise through the flak-bruised sky. His Fw 190, the best fighter of the era, is four miles away from LeMay's formations. German pilots will brave their own flak to attack bombers, especially when the combined attack disrupts a bombing run, but they don't enjoy it. Today the fighters steer clear of Flak City and prepare to attack as soon as the air is clear of antiaircraft shells.

The fighter pilot arms the guns one pair at a time, flicking one switch and waiting three seconds to activate the other. The pause is needed so as not to overload the airplane's battery. The airplane's design takes advantage of new electric controls like this that allow the pilot to focus on fighting instead of the minutiae of flying.

Mayer, at twenty-five years old, is a highly decorated, experienced mankiller. He has a lanky, utilitarian frame that seems out of sync with his round, boyish face. His limbs have sharp angles that his face does not. He's been at war since 1939, with his first kill (a French MS.406) recorded in 1940. He is one of the reasons why the

Fw 190 earned such a fearsome reputation during the Battle of Britain: his record shows dozens of Spitfire shootdowns.

By August 1941 he's got twenty-one aircraft kills, and this grim tally reaches thirty-seven by July. Earlier that month, Mayer is promoted to commander of the 3rd group of *Jagdgeschwader* 2 (III/JG 2). The wing is named "Richthofen" after the famous World War I ace known as the Red Baron. By November 1942, Mayer is laden with medals from fighting on the English Channel front, where he has spent his entire combat career. Mayer is nearly killed in a crash into the Channel; he swims an hour to the safety of the French coast.

He's also watched the tide of war change, been on the attack and now the defense. He's flown in several *Gruppe* but always with JG 2; this *Jagdgeschwader* is his home and the French coast his hunting ground.

As of this fall there is something new in the air—the Americans and their B-17s. Flocks of them are appearing, brazenly flying in the daytime. He knows that they eventually mean to attack the homeland, to cripple Germany. And Mayer knows it's up to him and his aviators to stop them.

The true strength of the Luftwaffe is not just the machinery; it's the people. There's a crop of pilots like Mayer who started flying in the late 1930s who form the backbone of the Luftwaffe. Mayer was born on a farm near Konstanz, in southern Germany. He fell in love with aviation at a young age, gravitating to the glider airfield at the Bellenberg. These airfields are repositories of national pride in an era when Germany was still bound by the Treaty of Versailles's ban on military development.

"German glider activity in the 1920s and 1930s had important implications," writes Jürgen Melzer, of Princeton University. "It led to significant progress in aeronautical science and technology, stimulated military aviation, and promoted a nationalistic air-mindedness.

Ironically, these were precisely the fields the Allies had wanted to crack down on with their ban on German aviation."

Joining the Luftwaffe is a logical step for an aviation-obsessed young man, since that's the only place where the airplanes are. Mayer joins the Luftwaffe in 1937 and in December 1939 *Fahnenjunker* Mayer is posted to the Channel front. He's steadily promoted as his flying skills combine with a talent for tactical adaptation.

Mayer's Luftwaffe comrades on the Channel front are some of the most experienced and deadly pilots in the world. They have first feasted on Spitfires and then British bombers. Many have experience ravaging substandard Russian warplanes as well, since an increasing number of pilots are being called back from other fronts to help defend Germany and France. The men in the cockpits of the German fighters are ready for the fight on levels that the Americans simply are not.

Still, the sight of so many well-armed bombers flying so close together is intimidating, even to a seasoned flier like Mayer. The British don't fly this way during their night missions, preferring long queues of bombers attacking in sequence. He knows the bomber's nickname, the Flying Fortress, and is reminded of it every time he's in range of the airplane's guns.

A German pilot who flew from 1941 to 1944, Gerd Gaiser, says in his 1960 book *The Last Squadron* that the B-17s made the air war an industrialized grind:

> It's mass we're up against now, and the mass flying in the enemy planes are not airmen; they're gunners strapped in their turrets, infantry of the air. So we too must create mass. From one day to another the era of sportsmanlike, chivalrous hunting had ended. The air space over Europe had turned into a battleground with fortresses and trenches—and it was our duty to storm those fortifications and break through.

There's more than one way to attack a sky full of bombers. Mayer keeps an eye open for damaged bombers that are falling out of formation, what the Luftwaffe calls "shooting out" (*herausschuss*). It's a predator's mentality: hunt down any prey that is too injured to stay with the rest. The German pilots have even dubbed the B-17 formations *"pulks,"* the German word for herd.

The German military didn't plan it this way and the Americans never predicted it, but the most effective air defense is a deadly combination of flak and fighters. Flak damages B-17s, which then fall out of formation. With no fighter escorts and no overlapping protective fire from the other bombers, the Fw 190 pilots are comparably safe to pick apart wounded bombers.

It's certainly less risky to face one bomber alone. Every B-17 in 1942 is defended by five .50-cal machine gun positions, and two of those are in ball turrets armed with twin machine guns. Flying into a formation of B-17s means exposure to clouds of overlapping fire. These gunfights are not extended; with a combined closing speed of 500 mph both sides only have a split second to kill each other.

A typical strafing run would begin above and away from the formation, followed by a slashing dive through the formation, riddling warplanes with bursts of 20mm cannon fire and 7.92mm machine guns. But this exposes the fighters to too much defensive fire, especially when the formations are flying tightly together as they are today.

The daylight raids have spawned fresh ways to attack. Small groups of Fw 190s approach from the rear of the formation, closing as fast as possible to eat away at the time the B-17s' rear gunners have to shoot. The pilots then blast the bombers before veering off, inverting and diving away from the airplanes in a quick split S maneuver. (The pilot flips the fighter over in order to decrease the G's and then dives, turning so the fighter is heading the opposite direction.)

Today, Mayer is trying something new. Instead of coming up from behind, Mayer pushes the Fw 190 about three miles ahead of the B-17s. Two wingmen follow in a V, positioning themselves ahead and to the left of the formation. As one, the trio turn to face the bombers head-on.

The view in Mayer's windscreen curdles the blood. He can hear the Fw 190's metal creak and groan. He's chosen one B-17 as a victim and aims directly at it. He knows the aircraft has no forward gun—the only direction the airplane doesn't have covered at the time—but the massive airplane itself is a threat and it's quickly filling his view. Mayer files these emotional reactions away for later consideration; as a former flying instructor he knows pilots will need training to keep fear from spoiling these attacks. He steadies his voice and radios the other fighters as the distance between predator and prey quickly shrinks: "Stay calm, do not open fire . . . Now."

He lines up the bomber with the modern and well-proven reflector sight (*Reflexvisier*). This gyro-stabilized system keeps his aim true, no matter what sort of maneuvers the aircraft is making during the attack. The Focke-Wulf has two Rheinmetall-Borsig 7.92mm machine guns mounted above the engine, firing through the prop at the rate of 1,100 rounds per minute. They are loaded with a candy cane mixture of incendiary and armor-piercing rounds. These are good for close-in work. The pilots are taught to target crew positions, engines, and fuel tanks with these machine guns.

The fighter has heavier armaments as well. Hits from the Fw 190's four 20mm cannons can down a bomber nearly anywhere they hit. The 20mm shells are fused to detonate after punching through the skin of an airplane, but before exiting the other side. High explosives can snap off wings, destroy tail sections, and cause other structural damage with a single good shot. They are also good for cutting crews to pieces.

Mayer fires just ahead of the nose, a deflection shot that he hopes will place streams of explosive shells and bullets where the bomber will run into them. A three-second burst of every weapon sends about 130 rounds toward the American airplane. Every time he fires the 20mms, two white bars on his console tick down, a simple visual reminder of his remaining ammunition. Jagged pieces of the bomber whirl past his airplane as shells and bullets impact.

Mayer's wingmen take their shots and the German pilots pull away, up and to the left, soaring through and then past the formation, only safe when out of range. Mayer feels the temptation to dive away from the danger, but he knows this will waste precious time and fuel if the fighters have to again climb above the bombers to reform for another head-on attack. It's another note to pass along to others.

Mayer's attacks disable the *Pandora's Box* (41-24503) and the B-17 drifts from the formation, going down in a slow-motion crash. The others watch helplessly as the aircraft descends and fades from view. "A/C 503 last seen badly crippled off Brest peninsula," the 91st BG's official report on the day's mission says, "First A/C lost in group. We lost our Sq. Commander, Sq. Navigator and a crew pilot."

The day is a professional and personal triumph for Mayer. He shoots down a second B-17 within twenty minutes of the first. A half hour after tangling with the Flying Fortresses, he's attacking a formation of American B-24s and is credited with shooting one of them down.

There's no totally safe way to attack a B-17. One U.S. combat report from November 23 details an encounter with B-17 #124448 during an extended gun battle: "E/A [Enemy aircraft] made frontal attack. As he came back, the tail gunner [Sergeant Parley Small] picked him up and saw bullets entering tail," the mission report reads. "As he turned, the tail gunner got more bullets into nose, and saw heavy smoke come out of nose. The plane disintegrated, the gunner clearly remembering seeing a wheel fly through the air. The pilot was seen to bail out."

The 303rd Bomb Group's combat report provides a glimpse of the deadly skills of Mayer and the rest of the Luftwaffe's Channel defenders: "Fw 190s made vicious close attacks in groups of two or three immediately after the bombers left the intense flak over the target. Group gunners destroyed two enemy aircraft with one probable and two damaged. The Group suffered its first crew loss in #41-24568. *Lady Fairweather* was on its third mission and was seen to hit the water while still in flames."

Other fliers in JG 2, flying in squadrons based in various air bases on the French coast, are adding to their tallies. Luftwaffe Second Lieutenant Walter Ebert is glad to be back in action. He downed a pair of Spitfires over England in 1940 but has not notched any victories since; Ebert likely had been injured and/or found a role as an instructor. But now the defense of Germany is paramount, and the flier is again fighting over the Channel with 8th Squadron of JG 2, operating from the Brest-Guipavas air base. Alongside him in the air is Lieutenant Friedrich May, a relatively new pilot to 8/JG 2. He only claimed his first victory in June 1942.

May and Ebert target a B-17 flying at 10,000 feet. It's always tough to match Luftwaffe records with the airplanes they claim to have downed. But based on location and timing, a B-17 named *Sad Sack* is May and Ebert's likely victim.

Sad Sack's commander that day is Major Victor Zienowicz, a West Point graduate who earned a medal there for rescuing two drowning cadets during a canoe mishap. He had survived a midair collision and emergency landing just five days prior to this mission, and is back in the air with the 322nd Bomb Squadron (part of the 303rd BG) in a new airplane.

Of the ten B-17s from the 322nd that take off that day, only half make it to France. When *Sad Sack* and four other bombers from the 91st reach the rendezvous, the sky is empty. They continue toward the target nevertheless. *Sad Sack* suffers an engine failure before even reaching the target and turns back for England, only to vanish on the way home. Zienowicz and his crew are labeled missing in action.

In total, the 8th Air Force loses four B-17s on November 23. Another B-17 is damaged beyond repair, sixteen others riddled by flak cannons and fighters. Three airmen are killed and sixteen wounded on these damaged airplanes; forty-three men are reported missing. Crewmen are only listed as killed in action if a body is recovered in an airplane or no parachutes are seen emerging from an airplane before its impact with the ground.

This is the fifth American bomber attack against the submarine pens in two weeks. The Germans at Saint-Nazaire shrug it off. The U-boat pens are beneath a massive bunker made of reinforced concrete and steel. By 1942 the British and American war planners know that no existing bomb can damage them. But Saint-Nazaire, situated near the mouth of the Loire River, is more than a submarine base. It has wet and dry docks that could bring marauding German raiders and even battleships to the Atlantic, making an already bad situation worse. The 8th Air Force (who is more interested in attacking fighter factories and enemy airfields) is whipsawed by conflicting targeting demands, and so the tightly guarded naval base remains high on the target list.

The mission of November 23 is presented as a win for the Allies. The official 8th Air Force record of the mission notes: "Admiral Sir Dudley Pound, First Lord of the Admiralty, writes to Lieutenant General Ira C. Eaker praising the effects of the US bomber attacks on disorganizing the servicing schedule of the German U-boat bases on the French W coast."

The dozens of men killed and wounded from the 8th Air Force pay a high cost for causing this fleeting scheduling delay. The 91st

BG's mission report sums up their day in a different way. They call it their "first disastrous mission."

BOY MEETS BOMBER

December 1, 1942. Maynard Smith is promoted to staff sergeant, another rung up the military ladder. The promotion comes just after his arrival at Pocatello Army Airfield in Idaho, where he's learning about the warplane that will save him or seal his doom.

A squadron of the 96th Bomb Group is familiarizing fresh crews with the ins and outs of the B 17 bomber. The training's scope expands beyond just gunnery. The ten men in each airplane must work together to survive in an alien environment against a savvy, high-tech enemy. Coordination only comes from training.

Smith has a penchant for powerful machines, and he's smitten by the Flying Fortress. "He loved the B-17, man, he *loved* it," says Maynard Smith Jr. "He said it was the most stable, unbelievable airplane that they ever built. Incredible."

The bomber, even on the ground, exudes a mixture of elegance and brute strength. The 104-foot wingspan is intimidating but also comforting—the more surface area, the more lift the wings generate. Shoot holes in these endless wings, and they'll still keep the airplane airborne. The beefy control surfaces at the tail seem ready to take damage, as well. The Texans he's flown in seem like flies in comparison. And those trainers didn't bristle with multiple gun positions.

Only from inside does he realize how thin that metal skin actually is. The circular ribs of the airplane make him feel like he's inside a living creature, one bred only to fight. The cables that control the flight surfaces are exposed tendons that stretch along the length of the fuselage's interior. When the guys in the cockpit move a control stick, those in the back can watch them slide back and forth in response.

The airplane is organized more like a centipede than a bird, broken into segments that are separated by bulkheads. The airplane's tip is mostly transparent Plexiglas, where the bombardier and navigator sit in metal swivel chairs. This makes sense, as they need the visibility. The second segment is behind and above these positions, and contains the pilot, co-pilot, and engineer/top turret gunner. This is sort of analogous to the arthropod's brain.

The next segment is the bomb bay. Crews can use a catwalk with hand ropes to cross over the doors, a terrifying tightrope walk between the racks of bombs. Since the bomb bay doors are made to open under very little pressure, slipping from the catwalk onto them could cause a fatal drop.

After the bomb bay segment comes the radio room. It's a cramped space, dials and switches on the walls, and the operator sits on a metal seat bolted to the floor in front of a wooden tabletop. The hatch to the dangling ball turret is directly behind the radio room. Behind that is the domain of the waist gun positions, who stand nearly back to back. The final segment tapers off past the rear wheel well, which juts into the fuselage, and ends with another transparent dome holding the tail gunner.

Smith and the other airmen soon find out that the people who are teaching them have not flown in Europe; indeed, the 96th are *themselves* shipping out in January to train for combat. Smith is being given a tour of an Army that's rapidly metamorphosing, reforming itself in reaction to the demands of a global war.

And before you know it, Smith is done in Idaho and sent to Wyoming, his last stop before the carnage of Europe.

CHAPTER 2

"A ROUGH SHOW"

December 20, 1942. Lieutenant Lewis Page Johnson Jr. sits in the co-pilot's seat of the B-17 *Unmentionable* (42-29631), eyes scanning the bright midday sky. This mission is meant to poke a hornet's nest, and those dark spots marring the sky are the angry insects coming to at-tack.

Johnson is part of the 306th Bomb Group, serving in a new B-17 but alongside a familiar flight commander. Captain Mack McKay's usual B-17, the *Lil Audrey,* is still being repaired after the airplane's life raft broke loose, snapped an antenna, and wrapped around the horizontal stabilizer during a late October mission.

These days missions are getting steadily larger, but not enough to satisfy the fliers or their commanders. Today's strike is a ma-jor effort—one hundred bombers are approaching the Romilly Air Park and Aerodrome east of Paris. It houses the reserves of German aircraft of all types, as well as serving as a repair and modification depot. Even destroying the stocks of extra parts could help keep the German fighters out of the sky. The 8th Air Force commanders always prefer to attack Luftwaffe fighter bases and airplane factories, seeing air supremacy as a key to scaling up attacks into Germany itself.

The airplane may be unfamiliar to Johnson, but the men are not. He's been with McKay and most of this tight-knit crew since July, when the 306th deployed to Europe. He was McKay's co-pilot during *Lil Audrey*'s flight to the United Kingdom that month.

Army Air Forces airmen are surrounded by random death, and there are precious few things they could do to control their fates. Picking the men you fly with is one of them. "Casualties did strike at random," Colonel Lester Rentmeester, a pilot of the 91st Bomb Group, will one day tell a historian. "But inferior crews had less of a chance of surviving in an emergency."

The noncommissioned officers, staff sergeants all, make up the bulk of the crew: Henry Bean, the radio operator; James Hobbs crammed in the ball turret; Roy "Hoot" Gibson serving as tail gunner; Donald Bevan manning the right waist gun; and Raymond Henn on the left. They are a cross section of American youth.

Henn hails from Queens, where he worked as a plumber after two years of high school before enlisting in January 1942. Gibson, born in Minnesota, finished high school but headed to San Diego to become an auto mechanic. He enlisted on January 1, 1942, at Fort Rosecrans as a AAF private.

Sergeant Henry Randall Bean hails from the small town of Dos Cabezas, Arizona. He wanted to be an electrician before the war changed his plans. According to local news articles quoting his family, Bean writes from overseas to push his younger brother to stay in school. "There is nothing you can do without a high school diploma—not even in the Army," he advises.

Bevan, from Massachusetts, is the only one who didn't fly over the Atlantic with the *Lil Audrey*. He's a replacement gunner; he's not part of that circle. But the crew knows he's solid; he's a driver who volunteers for combat missions as a gunner. He shot down a German fighter on a mission with McKay just the week before.

L. P. Johnson Jr. is far from his native Harlan County, Kentucky. His father runs a local coal mine in the town of Crummies, with all that entails—violent clashes with unions, responses to belowground accidents, and a prosecution in 1938 for threatening organizers. Johnson Jr. doesn't seem to want to go into the family business: when he joins the Army Air Forces he notes his profession as "actor."

Johnson discovers aviation while at the University of Kentucky, when he becomes an Air Corps cadet. He went to college early, and the awkward and sometimes bullied young student becomes taken with the slate-blue uniforms and the reactions it inspires on campus— from girls. Aviation gives him a sense of place and purpose, and after graduation in 1941 he joins the Air Corps.

All of these decisions have brought him here, in the air over France with Germans ready to kill him. He's not alone—101 aircraft have taken off from England that day.

The numbers of airplanes, the crews assigned, their formations, and even the flight routes are carefully chronicled in the mission records of the 8th Air Force. After the mission ends, more paperwork is filed by everyone from the engineers reporting combat damage to the munitions officers who tally the bullets fired. Crew Interrogation Forms became part of the surreal post-combat routine.[4]

---

4 Group mission reports and squadron combat diaries cited in this text have been preserved by the U.S. government and spread online, providing a treasure trove of primary sources, descriptions of actions, and statistics for those not near Maxwell Air Force Base or other archive locations. The 8th Air Force Historical Society's website (www.8thafhs.org) has a database that organizes the AAF primary source mission data in a highly useful way. The 306th Bomb

Of the hundred-plus airplanes, seventy-two have turned around citing mechanical issues. With such statistics, it's tempting to assume that some crews faked maintenance issues to avoid the deadly combat ahead. The British even have a term for it: creepback. The most common practitioners include "fringe merchants" who fly higher than the mission states and scatter their bombs wildly from up where flak and fighters are far less dangerous.

But creepback doesn't plague the Americans like it does the British. There are morale problems, and they are going to worsen, but the 8th Air Force crews don't tank their missions. There are some logical reasons for this. British bombers fly independently and at night, good conditions for a fringe merchant. In contrast, the clustered daylight U.S. bomber formations put everyone's actions in plain view.

Mechanical issues are real and more dangerous than enemy action. Inside unpressurized airplanes at above 20,000 feet, a malfunctioning oxygen system can be fatal. A ball turret on the fritz not only leaves a gap in defenses, it could lead to an airman being trapped inside of a crashing airplane instead of bailing out. A broken cockpit heater can cause frostbite and crash airplanes. Returning to base to tend to these things is not only humane; it's militarily smart. And if the crews feel some sense of relief, so be it. There will be another chance to get killed soon enough.

Johnson knows the day will be a long one just after they cross the French coast, when he spies dozens of enemy fighters forming up. They fall on the eighteen B-17s of the 306th over the city of Rouen. Waves of Fw 190s with silver fuselages are diving into the formations. They are approaching level with the bomber, as opposed to

---

Group Historical Association has also organized these primary documents for easy public access (306bgus.apollohosting.com) and they make for very interesting reading for those seeking raw reports from the time.

more effective 12 o'clock high, a Mayer tweak of his attack that is widely adopted by the Luftwaffe.

The gunners start to cry out directions of incoming fighters, and the call over the radio is "12 o'clock." Without such directional warnings, there's almost no way for a gunner to track and shoot at a fighter as it streaks in to make an attack.

In the *Unmentionable,* Hoot Gibson hears the directional calls over the radio from his crewmen. He fires and sweeps the barking barrel well ahead of an incoming Fw 190. The German's smooth flight takes a jarring angle and it corkscrews down and out of sight, with only a short-lived line of black smoke to mark its passing. Gibson winces because he doesn't see it crash. His crewmen watch it plummet and chronicle its decent, each trying to make the kill official. None can. Gibson chalks it up as a "probable" (as noted in the mission report) and scans for another fighter.

But the Luftwaffe has broken off the attack. The breather is tense as they pass north of Paris—everyone knows the fighters will be back. In the cockpit, Johnson and McKay see a tempting airfield below, but on closer scrutiny they recognize it to be a dummy target. The Germans have been setting these up to confuse recon flights and bombardiers.

As the next wave of fighters begins their attack, Johnson is close enough to them to see that these have leopard spot decorations on the fuselages. Then the airplanes close the distance nose to nose; even in this era of high technology, warfare can still be as personal as a knife fight.

The fighters seem to all be taking advantage of the lack of firepower in the B-17's front. They have Egon Mayer to thank for that. "All crew report there is no way to handle frontal attacks due to limited arc of .50 cal guns," reads the 306th's mission report for the day.

Johnson watches in horror as the fighters sweep over the B-17F *Terry and the Pirates* (41-24489) and stitch it with cannon fire. The crippled airplane falls ponderously out of formation, rolling like a fatally harpooned whale. The German fighters circle like sharks as it falls. Inside, First Lieutenant Lewis McKesson orders a bailout. McKay and Johnson can only watch and hope. There's a surge of relief when the crew begins to appear, parachutes blooming. But there are not enough chutes in the air. One man is killed onboard, two others die in the jump, and the remaining six, including McKesson, are taken prisoner.

The flak starts just before they reach the target. They consider it light, although it damages at least one bomber in the 303rd called the *8 Ball* (41-24581) badly enough that it later crashes in Britain. Its captain, W. R. Calhoun, doesn't think the emergency landing will go well, so he orders his crew to bail out before he tries. Calhoun sticks a belly landing, despite having a wedge of shrapnel in his knee, and he and his crew all return to their air base at Molesworth the next day.

Payback comes at twelve thirty in the afternoon when the formation reaches the German airfield. Each bomber carries ten 500-pound bombs, dropped from 20,000 feet. By the end of the overall attack, 165.5 tons of bombs fall. Workshops and shelters are swept by violent blast waves. One punches through the top of a large hangar, while four smaller airplane shelters are damaged by near misses. Johnson is happy to see his squadron score hits on buildings, exposed aircraft, and the landing field.

But the formations have to get home, and the silver Fw 190s return to harass the bombers all the way back to the coast and beyond. The fighters riddle the *Zombie* (41-24566) after the 303rd clears the French coast, and pilot O. S. Witt ditches in the English Channel. All crewmembers are killed; one airman's corpse washes ashore in Dieppe the next year.

The 306th is likewise ravaged. A second B-17 goes down in flames. The frontal attacks leave terrible wounds on the airplanes. One of the B-17s in the group takes incomprehensible damage: a clipped horizontal stabilizer, a mostly disabled engine, a total loss of the hydraulic and oxygen systems, a shattered nose, and a lack of elevator control. That airplane somehow makes it back to England, a striking testament to the Flying Fortress's toughness. But the group is taking losses; five men are injured, one fatally, when fighter gunfire rakes four bombers. Two crewmen suffer from frozen limbs.

Johnson and his men have survived, unharmed but haunted by the sights of the bombers plummeting from the sky, and the helpless feeling that they can't defend against new attacks. Overall, six B-17s fall to German fighters that day. Luftwaffe fighters drop, too, and bomber crews will claim fifty-three shot down or damaged. (These numbers are always way too high, usually by a factor of three.) The carnage eats away at the nerves. Even the bonds between the crewmen grow, as does their fatalism.

The 306th feels obliged to add a coda to their mission report: "Crews agree this was a rough show."

EAGLE MEETS BULLDOG

January 19, 1943. General Ira Eaker breathes deep as Winston Churchill enters the room. He has thirty minutes to convince the prime minister that he and the entire British senior air staff are flat wrong about U.S. bomber strategy.

Eaker is trying not to be intimidated, but it's hard not to feel overwhelmed while sitting in the prime minister's villa. Churchill himself arrives ready to impress, his bulky frame tucked into a bright blue Air Commodore's uniform. The American general finds Churchill "resplendent."

"Eaker is a soft-spoken Texan with an agile, athletic body," *New York Times* writer Raymond Daniell describes him. "His features, like those of so many men who have devoted most of their lives to flying, have set themselves into sharp, firm lines that make one think of an eagle. He is modest and retiring almost to the point of shyness and he has that unconsciously thoughtful courtesy usually associated with the antebellum South."

After a night of cramming like a student before a test, Eaker is facing one of the most formidable men of the age. Churchill opens with a salvo seemingly meant to wither his opponent: "I understand you are very unhappy about my suggestion to your president that your 8th Air Force join the RAF in night bombing."

So begins a literal armchair debate that will set the course for tens of thousands of airmen, including Maynard Smith.

This is Eaker's big moment, and there are a lot of people depending on his performance. Eaker's mentor, co-author, and boss, Hap Arnold, has manipulated the schedule at Casablanca to make this meeting happen. He's crafted a vision of air warfare over more than a decade, and now it's slipping away.

Franklin Roosevelt doesn't want to cede control over U.S. military personnel and needs Eaker to win this argument. The commanding general of the European theater, Dwight D. Eisenhower, likewise wants as much American control over the eventual invasion of occupied France as possible, and is also counting on him. (He told Eaker that very thing earlier that day.) Eaker's underlings who are putting their theories to the bloody test from English airfields—most notably LeMay—are also expecting him to save the day.

Even General George Patton, in charge of the security at Casablanca, stops by during Eaker's study session to wish him well. Lieutenant Colonel James Parton, Eaker's aide and future 8th Air Force historian, stays up with him to prepare, and the "James Parton Papers" kept by the U.S. Air Force Historical Research Agency provide the descriptions of the events of the critical day.

The crux of the debate centers on the continuation of daylight bombing by American warplanes. The British abandoned the tactic in favor of nighttime raids, accepting the more dangerous formation flying and lack of accuracy for the security of darkness. (German radar will continue to plague day and night efforts.) The Americans have other plans, and trained their crews to fly and fight in the sun. So far, they have hundreds of dead airmen and few signs of progress to show for it. They haven't even bombed Germany yet.

So the British are now asking—close to demanding—that the 8th Air Force join them in nighttime attacks, preferably under RAF command. The idea is to set up an Eisenhower-esque figure to oversee the entire air effort. The prime minister has gone so far to suggest the Americans stop building B-17s, and use its industrial might to produce waves of British bombers instead. Stocked with American crews, this overwhelming air assault would incinerate German cities.

This is distasteful to the 8th Air Force leadership, who doesn't think this unrestricted style of warfare jibes with the nation's values. "The bomber, like the snake in the grass, is a particularly nasty fellow," Eaker writes before the war. "He was unpopular with all and sundry because of his ability to drop high explosives, not always well aimed, at some establishments and peoples heretofore believed safe from molestation of warfare."

Precision strikes from heavy bombers are the American solution to make bombing palatable and effective. But the 8th Air Force cannot fight without British support on the ground, giving the PM enormous leverage to have the campaign unfold his way.

Arnold himself has spoken to Churchill to plead for daytime bombing, but failed to convince him. So he places a "panicked" call to Eaker in Europe to come to Casablanca. "The president is under pressure from the prime minister to abandon day bombing," Arnold tells Eaker.

"If our leaders are that stupid, count me out," Eaker says, losing his characteristic calm. "I don't want any part of such nonsense."

Now, after a day of travel and a night of preparation, he has to coolly plead his case to the one man who can make all the difference. This half-hour interview will decide the fate of tens of thousands of aviators, and set a course for American airpower forever.

Eaker digs into his notes, a point-by-point rundown of his view from the front and the latest tactical experiments. He hands the prime minister a memo called "The Case for Daylight Bombing." It concludes:

> Day bombing is the bold, the aggressive, the offensive thing to do. It is the method and the practice which will put the greatest pressure on Germany, wreak the greatest havoc to his wartime industry and the greatest reduction to his air force. The operations of the next 90 days will demonstrate in convincing manner the truth of these conclusions.

The PM doesn't seem especially receptive, but at least he's showing a real interest. "If the RAF continues night bombing and we bomb by day, we shall bomb them round the clock and the devil shall get no rest," Eaker says dramatically.

Churchill doesn't need to be sold on the idea that bombers can cripple Germany. He's been espousing that line for years, in part because that was the only thing his nation could do to hit back after they had been chased from France. But by early 1943 he and FDR are facing the reality that a ground invasion will be needed in Europe, as appealing as simply crushing the Nazis with airpower sounds.

"We look forward to mass invasion of the Continent by liberating armies," Churchill says scant weeks before Casablanca. "All the same, it would be a mistake to cast aside our original thought—which is strong in American minds—that severe, ruthless bombing of Germany on an ever-increasing scale will not only cripple her war effort, including U-boat and aircraft production, but also will create conditions intolerable to the mass of the German population."

What Eaker is promising today is what he and Arnold have been lobbying for since they co-authored books in the 1930s. Their theory: long-range aircraft can cripple an industrial nation with bombing campaigns without resorting to mass civilian casualties. The B-17 is built for this purpose.

It's important to note that there's no good evidence that daylight bombing is working at this point. One study commissioned by the Air Force in 1998 sums up the Army Air Forces' self-assessment of its strategic bombing campaign at the time as "illusory."

At the start of 1943 there are too few bombers available to cripple anything but the occasional submarine schedule. No one really knows how effective the results will be when the mission planners attack Germany, but Eaker nonetheless predicts the Nazi war machine could collapse under the bombers' onslaught. Their ace in the hole is the Norden bombsight, which promises unparalleled accuracy.

The U.S. will buy ninety thousand bombsights from Norden at a cost of $1.5 billion between 1933 and 1945. The device is trailblazing and smart, using a set of gyroscopes to stabilize the platform that the bombardier uses to aim. The Norden calculates the best course and aim point with direct communication between the bombsight and autopilot.

Despite the secrecy surrounding its creation, the Germans already have the design in hand. Herman Lang, a spy working at the Carl L. Norden Company, delivered one to Germany in 1938. He's been sitting in a jail cell since 1941 when the so-called Duquesne spy ring is exposed. It turns out the system is not too different than ones the Nazis are developing, anyway.

The Norden may automatically calculate the bomb release but it requires daylight to aim; the entire day bombing plan revolves around this piece of equipment. The Army Air Forces believes each B-17 has a 1.2 percent probability of placing bombs within a 1000-

foot radius of the target from altitudes of 20,000 feet. This statistic is critical, since that's how war planners extrapolate the total number of bombers—251 combat groups—they say they need to cripple the Axis. In other words, 220 bombers would be needed to achieve a 93 percent probability of one or more bullseye on any given target.

The early results are not promising, but Eaker chooses to call it growing pains. Combat trials from 1942 are indicating that cloudy weather and evasive maneuvering are hampering the bombsight's accuracy. There are a host of other problems that go undiagnosed. Military scientists didn't understand the aerodynamic subtleties at work on a bomb dropping at supersonic speeds. Even the paint can influence where they will fall.

Eaker has limited information on real-world use of the slick bombsight. The first widespread mission using the Norden isn't even expected until March. But he promises a groundbreaking campaign of heavy, precise strikes anyway.

As the war continues, the stats will never go the Norden's way. The 8th Air Force ends up putting 31.8 percent of its bombs within 1,000 feet from an average altitude of 21,000 feet; that's nearly the same as British night bombers that use targeting radar.

The biggest gap in Eaker's logic is the belief that the bombers can protect themselves. Since October, American pilots have taken over escort duties, but they are flying the same short-range British Spitfires. These can hardly reach Antwerp, Belgium, and really only provide protection over the English Channel and fringes of France. In other words, the bombers have to fly the most dangerous parts of the mission without any help. And the casualty rates reflect this, if one cares to look.

But Eaker is putting a positive spin on what he sees as the lessons of the air war in 1942. "Our bombing experience to date indicates that the B-17 with its 12 .50-caliber guns can cope with the German day fighter, if flown in close formation," Eaker says in October. "I think it is safe to say that a large force of day bombers can operate without fighter cover against material objectives anywhere in Germany, without excessive losses."

You can say that Eaker wanted to believe in the airplane and a more humane way of waging war, so much so that he lost the ability to be objective. But he presents statistics—indeed, uses them to correct the prime minister—that show the U.S. bomber losses are at 2 percent, almost half the British tally. But that statistic includes mostly short-range missions with fighter escorts. According to the actual mission records, losses on missions without escorts shoot up to 7 percent.

Eaker doesn't bring up this nuance. The long missions into Germany that he is promising will have no escorts, so one would assume the anticipated loss rate would be closer to the higher figure. But Eaker thinks that the loss rates will go down as the number of bombers on each mission rises. The larger formations mean more defensive guns to ward off the German fighters. This argument ignores the fact that the bombers he needs are being siphoned off to other theaters. The first year of the U.S. air campaign predictably will be hamstrung by the lack of aircraft. Missions will continue nonetheless.

Eaker's message to Churchill is that the lessons have been learned. "We have built up slowly and painfully and learned our job in a new theater against a tough enemy," Eaker finishes, according to Parton. "Now we are ready for the job we all cherish—daylight bombing of Germany. Be patient, give us our chance, and your reward will be ample."

Eaker is floored when Churchill hands back the memo—and yields. "Young man, you have not convinced me that you are right," he says. "But you have persuaded me that you should have further opportunity to prove your contention. How fortuitous would it be if we could bomb the devils around the clock."

Churchill may be giving the Americans a diplomatic win as part of a larger gambit at Casablanca, where he and Roosevelt continue to horse-trade as they form a strategy for the invasion of Europe. And he knows that a round-the-clock bomber offensive will take a toll on the Luftwaffe, and wresting the skies from them will be necessary for any impending invasion of France.

The political leadership is adamant when it comes to attacking targets in France. "Everybody at the Casablanca Conference concurred that two arms of German military might pose alarming immediate danger to the entire Allied effort—the U-boats and the Luftwaffe," Parton writes. "They were designated the first and second priority targets for both Eaker and Harris."

After some horse-trading, the Americans after Casablanca do enjoy a slightly freer hand when it comes to targeting. "Eaker was no longer obliged to pour bombs on the impregnable concrete sub pens in France but could go after submarine assembly yards wherever they existed," Parton writes.

Churchill remains unconvinced the B-17 is up to the task, or that precision bombing is possible. Churchill figures the Americans will at least start night operations with the RAF after their piles of dead airmen climb too high. "I had regretted that so much effort had been put into the daylight bombing," he writes after his meeting with Eaker. "And still thought that a concentration upon night bombing by the Americans would have resulted in far larger delivery of bombs on Germany."

If the Yanks want to fly into a bloodbath, Churchill figures he'll let them. They'll just have to learn the hard way.

LEAVING CASPER

February 7, 1943. It's the end of Maynard Smith's pre-combat training. The Army Air Force has shuttled him around the nation to get him ready for war, from Texas to Idaho and now Casper Army Airfield, Wyoming. But the funny thing is, although he has received a lot of training, he still doesn't feel all that prepared.

The 464th Bombardment Squadron (BS) here in Wyoming trains crews to work together inside the B-17. The training squadron has only been here since September, and the parts of the base that the bomber trainees use are a sprawling complex of quickly built houses and far-flung weapons ranges.

It's cold here, which he doesn't like, but as a Michigan man he's used to it. The effects of the base's 5,000-foot elevation and the ever-present vista of the towering Laramie Mountain Range on the horizon, however, are both new.

Casper itself is a small western town of about eighteen thousand people, most of them friendly to the Army. The Great Depression gutted two industries that kept Casper afloat: agriculture and oil. Last year's construction of hundreds of buildings put a lot of money in local pockets, and leaves a good impression with the locals. The airmen get a day a week to explore. The town has a theater and cafés, and a dance academy if you wanted to leer at some lithe young women. Casper Mountain is also close, for those who want to ride a horse to see the ice-shrouded waterfalls there.

But most of the crews' time here is spent training. There are six bomb and gunnery ranges, tucked in remote areas that the crews have to find. The airmen fly day and night here, often with little warning. The mess hall never closes for flight crews.

Smith enjoys the plane, but like most others going through the program, he's getting the feeling the Army is rushing its trainees. It's like they are just trying to get crews into the air enough times to check the boxes and then ship them out to fight.

He may think that, as replacements, they are getting cavalier treatment. It's true that replacement units run a shorter course here, one that skips all the "integrated" training events meant to bolster crew cooperation. After all, these guys are being dropped into combat with relative strangers in existing units.

But questionnaires filled out by AAF fliers in combat express frustration from both whole crews and replacements alike. The feeling is widespread in 1942 and 1943 that the training time in Casper didn't prepare them for the real show.

One glaring gap between reality and training are the altitudes from which the bombers are dropping their loads. In Casper the B-17s do not fly above 20,000 feet, but the average bomb run in Europe is considerably higher. (In the Pacific, the average altitude is even greater.) There are two very good reasons to fly so high. At those altitudes there are fewer flak cannons that can reach the formations. Also, Fw 190s lose a lot of their advantages in thin air.

There are trade-offs. Bombing equipment acts squirrely, guns freeze, unprotected skin sticks to metal surfaces. At 25,000 feet and above, the B-17 tends to spew oil from the crankcase. Aside from the danger of losing that much oil, the leak accumulates on the tail and freezes the control surfaces there. And 11 percent of the bombing missions at the time are taking place between 26,000 and 28,000 feet.

The flight surgeons have been writing reports regarding the average bomb run altitude in Europe since 1942. In '42 and '43, 78 percent of the bombs are dropped from over 23,000 feet.[5] But there's not a lot of concern shown by command.

Part of this is just plain ignorance. There's little understanding of the problems caused by putting unpressurized aircraft at 25,000 feet and expecting the crews inside to function. There's almost no medical literature; the flight surgeons are too busy qualifying crews to bother with academia. Hell, the physiological department of the Air Surgeon's Office is not created until 1942, *six years* after the development of the B-17.

---

5   The USAAF finally recommends increasing the training altitude to reflect combat realities—in September 1944.

The training at Casper is inherently dangerous. On February 26, 1943, a second lieutenant and his crew of nine from the 61st Bomb Squadron took the B-17 *Casper Kid* on a training mission toward a bombing range northwest of Glenrock. The pilot, snow blind and lost, crashes the airplane into a mountain. All ten men are killed.

By the end of the war, at least 130 officers and enlisted men will die in crashes during training exercises at Casper. Pilots complain that they don't have enough relevant practice with formation flying and how to fly on instruments alone, which given the weather happens all too often in England.

Gunners have their own specific complaints about their training at Casper. There's too much classwork and not enough shooting. Instead of air-to-air gunnery, the crews have more air-to-ground practice than they'll need. There's not much call for strafing attacks—any B-17 fighting that close to the ground is in a lot of trouble.

Smith derives no comfort from the instructors who visit Wyoming from Europe. These jaded men are a source of gallows humor and ghastly stories, but their practical advice all too often points out the flaws in the preparations here.

All these men did was add ghastly details of all the threats they were learning they would face, as chronicled in official mission reports: Those bulky heated suits break all the time, so get ready for frostbite. Those guns will jam and freeze. Expect oxygen lines to clog; men quietly die from anoxia, without anyone even noticing it. Especially ball turret gunners, all alone in their Plexiglas ball. Not that he knows what that position feels like; Smith accrues the token number of flight hours by firing a .50 cal only from the waist gun position.

After training in Wyoming, Smith receives his orders; his military records show he leaves for England on March 3 to join the 306th Bomb Group at an air base called Thurleigh. He will later tell family that he left the United States for the front without ever having flown in a ball turret.

CHAPTER 3

THE "UNBEARABLE" NUMBERS

March 14, 1943. Dr. Thurman Shuller sits in his office at Thurleigh airfield in England. The lieutenant colonel and 306th Bomb Group surgeon knows what he's doing is right. But he's also putting his neck out and launching a punch at people way above his weight class. The doctor's letter is addressed to the 306th commanding officer, Colonel Claude Putnam, but it's aimed at the 8th Air Force's top commanders.

Shuller looks over the words he's just typed and imagines the reaction from General Eaker. He's telling them that the crews of the 306th are experiencing "unbearable casualties in personnel and planes, yet at the same time realizing their effort hadn't done one thing to further the war effort."

The twenty-nine-year-old flight surgeon is not one to buck the system. As a farm boy taught in a two-room schoolhouse in Arkansas, he's worked hard to first graduate from the University of Arkansas School of Medicine and later to qualify as a flight surgeon. He takes his role as a doctor seriously, and what he's seeing in Europe needs to be addressed.

He's been with the 306th for a year, joining the first crews as they trained in Wendover, Utah, in April 1942. Now those same men are dying in staggering numbers over Europe and the survivors are showing clear signs of cracking. A bold letter may put Shuller's career at risk, but the crisis is real and the responsibility to make a stand is his.

Shuller's "Combat Expectancy of Fliers" puts sobering statistics to the gaps in formations and empty beds in barracks. He finds that the average bomber crew of ten can expect to survive about fourteen missions. By the early weeks of 1943, the 306th had lost almost 80 percent of its original combat crews. "The fliers were actually saying among themselves that the only apparent hope of survival in the theatre of war is either to become a prisoner of war or to get 'the jitters' and be removed from combat," he writes.

Setting a mission limit "would be an invaluable morale factor in giving these men at least a small hope for the future and a goal for which to survive."

Since the letter is meant for the higher-ups, Shuller's report notes that none other than Eaker has already suggested a mission cap. "Of this I am certain and you can count upon it," the doctor quotes the general. "A combat crew must be told what their combat expectancy is. And they must be told that when they have completed that period they will never again be required to man a combat crew station in an airplane on operations against the enemy."

Shuller is clearly asking Eaker to make good on these words. Putnam now has a choice: endorse the letter and send it up the chain of command, or try to bury it. For him, it's no choice at all. Putnam is a frontline leader who is not shy about calling out the inferiority of other bombing groups. Some of his mission reports are nothing less than scathing. He also sees the same corrosion of morale among his men. He endorses the letter and sends it to the 8th Air Force. He'll later describe Shuller as a "jealous guardian of rights and privileges of combat crew personnel."

Eaker knows the 306th well; earlier that year he personally inter-vened to replace the group's leadership. Back in November, as the VIII Bomber Command commander, he visited the 306th at Thurleigh with Major General Carl Spaatz, the 8th Air Force commander. They can't help but see lax security and the overall sloppy condition of the crews.

When Eaker becomes head of the 8th Air Force in January, he targets the 306th for change. "Eaker waited six more weeks, during which the group's record, measured by number of bombs on target and by B-17s lost, became the worst in VIII Bomber Command," ac-cording to Eaker's aide, the ever-chronicling James Parton.

The man they blame is Colonel Charles "Chip" Overacker, the 306th commander. He's been with his crews since they formed the group in Utah, and he enjoys being close to his men. He drinks with them at so-cial events, makes sure to fly the dangerous missions, and makes every attempt to be liked as well as respected. And his men do love him.

Eaker perceives this as a problem; his diagnosis is that Overacker is too emotionally close to his command, too tightly bound with his men to enforce the strict, nearly murderous discipline needed to get the job done. Overacker feels each KIA and MIA, maybe too much.

On January 4, 1943, Eaker—by then promoted to major general and moved up to succeed Spaatz as commander of 8th Air Force—returns to Thurleigh. With him is Colonel Frank Armstrong Jr., former commander of the 97th Bomb Group. Armstrong is Eaker's turnaround expert. He led the first B-17 mission over Europe in August 1942.

With zero ceremony Eaker relieves Overacker and installs Arm-strong as the group leader. "In the next 40 days, Armstrong's strong, steady, disciplinary hand turned the 306th around completely, mak-ing it the best group in the VIII Bomber Command and the first to drop bombs on Germany itself," Parton writes.

Beirne Lay is also on the trip as an aide. He will later co-write the novel *12 O' Clock High*, which fictionalizes these very events (and makes Egon Mayer's frontal attacks famous). Names are changed, and the 306th is tripled to become the 918th, but the depiction is fairly close to the real events. It's also emotionally accurate, capturing the despair and psychological damage of aerial combat in ways media at the time—and now—usually fails to capture. "We're in a war, a shooting war," the Armstrong stand-in tells an assembly of men. "We've got to fight. And some of us have got to die. I'm not trying to tell you not to be afraid. Fear is normal. But stop worrying about it and about your-selves. Stop making plans. Forget about going home. Consider your-selves already dead. Once you accept that idea, it won't be so tough."

Armstrong never suffers a nervous breakdown, as happens to his fictional analog. He returns to bomber command headquarters af-ter a few months and is promoted to brigadier general. Colonel Claude Putnam replaces him, filling some big shoes.

And now it seems the morale problems persist, even within this supposedly fixed bomber group.

The letter from Shuller prompts Eaker to act; he also knows mo-rale is an issue that can ruin daylight bombing. He also knows that this new form of combat is asking a lot of his men. For a leader so determined to put his crews in absurd danger, he's also attuned to their needs and they count on him to be a reliable advocate.

Three weeks after the report is issued, Eaker announces that any flier who reaches twenty-five missions will be done with combat flights, if he so chooses. There is now a reason to hope, as the number becomes a goal for crews to focus on. But the fatalism doesn't recede. The math still leaves a flier feeling hopeless—no crew has finished twenty-five missions without losing a man—but a long shot is better than none.

SPIRITS CONSIDERABLY DAMPENED

March 22, 1943. Lewis Page Johnson Jr. sits in the cockpit of his B-17, scanning the area ahead. Johnson, now a B-17 captain, is closing in on the docking area of the docks at Wilhelmshaven, Germany. Although the clouds are thick, he can see pillars of dark smoke rising from the ground ahead, coming from the target area.

Other bomb groups have preceded the 306th Bomb Group's attack, and the fires are encouraging signs that they hit something important. But there is lighter, white smoke drifting over the target area as well, and Johnson surmises that the Germans have ignited smoke screens to obscure the docks.

The expanse of sky outside the windscreen is a relief compared to a busy B-17 cockpit. Switches, dials, levers, maps, and radio equipment crowd Johnson's world. The B-17's interior seems designed to create fatigue.

"The coordinated operations of all these gadgets would be difficult in the swivel-chair comfort of your office," the Army Air Forces' surgeon general, Major General David Grant, says in 1944. "But reduce your office to a five-foot cube size, engulf it in the constant roar of engines, and increase your height to around five miles . . . that will give you an idea of the normal conditions under which these men worked out the higher mathematical relationships of engine revolutions, manifold and fuel pressures, aerodynamics, barometric pressure, altitude, wind drift, airspeed, groundspeed, position, and direction."

This inhuman demand stems from the need for longer missions into enemy territory, and the development of warplanes that fly longer, farther, and higher. These tech trends put the aircrews into almost otherworldly horrific combat conditions. It's unbearably cold at bombing altitudes; temperatures could reach 55 below zero Fahrenheit.

Johnson can see the flak clouds hammering the sky at his planned altitude of 27,000 feet. Most of the bursts are below and to the rear of 306th planes. He's glad for this, since the tactic is to fly straight at the target. After "bombs away" the airplanes lurch slightly, rising as they are relieved of their loads.

When Lieutenant Johnson becomes a command pilot, he plucks crewmates who have served with him in McKay's crew, and with each other, to fight alongside. "Hoot" Gibson, James Hobbs, and Raymond Henn are all onboard. Joining them are Stanley Kisseberth and Kenneth Powell.

Henn, the plumber from Queens, is manning a waist gun. This attack on this dockyard is his twentieth mission; he's nearing the end of his tour. But he can see shapes following the formation at a distance, predators stalking the herd. These are German airplanes, gathering by the dozens just out of range of their own flak. The full diversity of the Nazi fighter family is on terrifying display: Fw 190s, Messerschmitt Bf 109s and Bf 110s, and Junkers Ju 88s. The response sends a message: this is the reception you can expect when you try to bomb Germany.

And then they attack, a swarm of thirty fighters wheeling and diving in groups of three as the bombers approach their target. Four enemy aircraft are reported hit, three confirmed killed. Henn sweeps his .50 and sprays an oncoming fighter; it spirals away spewing dark smoke, and he's credited with a shootdown. The record shows that the Bomb Group alone fires 38,637 rounds during the mission.

When the crew makes it to the target, the fighters peel off and the flak begins. The shells detonate toward the rear of the 306th airplanes; Johnson sees that the antiaircraft gunners are also shooting a little high, which is bad news for those at the top of the formation.

Across the whole mission, sixty-nine B-17s and fifteen B-24s drop 224 tons of 1,000-pound high explosive M44 bombs. Despite the smoke and the clouds, the 306th crews watch the bomb impacts and see some blasts close to the German vessel *Sheer*. Now it's time to go home, and that means wading through the swarm of re-forming fighters.

Henn and Powell hear the other gunners call out the direction of an approaching fighter, and the fuselage suddenly fills with a whirl of fragments and the powerful rush of freezing air. Powell feels an impact on his leg and collapses. He numbly sees a new, gaping hole in the fuselage, and then sees Henn in a bloody heap. His face is gone, blown off by a 20mm shell. The stricken plane continues home.

One B-17 and a pair of B-24s are shot down. Ten B-24s and a dozen B-17s are damaged, wounding eighteen airmen, including Powell. Some are hit badly enough to inspire bailouts; the mission ends with thirty-two "missing" airmen, most of whose deaths can't be confirmed.

About half the airmen who leap from the bombers fight again. Those who do return are temporarily assigned to tour other air bases to share their survival stories of escape and evasion.

With Henn gone, Johnson and his crew have lost a trusted friend. The rest of the squadron also feels it keenly, especially since he was on the cusp of going home. The Combat Diary of the 423rd Bombardment Squadron records the final verdict: "Though this was a successful mission, our spirits were considerably dampened when we learned Sergeant Henn had been hit."

Just five more missions to get to twenty-five, Johnson thinks. Just five more.

MARCEL'S MONKEY

April 11, 1943. It's Maynard Smith's first full day at Thurleigh airfield. He's a staff sergeant, making $96 a month, nearly double what a private makes, with a foreign country to explore. The excitement of promotion and travel is tempered by the mood at the base. Mission cap or no, the men here are grim.

Any new arrival catches the doomed vibe early. Smith hears about the stats from airmen who figured they were going to die. "The saying went: the first time out you were due back, the second time out you're not coming back," he says.

Smith got his first glimpses of England at war in April as he shuttled the 125 miles from the 11th Combat Crew Replacement Center at Bovingdon, close to the Isle of Wight, to his home base of Thurleigh. Spitfires streak overhead and barrage balloons stand alert on the horizon.

Thurleigh air base isn't *in* the English countryside; it *is* the English countryside. The bombers are tucked into protective revetments that are spaced out between fields and farmhouses. In between these rural homes are stretches of pastoral land, straight from a Robin Hood picture book.

The revetments, holding two to four planes, are about a quarter of a mile apart. The layout helps hide the air base from the Luftwaffe and will limit the damage from German aerial attacks. Airplanes land on a main runway, and then taxi around a perimeter track to their homes. Jeeps, trucks, and ever-present bicycles shuttle airmen around the base. Any vehicles with lights are fixed with slats to keep their telltale glare to a minimum.

Crews are tucked into barracks, mostly Nissen and Quonset huts, with each window draped with a blackout curtain. There are fourteen other men with Smith in his hut. Inside are metal bed frames, wooden tables, coal stoves, dented coffee pots, and radios broadcasting the BBC and, when that went off air, the German's *Nachtsmusik* program. Airmen catch that two-hour, nightly broadcast from Berlin, piggybacking on the Nazi effort to entertain night-shift workers at factories. Any morale boost is welcome: the muddy roads and crude facilities are a constant—and valid—source of griping.

The British trained its pilots (and Polish airmen) at Thurleigh until December 1942, when the RAF handed the entire base to the Americans. It's one of the first to host U.S. bombers, part of the overall British red-carpet treatment. Churchill is demanding but he's also appreciative. More and more real estate is being handed over, and more bustling U.S. air bases spring up like boomtowns.

The village of Thurleigh has a few small pubs, but many bomber crews prefer to venture five miles into the nearby city of Bedford to unwind. There's even a Liberty Truck to taxi the men there and back. There are also bicycles, everywhere. Smith has been trapped with teens since he was forced to enlist. The allure of spending time with people of his own age is undeniable. And the towns are where the women are.

But being so close to the war, it's hard for a new arrival to do anything but try to fit into the surroundings, pay attention to the new cycle of between-mission training, and keep the growing fear under control. Or at least under wraps.

The trip here was an adventure in and of itself. Crews who train together usually travel together, but replacement airmen hitch rides as passengers in new B-17s to get to their assigned air bases in England. The replacements are assigned to squadrons as full ten-man units, with each position accounted for. So Smith arrives as a gunner with First Lieutenant James Lear, with each man inside assigned to the 423rd squadron, the "Grim Reapers."

Staff Sergeant Robert Folliard, a twenty-seven-year-old from Queens, is one of Lear's crew. Until the war erupts he works as a repairman in New York City after three years of high school. He enlists in January 1942, volunteers for gunnery school, and a little more than a year later, he's a B-17 replacement on the way to the air war over Europe.

The flight across the Atlantic is a long one for a B-17 and requires stops for refueling. There are several ferry routes, and many of them go through Africa. Once the Allies took desert air bases in North Africa from the Vichy French forces, they became vital links in the American soft invasion of England. Obscure airfields like Atar and Tindouf become bustling hubs of transiting military aircraft.

Among Smith's memorabilia is a faded photo of a desert scene, so picturesque that it belongs on a movie set. Smith has scrawled the name of the oasis, but the image is torn and the words lost. On the top, complete with an arrow pointing at a building on a hilltop, it says "MY QUARTERS." The back identifies the shot as taken at Tindouf. This was most likely taken during a stop during his flight into England.

All the travel and excitement has occupied his mind. But now that he's settled down in Thurleigh, Smith finds the air base claustrophobic and unwelcoming. He and other new arrivals are at a social disadvantage. As replacements, the Lear crew won't stick together, but rather will be assigned to various airplanes when needed. So there is no inherent crew bond to rely on.

The bombing has only gone on since February but callousness has already formed. No one wants to befriend the new guys since they may be dead soon. Some are literally heckled on the way in, called "fresh meat."

Smith finds that death is nonchalant and impersonal. He'll later tell his son: "If somebody got killed and didn't come back, everybody would just go over to his bed and open up his locker and just take what they wanted. You know? It was just like, 'Well, okay. You know, John can't use it anymore, so you know, I need these shoes, and you know, you need these socks.'"

Happily, there will be at least one familiar face here in England, if he ever gets here, that is. Marcel St. Louis's ferry flight has been delayed, but he and his crew of replacements should be here any minute. Smith's eager to hear the story of what happened. When the two gunners reunite at Thurleigh, he's not disappointed.

St. Louis catches a ferry flight from the United States that connects through Marrakesh as an unlisted passenger on the B-17 *T'aint a Bird* (42-3090). He's not the only one; the crew has picked up a spider monkey as a mascot, and they leave for England with "Tojo" onboard.

The *T'aint a Bird* leaves Africa for England on April 7, but the navigator follows an errant radio signal and gets the airplane good and lost. Bad weather compounds the problem. The pilot, First Lieutenant Willie Thomas, is running out of fuel. He thinks they may be over Nazi-occupied Norway, and foresees a disaster. But he has to set the bomber down, and he circles a stretch of bog near the shoreline. There's a town nearby and he knows that its residents can see the massive airplane circling overhead—the reception when they land could be hostile. Out of options, Thomas safely sets the airplane down in the soft earth.

Local militiamen arrive on the scene, and the crew sighs with relief as they realize that the B-17 has landed in neutral Ireland. This neutrality is routinely broken in many ways, most significantly through use of select air corridors, sharing Irish intelligence reports with the Allies, and providing weather reports.

The town Thomas spotted is a sleepy seaside town called Clonakilty. Irish home guardsmen from there gather up the crew. The official policy would be for the crew to be brought to officials and locked up. Instead, the guardsmen deliver the B-17 crew to a hotel, where they are to be "interned." The unexpected arrival sparks a multiple-day party. Locals swarm the hotel to meet the crew, and to buy them and their monkey a drink.

It only takes a day of this before Tojo drops dead. The cause of death is unknown, but the cold weather and alcohol are certainly suspect. The crew lays the simian out on a freshly made bed and the town lines up, state funeral–style, to file past the little corpse and pay their respects. The scene in the small town is getting surreal. But the airplane can't take off in the soft ground, so they have nothing to do but wait for permission to leave for England, and keep drinking.

Four days after the emergency landing, the crew of the *T'aint a Bird* leaves by truck. In the weeks ahead, locals will help build a makeshift runway for a new crew, which arrives weeks later to fly

T'aint a Bird to England. The landing inspires a local legend, one the Irish will enshrine in folklore, romance novels, and even a musical. One day, decades after St. Louis's adventure, city officials will even erect a statue of Tojo in downtown Clonakilty.

APEX PREDATOR

April 16, 1943. Lieutenant Josef "Sepp" Wurmheller takes a deep breath as he begins his takeoff from the Luftwaffe airfield at Vannes-Meuçon, sixty miles north of Saint-Nazaire. The fighter increases speed down the 1,600-yard grass runway. The Fw 190 is built for such unimproved landing strips. When the fighter reaches 170 mph, Wurmheller pulls back on the control stick and the fighter lurches into the air.

He's an ace with more than sixty victories in his ledger, so he's not nervous. He's eager. This is his first significant attack since he became the *Staffelkapitän* (squadron leader) of 9/*Jagdgeschwader* 2 two weeks ago.[6] It's his squadron and he's ready to make his mark. But the weather's been bad and the enemy bombers haven't been approaching the Lorient area, including Saint-Nazaire, which the 9/JG 2 is tasked with protecting.

But to Wurmheller's delight, there is now a formation heading into his clutches: dozens of B-17s dispatched to strike a power station serving a naval base in Lorient.

Wurmheller has a handsome, brooding look. His eyes are set slightly apart, nearly lazy but instead somehow predatory, like he can see more sky than anyone else. He's comfortable in the air, despite working for years as a miner in Bavaria.

Wurmheller's an accomplished member of the glider movement

---

6   *Gruppen* are designated with Roman numerals, then comes the abbreviated *Geschwader* designation. For example, the third *Gruppe* of *Jagdgeschwader* 2 would be designated III/JG 2.

that swept through Germany in between wars. Military service means the chance to fly airplanes with engines, and by the summer of 1938, Wurmheller is serving with JG 2. He records his first victory—a British single-engine bomber—in September 1939. Wurmheller's also an accomplished dogfighter who claims thirteen Spitfires in four weeks in the summer of 1941.

By September 1941 his tally sits at thirty victories. The experienced pilot is taken from France to serve as an instructor and, briefly, to fight on the Eastern Front where he scores ten more kills. When he comes back to the Channel front in May 1942, he picks up where he left off—making life miserable for the bomber crews. In June alone he claims another eleven victories.

Wurmheller rises to Luftwaffe legend during the ugly Allied ground raid at Dieppe on August 19, 1942. Around 60 percent of the six-thousand-man ground force are killed, wounded, or captured that day; the RAF loses 106 aircraft to the Luftwaffe's 48. "Sepp" is in the thick of the action when he heads to base to rearm and refuel. He crashes on the way in, breaking a leg and suffering a mild concussion. The pilot receives a cast and then limps back to another Fw 190, where he takes off to continue fighting. Wurmheller claims seven victories during the day, scored before and after his painful landing, bringing his total number to sixty.

Government propagandists publish a photo of the grimacing pilot sliding from the cockpit in newspapers, making him a bona fide hero of Dieppe. "A broken foot in plaster and his first sortie curtailed by an emergency landing during which he sustained a slight concussion, then climbing into another aircraft and dispatching seven opponents," the caption reads. "That's *Oberleutnant* Wurmheller."

He's quickly promoted to lieutenant, where he continues his aerial rampage along the French coast. When the squadron leader is promoted, he's tapped to replace him. Wurmheller reports to Egon

Mayer, the fellow glider alumni. By then, Mayer has sixty-two shoot-downs and downed a pair of RAF Hawker Typhoons in late February. A major since July, Mayer leads the entirety of JG 2 and right now is in the air near Wurmheller.

The Fw 190s climb quickly and head toward the expected track of the bombers. Wurmheller appreciates the radar and electronic intercepts that tell him when to take off, but all he needs to intercept the B-17s in the sky today are the vapor trails behind the fifty-nine bombers, long contrails at 25,000 feet that can be seen for miles.

That altitude is problematic. The Fw 190 loses a lot of potency over 20,000 feet. The radial engines suck in the thin air, sapping power and forcing pilots to go faster to compensate. The wings are also too short to handle the lack of air density, which risks stalls and makes sharp turns dangerous. This is why an otherwise inferior fighter, the Bf 109, remains in the air. It has a variable speed super-charger that gives an extra oomph needed at high altitudes.

That doesn't stop the Fw 190s from trying. Wurmheller climbs to take a position just outside the formation's range. He knows Mayer is eyeing the formation, looking for opportunities. Some of the formations are loose, leaving gaps in the defenses that a talented fighter pilot can exploit.

Wurmheller is seeing the results of a new tactic that the B-17 pilots have been ordered to try: fly to the target at a lower altitude and then climb steeply to 24,000 feet at their top speed of 170 mph to set up for the bomb run. The bomber pilots know this plan is impossible as dictated to them—the pitch of the nose can only go so high before the airplane stalls in the thinning air. They try anyway.

The result is disabled engines. Those that make it, like the *Memphis Belle,* have to reassemble to fill the gaps left by all the airplanes that abort the mission. "We burned up a lot of precious fuel in that maneuver, we wandered out of formation, and we arrived at the target low on gas and scattered across the sky," recalls the *Belle*'s pilot, Robert Morgan, in his memoir *The Man Who Flew the Memphis Belle*. "Luckily for us we were able to reform into tight formations before they came after us."

The B-17s are on their straight and level bomb run. The flak isn't thick and it isn't inaccurate, and the German fighters duck in and out of it. The bombers and fighters exchange shots in gunfights that are each just a few seconds long. The 303rd BG notes: "There were 20–25 single engine enemy fighters that attacked the Group in the vicinity of Lorient. *Old Faithful* (42-5360), piloted by First Lieutenant James McDonald, was badly damaged, but fought off the enemy aircraft, shooting down two."

The bombs drop, but not from all the airplanes. It seems many B-17s have overshot the target and won't be doing their jobs today. Wurmheller sneaks a glance at the ground and sees a large mass of white smoke forming a crude but effective defensive screen. He also sees impacts blossoming short of the target; the enemy is aiming poorly. The fighters don't knock any B-17s down before they reach the target, but the harassment is spoiling the attack nonetheless. And there's plenty of time to make it hurt as the bombers head home.

Wurmheller positions himself above a B-17 flying at 19,000 feet, and closes the distance to make his attack. The machine guns and cannons rip into the bomber's fuselage and it staggers out of formation. A handful of crew bail out under parachutes. The fighter pilots have no mercy: they know how hard it is to knock out a B-17 even if it's crippled, and they follow the stricken airplanes to ensure its fate.

German records show Mayer downs a B-17 flying at 3,000 feet at the same location and nearly the same time as Wurmheller. This is Mayer's second claimed B-17 of the day, but the 8th Air Force only records one as missing—a nameless B-17 numbered 42-5220, of the 305th, in which half the men onboard die; the rest survive a crash to become prisoners. Like everything else in World War II, the Luftwaffe's battlefield statistics can be murky.

The Germans and Americans alike are amazed at the B-17's resilience; airplanes that they write off as destroyed fly home, albeit missing pieces. Eight B-17s are badly damaged; seven men are wounded.

It's another day of failed experimental tactics. "We never tried rapid climbing again," Morgan says.

About eighty-five miles away, Friedrich May is also on the prowl. He's flying with the 8th squadron of JG 2, based at the Brest-Guipavas airfield. The young pilot has been fighting, and killing, airplanes steadily over the past six months. Now he has a cluster of twenty-five B-24 Liberators heading toward the naval installations at Brest, the exact facilities that 8/JG 2 is tasked to protect.

B-24s don't fare well against Fw 190s. The Luftwaffe considers them easier targets than B-17s, since they have fewer weapons and weaker fuselages. There's a number of ways to attack them: one favored tactic is to approach from behind and above and diving down to hammer at the B-24's rear gunner with 20mm cannons. Without that gunner, other planes can take extra time to safely riddle the bomber from the rear. Frontal attacks also prove brutally effective. And it's even worse when the fighters swarm from multiple directions. As an 8th Air Force mission report from April 16 puts it: "Formations are too small to cope with new attacks of many aircraft at one time."

May gets his kill six miles northwest of Brest, one of three Liberators shot down that day. Nine others are damaged, and one will never fly again. Thirty-one men on B-24s are missing and three wounded.

It's another ineffectual raid for the Allies and another good day for the Luftwaffe. The 8th Air Force lists eleven fighters destroyed, but the usual rule is to divide that number by three for a more accurate tally. That's a handful of German pilots, at best, shot from the sky as opposed to the dozens of Americans who are most certainly gone.

Within days of the mission, the word comes from Luftwaffe command: Mayer is to be awarded the Knight's Cross of the Iron Cross with Oak Leaves (*Ritterkreuz des Eisernen Kreuzes mit Eichenlaub*). He's been summoned to receive the award from Adolf Hitler himself in Berlin.

Wurmheller, who has a front-row seat from which to observe the major's lethal ability, doesn't feel jealous. Without Mayer in the air over Saint-Nazaire and Lorient, there will be more targets for him.

BLOODBATH OVER BREMEN

April 17, 1943. It's 4:15 P.M. Maynard Smith is watching the clock and the skies over Thurleigh. He's not alone—this is the expected time for the airplanes to return from a sizeable bombing raid against Bremen. The crew chiefs, maintenance workers, medics, and firefighters stand quietly, anxious but ready.

Twenty-six bombers of the 306th are assigned to attack a Focke-Wulf factory in Bremen. The group also leads the attack. The 423rd squadron flies, neither he nor Folliard have been assigned to replace a crewman.

This is the squadron's first mission since Smith arrived on April 11, since the Grim Reapers were not tasked to fly the previous day's attack on Saint-Nazaire.

So for now the replacements are watching for the bombers' return. The mission is supposed to be just over six hours long, and the planes left at 9:45 A.M. Two have come back already; one with a blocked oxygen line, the other with engine trouble.

The bombers appear as small specks. And then the red and yellow flares ignite. There's a socket in the pilot's compartment that fits the barrel of a Very pistol. A pull of the trigger sends a flare cartridge out the top of the B-17. It's a simple but effective way to get the ground crews ready for what's coming in without creating unnecessary radio traffic. There are wounded onboard (red) and the aircraft is damaged (yellow). The medics, firefighters, and crew chiefs prepare for the worst.

The B-17s land one by one, those firing flares given priority. Smith counts nine bombers returned. Just nine.

It doesn't take long to hear what happened. The mission went smoothly until the formation began its bomb run, when (according to the squadron's combat diary) "everything popped loose at once." The Germans blanketed the sky with shells, "the most flak ever seen by anyone. It wasn't as concentrated or as accurate as at Saint-Nazaire, but there were many times as many bursts."

This is a classic "barrage" technique that antiaircraft gunners employ. Instead of tracking a group and firing clusters of shells at them, the Germans just choose a sector of sky and fill it with as many shells as possible at as many altitudes as possible. Flying toward a fixed target protected by such a barrage, with orders to stay on a straight and level approach, means plunging into a shrapnel maelstrom.

Today the barrage claims a B-17 piloted by First Lieutenant Warren George. The airplane takes a hit from a flak shell and falls out of formation, to be beset by fighters. Another pilot sees an attacking Fw 190 collide with the bomber's stabilizer before "bombs away." It was last seen on fire, but still under control. Onboard is L. P. Johnson's former crewman, the driver turned gunner Donald Bevan.[7]

---

7 Bevan survives his capture and will one day author *Stalag 17*. The story revolves around American airmen held in a World War II camp, rooting out an

One of the missing airplanes has made an emergency landing at another air base. That leaves ten more missing. Two are downed before reaching the target, six more over Bremen, and two more (including George's) are missing and presumed crashed. The 306th combat diary calls it "the day of the most disastrous raid for the group. In all, ten crews and 100 men were lost."

It could have been worse, if not for the nearly routine acts of heroism inside the formations. A B-17 from the 423rd squadron, piloted by Lieutenant P. E. Youree, limps away from Bremen, motors all but burned out, the hydraulics malfunctioning, and the internal control cables severed. Lieutenant Leroy Sugg, "through his own ingenuity," rigged a parachute harness to the cables so the pilots could steer the bomber back to England.

The 306th takes the bulk of the casualties that day; German fighters tend to focus on one group. The entire 8th Air Force suffers two killed, four wounded, and 159 missing. A day goes by before the pilots and crews receive word on the eighteenth: "Because of our large recent losses, the group was made non-operational in order to give us time to train our new crews and to lick our wounds."

Between January and April, the 306th has the highest casualty rate in the entire 8th Air Force.

New squadrons are coming in and the replacements will be tested for the first time; the bomb group uses the time for intensive training. They are filling the void between training and the actual fight. One 306th combat diary entry describes the pace: "The balance of this month was spent receiving newly-arrived members of the 94th, and teaching them as well as our new crews, morning, noon and night. Classes begin at 8 in the morning and run until 10 at night, seven days a week."

---

informant. The Broadway play by Bevan and Edmund Trzcinski is based on their experiences as prisoners in Stalag 17B in Austria.

So much for exploring the town, thinks Smith, his apprehension growing. It seems that all that gallows humor and fatalism is well deserved.

The Bremen raid is a breaking point for the entire 8th Air Force. It will bring the entire debate over escorts to a head. General Frank Hunter, commander of VIII Bomber Command, uses the mission to lobby for twenty fighter groups to counter growing German fighter opposition. But he wants lots of long-range planes to do the job.

The fighter available in Europe at the time is the P-47 Thunderbolt; Lockheed P-38s in England have been reassigned to North Africa. The 56th Fighter Group is taking their sweet time flying actual missions. They arrived in England in early 1943 but don't see combat until April. His men hate the bulky P-47, preferring the nimble Spitfire. Hunter agrees and has decided that the airplane needs extra armor and his men need more training before they can escort the B-17s. The experimental flights with the P-47 have been lackluster training sorties. Only one German has been shot down by a Thunderbolt, in an April 15 surprise attack from above, taking full advantage of the P-47's ability to dive fast. (Climbing is another story.) In the meantime, one P-47 is shot down and two others lost to engine failures during these early test flights.

But there are hundreds of American airmen dying every week in B-17s and B-24s. Eaker's patience runs out after Bremen. In late April he demands Hunter's P-47s install drop tanks and fully join the fight.

Easier said than done. Hunter's people have been working on a P-47 drop tank, and the results are dismal. The tanks are made of paper, reinforced with resin to make them more resilient. Instead, they leak. Even worse, they don't work at high altitudes because the tanks are unpressurized, preventing the fuel from flowing.

Hunter refuses to adopt drop tanks and so Eaker relieves him, eventually sending him back to the United States to assist fighter training. There, Hunter will do his best to maintain racial segregation in the Army and help foment the so-called "Freeman Field Mutiny" of the Tuskegee Airmen.

It will be the first week in May before the P-47s are assigned to escort missions; a partially pressurized drop tank is also made a research priority. The 306th isn't privy to this political dogfight. They must live with its reality; the stand-down will end soon and they will still be on their own when it matters most.

PICKED TO FLY

On April 23 Marcel St. Louis is officially assigned to the 367th squadron of the 306th. The timing couldn't be worse: the next day Jack Alexander publishes a story in the *Saturday Evening Post* called "The Clay Pigeon Squadron."

It's a surprisingly candid visit with Major Harry Holt, the red-haired, pinched-face squadron commander. The 367th (never identified in the article by its actual number) only deployed in November, and by spring 70 percent of its original crews are gone. "The three nearest neighbors he had in the officer's billet, where he lived until recently, have been killed or otherwise lost to the squadron, and he has seen them all go down over enemy territory," the article says. "The replacements report bright and eager, and pretty soon the vacancies begin appearing among their bunks, too."

This is not what a new bomber crewman wants to read before his first mission. And it's not what their families at home want to hear, either.

The *Saturday Evening Post* is a steady source of flag-waving coverage of the war, but even the best spin can't ignore the realities of the carnage happening in the air over France and Germany. "This is, indeed, bitter, murderous warfare, full of flame and sudden death, and a far cry from the training fields of America," Alexander waxes. "But when one hears griping in the Nissen huts, it is not of this but of the public men at home who snipe at the war effort, of civilians who seem to think that bombing work is just a series of clean-cut triumphs, of the dearth of spare parts with which to patch up the flak-riddled planes, and of the relatively insignificant size of the American bomber forces here."

The airmen know Eaker and Arnold are lobbying—hard—for more aircraft in Europe. More bombers mean more defensive guns, more protection, more damage done to targets. So as their chief advocate, Eaker in particular earns their admiration.

"It didn't help our morale any that the British government and the British military considered us mad for persisting in daylight strategic bombing, and the British press was fanning the flames of this sentiment," Robert Morgan later writes in *The Man Who Flew the Memphis Belle*, summing up the prevailing attitude. "Against this tide of pressure, public opinion, strategic level skepticism and plunging morale, the 8th Bomber Command drew on a weapon even more devastating than the Norden bombsight. This weapon was our Commander, Gen. Ira Eaker. The strapping, dark-browed, purse-lipped Ira Eaker believed in the mission, and he had the stature, nerve, and credentials to blow cigar smoke into the face of anyone who believed otherwise."

Smith and St. Louis have to fret while they await their first mission. Missions are being scrubbed because the weather in April is awful. But the missions that have flown produce plenty of casualties, and that means opportunities for replacements.

L. P. Johnson is in need of crewmen. Not only is Henn dead, two of his stalwarts—Eugene Pollock and James Hobbs—both complete their twenty-fifth missions in late April. Now he has to complete his final mission with green replacements onboard. He chooses Maynard Smith as a gunner. Smith has one familiar face on the airplane with him, as Johnson also taps Folliard to man a .50 cal.

Later, when Smith becomes a household name for the wrong

reasons, there will be an impulse to claim that a bad reputation made the crews hesitant to fly with him. There's no evidence to support this.

It does make sense that Smith—known for his brash, anti-authoritarian attitude—may have rubbed crews the wrong way or developed a reputation during training. His outlier age alone could cause hesitation. But inferring that his wait for a mission is connected to his personality is a stretch. With the bad weather, the arrival of full, unbloodied crews, and the post-Bremen stand-down, there has not been much opportunity for the replacements to fly. Folliard and St. Louis haven't flown in combat, either.

His family doesn't recall him describing any problems. "He was just pretty good buddies with all the guys on the plane," Maynard Smith Jr. recalls him saying. "He had a pretty good relationship with all of them."

On April 30, the seasoned crewmen recognize the signs that the air raids will restart. There's never an announcement the night before a mission that one is coming the next day. But Smith sees how the experienced fliers keep an eye on the Operations area; when the mission planners gather there, it's a good idea to get some extra rest in anticipation of that 4 A.M. wake-up.

Smith feels something turn in his stomach. He's about to see combat.

PART 2

MAY 1, 1943

CHAPTER 4

SYNCHRONIZE YOUR WATCHES

Maynard Smith never thought something as simple as getting dressed could be such a challenge. Every motion seems dreamy and unreal. It's hard to reconcile the banality of dressing with the extreme circumstances. It's 4 A.M. now and by noon he'll be flying somewhere—he doesn't know exactly where, but when he gets there he'll face the most advanced military on the planet, dedicated to killing him.

He first dons his woolies, then slips the standard Army pants and shirt over them. The summer flying suit goes on over that. Heavy wool socks—two pairs, he's learned—and the same old general issue brogans on the feet. Cap on head and a flak jacket completes the morning's ensemble.

His legs are on autopilot. They carry Smith outside into the dark morning, where others in the Grim Reaper squadron are clustered. A jeep arrives, headlights fitted with blackout slats, and behind it is a GI truck with hard wooden seats and no lights at all. The driver

doesn't want to get behind schedule, so the truck just slows to a crawl
to allow the men to hop inside.

The truck rumbles through the base, past the lightless farmhouses and airplane revetments. After five minutes a smell fills the
truck—frying bacon. The mess hall is close; time for breakfast. With
missions running as long as nine hours, a good breakfast is just common sense. But Smith wonders if he'll have an appetite. If you're having your last meal, do you enjoy it or just give in to the fear-inspired
nausea?

Inside, there are fresh eggs instead of powdered, made to order. This indicates a tough mission ahead instead of a "milk run,"
which refers to that ingredient's use in powdered eggs. There's bacon
in heaps, coffee by the cupful. Pensive conversations, sweaty hands
gripping forks. The mechanical act of inserting food, chewing, swal-
lowing. The act becomes another reminder that the human body is
just a machine, one that can be damaged in all sorts of terrible ways.
The B-17 can take a direct hit from a 20mm shell and keep flying,
but it only takes a tiny piece of well-placed metal to end one of the
people inside.

The grim lectures and horror stories of experienced crewmen,
accumulated since gunnery school, come unwanted: limbs clipped
off by machine gun fire, entire crews immolated in an instant by
a flak hit, midair collisions of bombers, blood congealing in frozen
fuselages, trapped ball turret gunners crushed during emergency
belly landings.

A whistle trills. The thoughts recede, but leave what feels like a
stain on his mind. Just do what everyone else is doing; pick up your
gear, take a last swallow of coffee, and file out to where the makeshift
shuttles are waiting to take them all to the mission briefing.

Everyone in the 306th who is flying today is in one room. There
are 180 men clustered in squadrons and aircrews, chattering among

themselves in rows of chairs facing an elevated platform. The math is easy: there are the group's eighteen bombers tasked to the mission, wherever it's destined to go. On the wall behind the platform are hinged panels, and Smith wants to leap up and throw them open to reveal the maps of the day's flight route. But the security is so tight that even the flight officers are kept in the dark until the morning of a mission.

There's a lot of chatter going on, nerves and bravado on display. Smith gathers with Folliard and the others in L. P. Johnson's crew, but he scans the room for a more familiar face. There's Marcel St. Louis, standing with his Clay Pigeons. The two, together since gunnery school, will remain together on their first combat mission, albeit in different squadrons.

A whistle sounds three shrill blasts and everyone shuts up. The room stands at attention as Group Commander Colonel Claude Putnam enters the room, flanked by his operations and intelligence officers. Putnam is the epitome of military bearing—the Texan volunteered for the National Guard at age twelve and became a sergeant by eighteen.

The room gets pensive as the panels open and the mission is revealed: the submarine pens at Saint-Nazaire. The mood darkens. They are going to Flak City.

The submarine pens and shipyards have been bombed for years to no avail. Even the more vulnerable rail yards that service it seem to reassemble soon after being bombed. The only thing the missions produce are frustration and reports of missing airmen.

On February 28 the British, following their blanket night bombing ethos, had launched an incendiary raid on the town itself, burning about 85 percent of the buildings. (They courteously spend three days dropping leaflets warning the residents to flee.) The Germans ordered a general civilian evacuation on March 1, scattering any remaining residents—now refugees—across the Guérande Peninsula.

The May 1 mission plan unfolds in front of the men. The group's eighteen bombers will be among the seventy-eight B-17s from four bomber groups, tasked with hitting the shipyard and nearby sub pens with a pair of 2,000-pound bombs per aircraft. "Wheels up" is planned for 8:45 A.M.; the operations officer gives the specific times and order of takeoff for each squadron. They'll gather above Thurleigh and then rendezvous with four squadrons of bombers of the 91st BG. That group will be in the lead for the mission.

That elicits some grumbling; Putnam has earned a reputation as an excellent pilot and naturally would be these men's preferred overall mission leader. But since there are not enough bombers to make the formations large enough to be effective, these composite groups are common. And leadership rotates.

Bombers of the 91st and 306th groups will combine to form two mega-formations called combat wings. Such organization is needed because the bombers do not all fly over the target at the same time in one solid formation. As one AAF training video explains: "It would be desirable to stack as many planes as possible in one defensive formation. However it has been found that the largest practical defensive formation is the combat wing of three groups. Any formation of aircraft larger than this has been proven to be unwieldy."

Johnson's plane will follow his squadron lead, piloted by Captain Raymond Check, who will in turn follow the 306th leader, Putnam, who in turn will follow other bomb groups when they rendezvous with them. Marcel St. Louis won't be too far away; he's flying with pilot Alden Mann, flying with the lead squadron in the center of the formation. It's a better spot than Smith's got: Johnson's airplane is on the fringe and lower than the lead squadron, and therefore a more popular target for fighters.

A diversionary flight along the Brittany coast by twenty-four B-24s will, hopefully, confuse the Germans as to the true target. There's no reaction when the 306th hears that there will be six squadrons of Spitfire escorts providing very limited cover for the Liberators. They'll peel away from the bombers to sweep the area north of Brest for fighters. This is of zero consequence to the B-17s, which will be nowhere near Brest. Thanks for nothing, as usual.

The route to the target approaches by land, a half-hour tear across France to approach the submarine base from the east. It's hard to aim the Norden when bombing a naval base if you're approaching over a featureless sea. By 11:30 A.M. the formation will be bombing Saint-Nazaire. The escape route after the bombing heads straight out to sea, at a low altitude that is both comfortable and harder to spot on radar, and eventually turns northward to England.

The intelligence officer then steps to the platform and lays out some details on what they are trying to destroy and how the Germans plan to stop them. The chief target is the shipyard in Saint-Nazaire. The charred remains of the town are empty but the military facility is a city unto itself. There are sixty-two workshops for equipment repairs, nearly a hundred spare-part warehouses, myriad offices, and more than ninety dormitories. So there is plenty to bomb, even if the submarines themselves are protected by their massive, reinforced enclosure.

Saint-Nazaire is known as Flak City for a reason. The constant attacks from the air prompt the Germans to emplace more and more AA guns. The German navy operates the defense of coastal installations, so you can abandon any hope that some fresh-faced Hitler Youth is manning the guns, as is increasingly the case in Germany. There's an entire naval brigade protecting the base, with nearly eighty anti-aircraft guns at the ready.

The 306th has a special hatred of Saint-Nazaire, and this mission has echoes of the one that earned their loathing. On February 16 the 306th flew into the port. The leading-edge squadrons sailed through nearly unscathed, but by the time the follow-on 306th was over the target the 88mm gunners below had their correct altitude and speed. Shells exploded inside the formation, hitting every aircraft in the group. Three B-17s were shot down that day—one from a direct and devastating nose hit—and dozens badly damaged.

There are almost twice as many flak cannons around Saint-Nazaire now as there were in February, and they're of a higher caliber. The crews today can expect more 105mm shells that, like the 88s, can reach high altitudes well over 20,000 feet. The plan calls for the bombs to drop from 25,000 feet, but that height doesn't afford as much safety as it once did. Lovely.

The briefing ends as they all do, with a communications officer laying out the radio frequencies of the mission, various call signs, details of the meanings of flares, and a stern reminder to maintain radio silence except for an extreme emergency. The last commandment is "Synchronize your watches."

The sun's barely up when the crews file out of the briefing room. It's a little more than an hour before the bombers will begin to taxi. Smith and the other gunners head to the armory to collect their .50-caliber guns. They board the buses that circle the base and drop the crews at their aircraft.

This ride is the worst time—when there's nothing to do but think about what's ahead. "Being underway is actually a relief. It's that damned ride to the planes that will kill you," says Robert Morgan, pilot of the *Memphis Belle,* which is preparing for the May 1 mission at a nearby airfield.

For a rookie like Smith, the unknown dangers bleed into personal examinations and self-doubt: How will I react when the shells and bullets are flying, when the cold air is too thin to breathe? He'll soon find out.

BLUE BUNNIES

Smith strips down to woolies and re-dresses for combat. It's a process of applying layers, too many damned layers. Over the wool underwear comes the Blue Bunny, an electrically heated suit made by General Electric. There are two-pronged electrical plugs on the hands and feet that connect to heated glove and boot liners. There's a flap on the ass.

Smith has already heard the horror stories of burns from malfunctioning suits, but the more common gripe is that they don't work at all. It doesn't take a brilliant engineer to figure out why: It's wired in series, like a string of Christmas lights. If any of the wiring breaks or shorts out, which usually happens in the limbs, the whole blue-colored suit fails.

When your flight plan calls for many hours above 20,000 feet—as today's does—it's a good idea to plan for this malfunction. So layers of heavy clothes go on over the Blue Bunny. The heated socks slide into fur-lined boots.

As a gunner, his hands are everything. He needs dexterity to operate the .50s, and repair them if need be, but frozen fingers are just as useless. The solution is silk gloves with another, heavier pair over them. When it's time to shoot, Smith will take off the heavy gloves, leaving it to the silk to prevent his sweaty hands from sticking to the cold metal.

He makes sure to empty the coffee from his bladder into the latrine. It'll be a nine-hour flight not including the wait for takeoff, and unlike the other B-17s in the States, there's nowhere to take a leak. B-17Fs come out of the factory with a receptacle in the bomb bay that the crews use to relieve themselves. This is one of the first things the crew chiefs usually tear out of the airplane when they arrive in Europe. The device routes the urine through a hose and into the air. Doing this, however, splatters the window of the tail turret and when this freezes it blocks the view. The most popular alternative is to just use an empty ammo can.

Smith slips back into the A-4 coveralls and shrugs on the heavy wool-lined flying jacket, and that's the basics taken care of until he's onboard.

The B-17 waits serenely, being fussed over by mechanics and bomb-load crews. She doesn't have a name, just the number 42-29649. The aircraft has not seen much combat, if any. The bomber enters USAAF service in January that year and reaches Thurleigh on March 24.

Smith steps to the ball turret to examine it in a routine that's part ritual, part checklist. He's hand-delivered the .50 cals to ground crew, who are affixing them to the ball turret.

Standing with the crew makes Folliard and Smith feel like outsiders. Johnson has stocked the airplane with as many familiar faces as possible. In the front of the airplane he's got co-pilot Second Lieutenant Robert McCallum, engineer (and top turret gunner) Sergeant William Fahrenhold, and bombardier First Lieutenant Stan Kisseberth. The navigator is not as well known: Sergeant Joseph Melaun is from the recently arrived 410th squadron of the 94th Bomb Group. That group hasn't flown any missions yet; that will come in weeks. He's part of the two squadrons in training at the base in late April, and so he's as green a replacement as Smith and Folliard.

Johnson has stocked the back of the B-17 with as many men he knows as possible. That includes Sergeant Henry Bean in the radio room and Sergeant Hoot Gibson manning the all-important rear turret. Rounding out the crew are gunners Joseph Bukacek Jr., Folliard, and Smith.

Bukacek, from St. Clair County, Alabama, is the son of Czech immigrants. The household is bilingual; his mother never learned English. His father graduated from the University of Prague in Czechoslovakia in woodworking. "When they got to the United States, they went to Chicago and he was doing the interiors of the Pullman trains," says his niece, Roxanne Bukacek. Bukacek is married, with no children. He and Roxanne's father, James, are fighting for the United States on opposite sides of the world, one here in Europe and the other in the Pacific.

Lieutenant Kisseberth was working his way through the University of Arizona as a filling station attendant when Japan attacked Pearl Harbor. By 1942 he's flying as a B-17 bombardier. Kisseberth has scars to prove his veteran status. He's wounded for the first time on February 16, 1943, over Saint-Nazaire and again on February 23, 1943. He had been promoted to first lieutenant just a month ago.

Johnson assigns Smith to the ball turret. Short guys, he now sees, *always* get the ball turret. He's never fired a gun from inside that Perspex globe, but there's no complaining now. Statistically this position is actually the safest from enemy attacks, but no one believes this. It's certainly the most uncomfortable position in the B-17—all the bitter cold and violence of a waist gunner, but inside a lonely and inhumanely cramped space.

It's time to finish dressing for the mission. Smith dons the soft but warm B-6 helmet, parachute harness, earphones, throat microphone, oxygen mask, and Mae West inflatable life preserver. Now there's nothing left to do but climb into the bomber, communication cable dangling as he walks.

Ball turret gunners don't enter their fighting position until the bomber is in the air. Smith will have an expected eight hours inside there, so he's in no rush. He climbs onboard, takes a seat on the floor near a window, and listens to the aircrew test the engines one by one.

RENDEZVOUS OVER ENGLAND

L. P. Johnson goes through the takeoff procedures with rote efficiency. He follows the checklist faithfully but makes sure not to fall into any casual routines—it's up to him and McCallum to spot any signs of trouble. Even a small malfunction could scrub a mission or kill the whole crew. In the cockpit, details matter.

The aircrew checks the compass, comparing its heading against the orientation of the runway. In an age of electronic miracles, this is decidedly old-school. There are too many ways the Germans have discovered to jam or spoof radio signals to trust navigation beacons while over France.

Weather is as great an enemy as the Germans. Not only can clouds obscure a target from the view of a Norden bombsight, those same clouds can rob a formation of its best methods of knowing where they are. "Generally they're trying to navigate visually," says Roger Connor, a curator within the aeronautics department of the Smithsonian National Air and Space Museum. "It's a combination of dead reckoning and pilotage once they're over the continent at this time, basically pinpointing landmarks and then using a precomputed path based upon the wind, time, distance, working out their intended airspeed and wind correction angles."

So the compass may be the only tool that can save them from getting lost in or above the clouds, but experienced pilots know that the ones in cockpits are unreliable. Navigators gripe about them and pilots ask for more stabilized, reliable versions in their postmission reports. But there's been no upgrade. On a day like today, about to start a mission into cloudy skies, it's hard not to feel angry.

Johnson and the rest of the pilots see a flare floating over the assembled B-17s: the signal to start engines. White exhaust belches from eighteen airplane engines sputtering rudely to life. The cold, quiet English morning is being torn apart by the simultaneous growling of seventy-two 750-horsepower engines.

The awakened B-17s roll out to the assembly area in their predetermined positions. It's a loud, creeping elephant walk, a procession of growling bombers eager to open up their throttles and take to the sky, where they are no longer ungainly, clumsy machines but graceful, powerful masters of the air. Johnson guides 42-29649 to her place on the flight line, close to the end of the line of B-17s. The squadron leader, Claude Putnam, is at the front of the line.

A figure appears on the balcony of the control tower, lifts a flare gun, and fires. It's the signal to take off.

Squadron by squadron, the line of bombers ease into the air and perform a synchronized turn toward their respective assembly areas. One bomber takes off every fifteen seconds. Close to the airfields there are low-power radio beacons called "bunchers" that help the navigators and pilots get to the right spot.

When it's the Grim Reapers' turn, Johnson pushes in the knob to release the brakes and works a handle on the center console with his right hand to get the engines to full throttle. At 50 mph he has rudder control, if he needs it, and at around 100 mph the plane lifts off the ground. The B-17, back in her element, immediately rediscovers her grace.

The mission has begun, Johnson's twenty-fifth and final one. Not that anyone mentions it—it's bad form to tempt fate that way. He's busy flying, working with the aircrew up front to safely get into formation over the air base. The gunners just sit and wait for their jobs to begin, and try not to think about midair collisions during assembly and rendezvous.

Johnson locks the tail wheel to keep it from spinning and then retracts the landing gear to cut down on the aerodynamic drag. The "LDG GEAR DOWN" light winks off but he and McCallum crane their heads and confirm this visually.

Fitting a formation of B-17s together is a matter of mathematical assembly. The key unit to it all is the number 3. A lead airplane has two wingmen on each side, one flying above and another below. Six of these airplanes form a squadron, with two to four miles between squadrons to avoid midair collisions.

After ninety seconds of flight the lead plane of each squadron banks sharply to indicate a turn is coming, and then slowly eases to the left. Each pilot turns when the plane in front of him does. Each squadron of six meets, takes positions, and then meshes with the other squadrons. They circle and climb in a wide circle so that all the squadrons can fit into their designated slots within the group's overall formation.

So three squadrons' worth of 306th B-17s, eighteen bombers strong, are now creating a large, staggered V in the sky over Thurleigh. Putnam flies in the lead bomber at the formation's center, with two other squadrons immediately behind, with one at an altitude above and one below the center.

The 306th climbs as one. They break through the mottled cloud cover at 3,000 feet and the sky brightens. Johnson sees the cloud mist clinging to the wings and propeller tips. The formation keeps climbing to 6,000 feet.

This same organizational system—wedges of airplanes each following a group lead—will be used to link up with the other bomber groups, which even now are forming up above their own bases. Some of the 306th squadrons will combine with those of the 91st BG. With so few B-17 units, these so-called "composite groups" are needed to get as many bombers in the air over a target as possible, which of course is critical to their defense since there are no escorts.

The 306th airplanes reach Bassingbourn, home of the 91st Bomb Group, at 9:15 A.M. Twenty-two B-17s join the formation, in the shape of a diamond-shaped four-bomber squadron and three-airplane wedge. The 306th takes position behind these squadrons, as per plan. Now it's time to meet up with the airplanes from other bases.

There's a system of radio beacons dotting the English countryside and seafront that are reliable points where the airplanes from diverse air bases can congregate. Today the rendezvous will be via Splasher no. 13, near Portland, at 10:30 A.M.

The formation steadily climbs as they approach this rendezvous, and Johnson and his crew slip on their oxygen masks as they get higher. The formation ultimately reaches 26,000 feet, the mission's prescribed altitude for the rendezvous with the other bombers on the mission, collected into their own combat wing. Within it are twenty-one airplanes from the 305th Bomb Group, flying from Chelveston airfield.

They've linked up with nineteen airplanes from the 303rd, flying from Molesworth. One of them is the *Memphis Belle,* with pilot Robert Morgan and his crew on their twenty-second mission. "The mission was ugly from the start," Morgan says in his postwar memoirs. He and his men are coming off a brief combat hiatus, including some leave time that they'd usually spend carousing in London. Instead, the men return to base early and stick to themselves, passing the time playing softball. They are at the point where they only want to be around each other.

By the time the bombers are poised to cross the English Channel, the strike force is seventy-eight airplanes strong. Johnson is starting to really worry about the weather. The clouds had obscured less than half the ground when they formed up, but they are getting thicker. If this keeps up, there will be no point in flying to Saint-Nazaire.

The English coastline is more than just an arbitrary border. After this moment, the mission will proceed in radio silence. This is also where the navigation aids that keep them from getting lost over England are now functionally useless—they are in range of the phony German emitters that mask and mimic the radio beacons.

Undaunted, the lead bomber signals with a flare—it's time to follow the prescribed flight path to France. The formations circle, enabling the bombers to tighten up their positions, and then head south.

THE CHANNEL BLUES

It's a hell of view, Maynard Smith admits to himself. The ball turret is terrifying in some ways, but from here he can see some amazing vistas of land, sea, and—especially—sky. Looking to the starboard he can see dozens of B-17s stretched above him in staggered lines. Four miles behind him is another stack of aircraft cruising in their well-choreographed geometry. Shimmering contrails expand and sparkle in the morning light.

Observing the mass of other bombers is not entirely a comfort. The air is bitterly cold even for 25,000 feet, and those thick contrails don't seem to want to dissipate. What's the point of radio silence and diversionary flights if the formation is going to hang a "KICK ME" sign like this for German fighters?

Puffy cumulus clouds stretch like a worm-eaten carpet far below him at 3,000 feet. The clouds cover nearly half of the view, but he can see when the countryside transforms to water. They've left the warm embrace of England destined for the desperation of France and the hatred of the occupying enemy there.

The transit time gives Smith a chance to get acquainted with the ball turret. The guns have the design priority here, leaving him squeezed between the twin .50 cals, knees cocked back in a near fetal position. His right foot activates the interphone switch. His left foot sits on the range pedal that controls the reflector gun sight hanging above his head. The seat includes a half inch of hardened steel for armor, which is *comforting* but not *comfortable*.

Smith tries the full range of the electrically powered turret's motion, using the hand control grips to revolve this way and that. The turret can turn a full circle in azimuth and can be lowered and raised from level (0 degrees) to straight down (-90 degrees).

Johnson's voice comes through his headphones: test the guns. This is standard routine for every bomber when they get to a high altitude. On top of the myriad typical malfunctions, any moisture in the guns can freeze and cause a jam. The time to find out is not when fighters are attacking.

Smith grips the handles on the side of the turret and pulls them back to cock the machine guns. There's no safety switch. He aims via a cruciform indicator projected on a glass screen that's mounted on the gun sight. The screen aligns with a circular window between his feet.

He points the twin .50s down and away from any fellow bombers and puts his hands on the grips, thumbs on the buttons that trigger the machine guns. Two cans of five hundred rounds each share the limited space inside the ball; the guns have been loaded from the outside, before takeoff. Smith fires a quick burst and the barrels spit an arcing stream of rounds. The bolt mechanisms are so close to his knees that he worries that his clothes will get caught in them and tear.

He dimly hears rattling gunfire above him but he doesn't really know the other gunners have finished their test fires until they report to Johnson over the intercom. The ball turret gunner doesn't know *anything*—it's the most isolated position on the B-17. The cockpit pilots obviously have each other, plus the navigator and engineer in close proximity. The radio operator sits in a cubby space, but at least he can lean out and see other crewmen. The waist gunners fight back-to-back, and the tail gunner can easily slip out of his position for some human interaction. Meanwhile, Smith is strapped inside this tiny aquarium.

This isolation can be dangerous. If there's a problem with the oxygen system of any other crewman, someone is there to share an oxygen mask and fix the problem. But ball turret gunners who succumb to anoxia do so alone, and can pass out and even die unnoticed.

The interphone is little help. There's little chitchat inside the plane as they make their way to the target, and what discussions happen tend to be terse, businesslike. That makes for a painfully solitary vigil, with nothing but the sight of the other bombers to keep him company.

And now Smith is seeing that the formation is losing airplanes. Just after they reach the Channel three B-17s from the 306th peel away and head north toward home. He doesn't know it but they are reporting engine malfunctions; three are out and one is experiencing severe vibrations. Five airplanes from the 303rd also abort.

Onboard the *Black Swan* (42-5780), Lieutenant Jay Sterling and his crew have a brief discussion about their no. 3 engine. It made some funny noises during takeoff but seems alright now: the B-17 continues on the mission. Of the seventy-eight airplanes on the raid, eleven head for home with mechanical trouble. Smith's view of the formation changes as Johnson and the others in the 306th re-form into a new box, filling the gaps left by the departed airplanes.

At 10:40 A.M. the formation changes its course to avoid the Isle of Guernsey. There's a flak battery there, set up on a golf course, with its own tracking radar. The guns are mostly medium- and close-range weapons—those that are more useful to use against ships as well as airplanes—but why take the risk and provide detailed radar data? Better to just steer away from the danger.

Smith knows the next milestone will come in just minutes—crossing over into occupied France. He keeps his eyes peeled on the horizon as they near land, but he can hardly see the ground below because the cloud cover keeps getting thicker. Aside from the overcast weather below, they are punching through some high-altitude cirrus clouds at 26,000 feet.

The formations are approaching the French coast near St. Brieuc at 10:54 A.M. It's time to dash across France, a twenty-minute run that will end with a final sharp turn toward Saint-Nazaire.

CHAPTER 5

ALARMBEREITSCHAFT

Josef Wurmheller is dressed and ready for action, waiting for the telephone to ring at the operations room at Vannes-Meuçon airfield. He's surprised that he and his *Staffel* are on a ten-minute readiness alert—the overcast sky looks awful for bombing. But then again, he doesn't understand a lot of things concerning the way Americans do what they do.

They're sending in manageable numbers of bombers, and without any escorts. It's a recipe for slaughter. The Nazi high command believes this, too. That's one reason why they are pouring resources into the nightfighters, who are tangling with the British bombers under the invisible gaze of radar and glare of searchlights.

Wurmheller, like all Channel pilots, wonders how much more damage they could do if the Reich would only pay more attention to its day-fighting force. A small number of his fighters are expected to bring heavy losses to the B-17s and B-24s. But those formations are getting bigger and ranging over a wide enough area to challenge the threadbare German defenses. The new fighter pilots are showing their lack of experience, and the ones with any are proving slow to adapt to the Channel front. And the response from Berlin seems to be: build more flak cannons.

Above all, the Americans don't seem to be deterred by their losses. It's insane but generates a tinge of respect and even jealousy from the Nazi fighter community. "In contrast to German High Command during the Battle of Britain, the USAAF command did not lose their nerve," Josef "Beppo" Schmid, a Luftwaffe general in command of the 1st Fighter Corps, remarks after the war.

The French never had much use for the improvised airfield at Vannes, but the Germans transformed it into a bustling bomber base in 1940. For two years the unpaved landing strips hosted the bombers meant to bring England to her knees. When this effort failed, the bombers left and the fighters moved in to defend the Reich. Wurmheller is glad he doesn't live on the base: aircrew and some senior officers from the base are quartered in hotels in the town of Vannes.

Two squadrons (*Staffels*) are based in Vannes: the 7/JG 2 and Wurmheller's 9/JG 2. Hangars, ammo dumps, and fuel tanks are sprinkled in wooded areas adjacent to the airfield, meant to mitigate the damages from Allied attacks. There are forty-one large and twenty-one small aircraft shelters, plus two larger hangars used for repair work. The entire complex is protected by twelve flak positions, radiating out three kilometers. This is one of several air bases hosting JG 2 fighters—dozens of Fw 190s and Bf 109s can rally like wasps.

Now it seems the Americans are at it again, with a bomber formation crossing the Channel as Wurmheller and his squadron wait for them to approach. There are only two degrees of readiness at Vannes—sitting in the airplane on *alarmbereitschaft* (instant readiness) or on a ten-minute standby, waiting nearby in a full flight suit. All he has to do is slip on his heavy leather jacket and trot to the nearby Fw 190A, which even now is being prepared for action by ground crews.

Knowing the Americans are coming is not magic. There's an entire enterprise, using the latest technology, to spot inbound raids. It starts with monitoring communications. The German's "Y Service" is set up to snoop on transmissions in England, and these frequently tip off an impending raid. But the information takes a tortured route through Paris and Berlin before returning to the Luftwaffe unit commanders, a process that takes a full day. It's useful for postmission analysis, but for the frontline troops it's just another annoying example of the Reich's clumsy bureaucracy.

Luckily for the interceptors, there are plenty of other indications the bombers are coming. The Americans make a lot of radio noise as they gather in their formations and tend to rendezvous in a handful of designated areas. The Germans know just where to point their eavesdropping antenna. "As the assembly would last a long time, there was sufficient time left for forewarnings and for preparation of our own operation," Schmid says.

The Germans have a very low appraisal of the Americans' subtlety. "The badly disciplined R/T traffic of the U.S. bomber units facilitated the plotting of the courses and the early finding out of the target," Schmid recalls. "Thus, messages like 'crossing the enemy coast' or '30 minutes to target' or 'no clouds over target' could be picked up again and again."

For years the British and Germans have dueled in the skies over Europe at night. One result of these desperate, blind battles is a system of German radar stations that line the Atlantic and North Sea coasts. There's a wall of invisible energy covering the Channel, and the American bombers are easily spotted, easing the preparation and direction of fighters.

The German radar techs are so good that they can pinpoint individual bombers and vector fighters to particular targets. Warfare always comes down to cat-and-mouse adaptation, and the history of electronic warfare is certainly no different. The British bombers have started to deploy clouds of foil strips that mimic the radar returns of an airplane. They also use jammers to overwhelm the frequencies of the German radar with noise.

But the U.S. daytime raids don't warrant this electromagnetic dueling—or at least the 8th Air Force leadership believes in early 1943. The Americans don't use chaff and they don't bother with jamming radar. The large formations are easy to spot from the air, especially given the contrails that clearly show the direction of the flight. Their diversionary flights are annoying, given the relative paucity of German fighters on alert during the day, but there's seldom any real doubt as to what target will be attacked and when.

The first radar to pick up the formation is the Freya, which can pick up formations at eighty kilometers. Two rectangular arrays stand on a mast, radiating energy at 250 MHz. Radar may be invisible, but the way it works is very physical. The antenna bathes the oncoming airplanes with radar energy at a 3.9-foot wavelength, the distance between peaks of the sine wave. The waves reflect off the surface of the airplanes, returning to the antenna's receivers and forming an image of what's approaching. So, the shorter the wavelength, the more detailed the return and the better the resolution.

A second kind of radar is also tracking the formation as it gets closer. The Würzburg-Riese FuMG 62D doesn't stand tall like the Freya. It's a squat, wide, 7.5-meter diameter parabolic dish. Along the coast these operate in tandem with the Freya, picking up the exact measurements of location, course, and height that the longer-range radar can't determine.

Wurmheller doesn't understand why the Americans don't try to jam the Würzburg, as the British do. He understands better than most that it's impossible for bombers to hide from fighters during daylight. But everyone on both sides of the Channel knows that the Kriegsmarine flak batteries protecting the coast also use the Würzburg to help aim their antiaircraft guns. Jamming the Würzburg seems like an obvious countermeasure when attacking the submarine pens, but it's one that the Americans simply aren't bothering to pursue.

Radar information about the approaching bombers winds its way through channels and eventually gets to Wurmheller's unit by phone. He knows an attack is brewing well before he heads to the hangars to wait out the alert. But timing is everything—the Fw 190s only have enough fuel for an hour and a half of flight, and it's vital that every minute is spent chewing apart bombers. Such advanced warning enables him to take off at just the right moment. The downside is the rise of adrenaline-fueled anticipation and the risk of a letdown that comes when the weather scrubs the bombers' mission.

As it should have today. He looks back into the sky—the cloud cover is thickening, forming a blanket between the ground and the bombardiers. They may be coming a long way for nothing.

The clouds don't overly concern Wurmheller. Up where he hunts, the sky will be clear.

A phone call confirms two sizeable formations are moving toward Saint-Nazaire, dozens of B-17s heading to once again strike the submarine base. The Americans will be in range of his fighters by 11:10 A.M., just southeast of the town of Châteaubriant.

Wurmheller and his 9/JG 2 pilots leave the ready rooms and head for their yellow-tailed airplanes. They're ready to meet them.

"A BEAUTIFUL SIGHT TO SEE"

From Colonel Claude Putnam's point of view, everything seems to be going well for the 306th until it's time for the hard left that will aim the formations toward Saint-Nazaire.

Sure, there's been some opposition but so far it's been token. A handful of fighters menaced the leading group as they approached France, and a few lonely ack-ack batteries took shots at them as they crossed the coastline. Even as the bombers traverse France, the fighters aren't present in enough numbers to press their attacks. There are a few fleeting gunfights but no bombers are damaged enough to fall out of formation. So far, so good.

But now things are going sideways, and on the verge of the most dangerous part of the day. Every mission includes what's called the Initial Point, where the formations will begin their bombing run. After that, it's supposed to be straight and level as LeMay intended.

The 91st just passed the IP and didn't change course. What the hell are they doing?

Putnam sticks to the plan and makes the turn. His navigator, Captain John Dexter, confirms that they are heading to the target as intended. C. H. May, his bombardier, even thinks there may be a cloud break wide enough to drop their bombs. This squadron will try to complete the mission. The interphone gives him updates from the crew, who are watching as the other groups make their belated turns. Now the expected leaders of the combat wing are *behind* the 306th as they close in on the submarine pens.

The 105mm flak is bursting at their altitude, but the cannons aimed at them have the wrong deflection and the bursts are popping harmlessly behind them. Other groups are not as lucky, and Putnam and his crew can see the damage mounting in other formations, bombers leaking black smoke or staggering to keep up with their formation. But that's not his problem. The only thing on his mind is getting the twin 2,000-pound bombs out of his plane and onto that damned naval base.

During the bomb run, May essentially takes the reigns of the airplane from the bombardier's seat. It's one of the effects of connecting the Norden bombsight to the airplane's controls. First, May has to "tell" the bombsight when the airplane is flying even. He eyes the two bubble sights mounted at right angles on the vertical gyro's frame—basically the same as a carpenter's level—to set this value.

This is easier said than done. May must do this while hunched over the bombsight in a B-17 being shot at by flak and bouncing around at 25,000 feet. There's another chronic problem—the size of the bubbles are influenced by temperature, which varies wildly from mission to mission. It's another example of something that should have been included in bombardiers' high-altitude training.

The Norden uses preset values that May input before they even took off. These include airplane speed, altitude, and the ballistic parameters of the bomb itself—all the variables needed for the site to automatically calculate the correct drop point. These are based on what the mission *should* be, not what it actually *is*. So there's a rushed period of calculation while May corrects these figures with a slide rule and a bombing table that is printed nearly too small to read.

The rest of the bomber's crew waits impatiently as the bomb run continues. A bombardier named Robert Hecker sums up the dynamic onboard, quoted in a 2017 issue of *World War II Magazine*: "I did feel sorry for our gunners, though. With no enemy fighters in the flak field to focus on, the guys at the .50 calibers were free to agonize about our vulnerability. I could hear them in my earphones. 'How much longer?' they would mutter from turrets and waist mounts. 'How much longer, for God's sake?'"

May moves his face back to the down-facing telescope. He's supposed to be steering the plane to the release point. The bombsight scans the area beneath the airplane, but today its crosshairs are over clouds instead of terrain. This is a real problem—he's supposed to use the bombsight's knobs to adjust those preset values the entire way to the target, using the view to fine-tune the upcoming drop. Without the target in the crosshairs, there's no way to do this.

There—a break in the clouds and Saint-Nazaire is in the literal crosshairs. The submarine pens look like the massive concrete slabs that they are. May has a scant ten seconds to trigger the bombs release. The bomber lurches suddenly as it becomes 4,000 pounds lighter. Behind the lead bomber, the others in the formation also drop their payloads. The view impresses Smith, watching intently from the ball turret. "It was a beautiful sight to see the bombs all falling in rapid succession," he says later. "Great splotches of brown smoke came rolling skyward."

May peers through the broken overcast at the impacts. It's a good grouping but the aim is short and off to the right. He sees bright white blooms of the explosive concussions striking the water and brown ones from hits on land. Their bomb run has largely missed the target.

THE HERO OF HAMM

Major Paul Fishburne at age twenty-two is the squadron commander of the 322nd, part of the 91st Bomb Group. He's leading the formations as they soar over Saint-Nazaire. Or he's supposed to be.

Fishburne is another whose early exposure to aviation turned into a career. He grew up in Montgomery, Alabama, and watched Claire Chennault and his Flying Trapeze practice at nearby Maxwell Field. Seeing those Boeing P-12s in action lit his desire to be an aviator. But making it happen wasn't easy: he can't get into West Point or Annapolis. After two years at Auburn University, where he waits tables to make ends meet, the Army finally accepts him to flight school, and he graduates in May 1941.

Fishburne feels an unwelcome but familiar sense of losing control of a mission. In March he led his men into what some in the 91st call the Hamm Massacre. That day, seventy-one B-17s from three groups took off from England and headed through bad weather to bomb the marshaling yards at the German city of Hamm.

The weather was awful on that day, too. The three bomber groups promptly lost each other in the clouds—one turned for home, another headed for a secondary target in Rotterdam. Fishburne and his sixteen B-17s were alone in the air. He could have turned back, with no reproach. But he plunged ahead to attack Hamm.

They met intense flak and nearly 150 fighters, but dropped their bombs anyway. Four bombers were shot down; all the rest suffered damage. Besides the downed aviators, one man was killed and five seriously wounded. Upon landing, Fishburne faced trouble; his only defense was a successful mission, but the bombers equipped with cameras to capture the results had been shot down.

But there was a combat photographer onboard with images of the bombing—somehow the crews performed a nearly picture-perfect run. At that moment, Eaker and the others lobbying for daylight missions wanted examples of bombs hitting targets, and here was one lone group taking the fight to Germany without fighter escorts. So in April, Fishburne received the Distinguished Flying Cross.

Until now, this May 1 mission is going comparably well for the 91st. The fighter encounters so far seem lackluster. Except for the maintenance aborts, there are no B-17s missing as they close in on their target. The 91st makes its hard left toward Saint-Nazaire when Fishburne sees something wrong. They are starting the bomb run, but now the 306th is *ahead* of them.

His crew is witnessing other bad things and reporting them to him via interphone. Two B-17s of the 324th have clipped each other, a collision that doesn't knock any airplanes out of the sky, but it is disrupting the entire formation's approach.

Even worse, Fishburne's bombardier is saying the weather is too bad to drop anything. There's near total cloud coverage at Saint-

Nazaire. The overcast has become unbroken and thick—there's not even a horizon, just a haze that looks like an empty, unpainted canvas. The 91st soars over Saint-Nazaire but the bomb bays remain closed. They won't be dropping anything today.

The mission plan calls for a steady drop in altitude after the release, a welcome change from the frigid high altitude and a harder target for German radar to spot. Most B-17s jettison their 2,000-pound bombs into the Bay of Biscay to lighten up for the trip home and relieve the crew of the ugly task of disarming the live bombs.

Fishburne and fifteen of the 91st airplanes descend through a layer of clouds starting 6,000 feet. The formation is in disarray, split into three unequal parts as they blunder through the overcast. When they emerge from the clouds, there are just six B-17s still with Fishburne. He continues along the planned route, leaving nine B-17s in the group on their own. By the end of May, Fishburne will be relieved from duty as squadron commanding officer.

Several of these orphaned B-17s find each other and make their own way along the coast. Others are left to fend for themselves. One of them is the bomber *Vertigo* (41-24547), of the 323rd squadron. "The group leader made no attempt to reassemble the squadron after breaking out into the clear," recalls Alvar "Al" Platt, the bomber's waist gunner.

This is when Putnam and the rest of the 306th head back to collect them. The combat diary for the 423rd squadron says the group "made a 360° turn to protect the 91st Group, which was in trouble." The airplanes form an ad hoc diamond shape, again giving each other the security of each other's .50 cals.

Inside the *Vertigo*, there's a sense of relief now that they're with other bombers, no matter which group they're with. The 323rd squadron's commander, Lieutenant Bob Rand, is piloting so Major Maurice Rosener is free to leave the co-pilot's chair. "Rosener came back through the waist area to use the porta-pot and I asked him how he had liked that one," according to fellow crewman Al Platt. "It had been an easy run. He said he didn't think he would have any trouble making twenty-five of those. I think he changed his mind before the day was over."

The other bomber groups are having less luck. The 303rd BG, flying over the target miles behind both the 306th and 91st composite groups, is finding out why the area is known as Flak City. The German naval gunners have them bracketed with accurate fire and the damages are mounting.

Inside the *Memphis Belle*, pilot Robert Morgan sees the explosion before he even feels it. A shell has struck one of the B-17's engines. He watches out the window as it spews smoke and oil. The airplane is injured but continues doggedly on, keeping in formation and dropping its payload. "We never knew if we hit the target or not," Morgan says. "We were toggling individually instead of releasing on the lead bombardier, and suspected that most of our bombs fell into the water. A few others, to our acute regret, landed on the city itself and did considerable damage."

Elsewhere in the 303rd the flak is a taking a bigger toll. Seven of ten inside the *Joe Btfsplk II* (41-24610) are on their first mission. That includes engineer Tech Sergeant David E. Lee Jr. Engineers double as top turret gunners, and from there he gets a good view of the flak tearing into bombers around him.

Joe Btfsplk II is a ghoulish name for a bomber, even though *it comes from* a character in the *Li'l Abner* comic strip. If anyone asks how to pronounce the name, they are treated to a wet, loud raspberry. Cartoonist Al Capp created Joe as a jinx, always well intentioned but plagued by terrible outcomes. On May 1 the bomber will live up to this namesake.

Shuddering impacts tells Lee they've been hit, badly. Inside the shrapnel-punctured fuselage, waist gunner Staff Sergeant Anthony

Peklinsky is down with a bad wound in his thigh. The bomber shrugs off the damage, flying level in order to drop its bombs. Then another violent vibration and a flak shell bursts at just the right spot in front of the right wing, destroying both engines.

Lee can see them from the top turret, sputtering and spitting jagged metal into the slipstream. The airplane is already slowing but she's still alive. "We were limping behind formation and badly crippled," Lee says. "But we were going home."

It's a hopeful outlook, given the promise of a long, dangerous trip. And the relief is short lived. The call comes over the interphone: "Bandits at 2 o'clock."

MYSTERIOUS SIGHTINGS

There's a strange airplane in the sky, flying level with the formations but well away from the flak. Several crews report its presence and give the same description: they say it's a B-17.

This B-17 has unidentifiable gray letting on the fuselage. Reading the icons and numbers on bombers is second nature to anyone in the sky over Europe in World War II. These identifiers help keep composite formations together, identify airplanes that are shot down, and limit the overall confusion that can reign where radios are deemed a security risk.

To the eyes of the crews, there are other suspicious details. "Waist gun windows were closed and the turret inactive," the 306th mission report reads. "All engines seemed in good shape and the aircraft was under control. This airplane acted very suspiciously in that it made no attempt to join the formation. It was last seen on a heading of 90 degrees into France. Enemy fighters did not attack it."

The Germans prize captured B-17s, and by 1943 several have been downed in reasonable condition. These are being repurposed by *Kampfgeschwader* 200, a Luftwaffe special operations unit that flies captured Allied airplanes on combat missions. They deal in deception, using purloined airplanes to spy on troop movements and insert paratroops. This would be the logical operator of a B-17 on May 1, 1943.

There's a chronological problem with this theory. The first B-17 operated by KG 200 is the *Wulfe Hound* (41-24585), a bomber with the 303rd that crashed in November 1942. Luftwaffe ground staff repair her in Germany and she's flying by 1943, but her first assignments don't come until September. The idea that the *Wulfe Hound* is in operations against her former unit is a long shot. The next B-17 that the KG 200 uses won't crash until the end of May 1943.

The crews not only think they know what the airplane is, they have an idea about what it's doing.

In reports airmen will theorize the faux bomber is gauging the formation's altitude and passing the information to a pair of German airplanes lingering nearby with another new weapon aimed at the Flying Fortresses.

There are two Bf 109Gs flying above the 303rd, shadowing the formation's level course just out of range of the guns. All of a sudden, they tip forward at steep angles aimed directly at the Flying Fortresses below. It's the signature maneuverer of dive-bombing.

The 109s pull up, sending sticks of 551-pound bombs to plunge into the 306th's airplanes. These bombs are time-fused to explode in the midst of the B-17s, causing whatever damage possible but more importantly to use the resulting chaos from the concussions to break formations apart.

Instead, the bombs fall through the formations to the ground below. They seem to detonate in bright geysers on impact with the water. The crews dutifully and morosely report this awful new tactic, but in reality it rarely works and soon will be abandoned for other more effective weapons.

There are other strange sightings reported on May 1. Crews claim to see some enemy aircraft painted to resemble P-47s. God knows there are not actual escorts nearby and none of the three captured P-47s flown by the Germans are available at the time, nor would they be flying near a hostile bomber formation. (They are more useful as photo reconnaissance airplanes.) But sightings like this are common in World War II—crews are convinced that the Nazis are sneaking in on them. Therefore, any fighter that acts strangely is deemed a threat.

This naturally contributes to fratricide, but there's little apology from the overstressed crews. "If the plane is friendly, what the hell is it doing looking like an enemy?" Maynard Smith will remark to a *New Yorker* reporter, crudely but effectively stating the gunners' prevailing attitude. "When you're up in the air, start shooting and *then* start recognizing."

A MURDER OF FIGHTERS

Josef Wurmheller and his wingman, Rudolf Gerhardt, scan the B-17 formations with an eye for weakness. A stream of radar updates regarding the position of the enemy aircraft had come over the radio and he's adjusted his squadron's course to intercept them. He's coordinating the effort on another frequency, spreading his planes around but making sure to concentrate the attacks on specific formations. The more fighters there are, the fewer B-17 guns will target individual planes.

His 9/JG 2 is just one of the squadrons responding to today's raid on Saint-Nazaire. More than forty fighters are closing in, climbing in wide circles to reach their targets at 20,000 feet. The bombers are dropping their altitude after the bomb drop, and the fighters are climbing to meet them. Wurmheller welcomes their descent and the return of the power that comes with thicker air.

Wurmheller's squadron approaches the 303rd "12 o'clock high," head-to-head and high. To the nearby B-17 aircrews like Johnson's who are watching the action, it seems like the fighters are harrying the bombers like gnats. One 8th AF mission report describes Fw 190s that "attacked in pairs, diving under the formation, coming up again or in from the side. Some were seen to roll up under the formation to attack."

Solitary contrails point the way to any stragglers. Wurmheller spots one, seemingly undamaged but nevertheless falling steadily below formation.

It's the *Black Swan*. The no. 3 engine that barked during takeoff isn't pulling its weight; the stress of a steady headwind seems to have overtaxed it. Without the engine, the bomber both slows and loses altitude. Now the crew is within eyesight of the others in the formation but functionally alone, at the moment when enemy fighters are looking for easy prey.

The damaged *Black Swan* is an obvious target and Wurmheller makes it a personal priority. He dives, first triggering bursts of 20mm cannons and, when closer, chewing into the bomber's fuselage with machine guns. He peels away, close enough to see the skull and crossbones painted on the side of the airplane.

Gerhardt is finishing his own attack on it. The pair turns and, instead of climbing for another head-on attack, roll to turn and attack another bomber right away, slashing at it from the sides.

Other German squadrons attack the easy target. *Unteroffizier* (literally, "underofficer" and used for Luftwaffe noncommissioned officers) Paul Rossner, of 7/JG 2, lines up for his shot, but he sees the B-17's top turret aimed directly at him. *Black Swan* gunner Powell Griffin has a bead on the German and the two men fire at each other like duelists.

Twin streams of .50-cal bullets reach toward the Fw 190. Then Rossner feels someone punch his leg and he looks down to see a ragged hole and the shocking appearance of flowing blood. The airplane starts belching smoke and resisting commands like a stubborn animal. Rossner wrestles with the yoke as the fighter screams toward the ground and falls out of view.

Inside the *Black Swan,* it seems like the Germans are everywhere at once. A cannon shell bursts through the aluminum skin near the radio room and detonates inside the fuselage, igniting fires. The electrical system shorts out and the intercom goes silent. Now anything can be happening, but the crew assumes the worst: the bomber is dying.

Co-pilot Second Lieutenant John Neill sees the smoke swirling into the cockpit and unbuckles from his seat to bail out, wincing because his leg is peppered with shrapnel. His pilot, First Lieutenant Jay Sterling, is slumped in his seat. Neill unbuckles the man and starts to drag him back through the fiery remains of the fuselage. He sees navigator Second Lieutenant Harry Roach, face bloody, at the forward escape hatch. Engineer Sergeant Powell Griffin, scorched and bleeding, is close behind. They both bail out.

Neill and the unconscious pilot reach the open bomb bay. The rear gunner is already there and leaps into the void. Neill is desperate: leaving his pilot here is guaranteed death. So he throws Sterling out the opening, hoping he'll recover consciousness on the way down and open his parachute. He doesn't.

As he readies himself for the jump, the entire plane banks at a sickly angle and starts a death dive. This pins him to the bomber's interior wall. Inside the nose, bombardier David Parker is likewise trapped by centrifugal force as he tries to bail out.

Wurmheller and Gerhardt have only seen two parachutes leave the stricken bomber, and they make the instinctive decision to confirm the kill. With no return fire to contend with, the pair can take extra time to aim. The pair mercilessly riddle the *Black Swan* and it explodes in a sudden flash, wings snapping off the disintegrating fuselage.

Everything changes for Parker and Neill in an instant. One second they are immobile as bugs impaled by pins, the next they are soaring wildly through the frigid air. Neill's brain processes that he's alive and falling, and he starts to struggle with his parachute. It opens, jerking his neck with a painful snap, but somehow he's alive.

Parker is also under a working parachute, falling amid the ragged pieces of the *Black Swan* streaking to the ground. One of the broken wings, falling like a spinning maple seed, clips Fields's parachute, fouling the lines. He plummets to his death.

There are only four survivors of the *Black Swan*. All but one will end up in German stalags; Roach will be taken in by the French resistance and ferried back to Allied lines. Wurmheller and Gerhardt are both credited with a B-17 kill. Ironically, the final attack that earns them the distinction actually saves the lives of two American airmen.

This is but one drama amid a running gunfight that steadily descends from 20,000 feet to 15,000 feet to 6,000 feet, started over land but extending for a half hour over water along the French coast.

The fighters are focusing on the 305th BG, and a 366th B-17 flown by First Lieutenant Einar Suomi peels from the sky in clear distress. The other bombers watch as Suomi and his co-pilot try to make a water landing but the airplane reels into the surface far too fast, an uncontrolled crash that kills all ten men. The most likely fighter pilot who downs the airplane is Otto Kleinert of the 7/JG 2, who claims a B-17 near Belle Île just before noon.

A refugee B-17 from the scattered 91st is also fighting for its life. Lieutenant James Baird and his crew of 324th squadron are flying alone when seven Fw 190s intercept them. The fighters see an easy target, but Baird proves to be a slippery foe. He drops into the clouds for cover, shaking off two Fw 190s that way. He now has to rely on his gunners to ward off the remaining fighters at sea level. Fighting low to the ground is dangerous but it robs the Fw 190s of a lot of tactical options. The crew claims to shoot down three fighters before the other two run low on fuel and leave.

The hunt for stragglers continues. The crew of the *Joe Btfsplk II* has been lulled into complacency. Their captain has dropped into the clouds at 4,000 feet, hiding from any lurking Germans as they guide their flak-ravaged B-17 back to England.

But even as the crew is handing each other cigarettes, the pale light coming from the windows brightens. Without the overcast the *Joe Btfsplk II* can be spotted at a dozen miles, and sure enough there is a pair of German fighters that even now are wheeling toward them. That break in the clouds is as good as a death sentence. "The plane and guns were in such condition that we were practically helpless," recalls its engineer, David E. Lee Jr.

The fighters tear into the B-17. "The pilot told me to tell the boys to leave their guns and brace for the crash because we were going to crash in the ocean," says Lee. "We did not have time to get braced for the crash and to release more than one rubber raft." The airplane hits the water hard enough to knock Lee unconscious.

When he wakes, the airplane has already sunk and he's on a life raft with Peklinsky. The men will wash up on Belle Île and eventually be captured.

All told, the fight over Saint-Nazaire costs four bombers. There's only been forty-five minutes between the start of the bomb run and the final fighter attacks. In that time, the B-17 crews estimate as many as fifty fighters in the air, and the 306th alone tallies twenty to twenty-five gunfights, or what they call "encounters." The aerial battle leaves wreckage and downed airmen falling across France.

"A BLUFF THAT ENDS WELL"

Marcel Bertho is a refugee in his own occupied nation. The seventeen-year-old and his parents fled their native Saint-Nazaire in February when the British made clear they were going to reduce the city with firebombs. On February 28 and in late March they did just that, leaving Bertho's family stranded in the village of Québitre, twelve miles from the ruined city. The village sits on a small island surrounded by marshes and is served by a single dead-end road.

It's not hard to tell that another Allied raid is underway this early afternoon: the sky is mottled with clouds but through the gaps Bertho can see the flak blooms high over the city. He and his cousin Philippe Belloit are among a small gaggle of villagers staring at the grim spectacle. Then they hear a sound—the whining growl of an airplane.

The distant fight 20,000 feet above them suddenly seems a lot closer when a small airplane cruises into view from the south, flying low and crossing almost directly over the village's center. The apparition disappears over the horizon as quickly as it appears. Then the spectators gasp and point as a stark white parachute appears, drifting toward the marshes north of the village.

Belloit doesn't hesitate: "It's an Englishman," he declares. "Come on, we'll get him back."[8]

The foot chase is on. The cousins dash to the north, keeping an eye on the man under the parachute as he drifts. They stumble through ditches and muck, alternating their eyes from the ground to their quarry in the sky. It takes awhile, with the parachute coming down more than a quarter of a mile away from the village.

Bertho and Belloit get closer, eyes peeled. They finally see a figure wading through thigh-deep marsh water, behind a thicket of brambles. The pair of Frenchmen call out to him: "Tommy?" The response comes back, *"Nein, Deutsch!"*

---

8   There are many excellent oral histories from World War II on French websites, including "Chemin de la Mémoire 39-45 en Pays de Retz" (http://chemin -memoire39-45paysderetz.e-monsite.com).

The cousins share a look. "Shit," Belloit whispers. "A *Boche*." But Bertho sees a pragmatic upside. The Germans have imposed a death sentence for any who help downed Allied airmen, and now the pair won't have the option to be dangerously patriotic. "Better a *Boche* than an Englishman," he quips.

The two Frenchmen meet the pilot, who they see is suffering from a bleeding leg wound. It's not deep but the man is in obvious shock and pain. The German tells them his name: Paul Rossner, fresh from his fight with the *Black Swan*. "He smells of gasoline and oil. He has a big hematoma above the eye and seems a little groggy," Bertho recalls. "He has a big pistol on his hip."

The two Frenchmen stomp into the mire and take supporting positions on either side of Rossner. It's an awkward and miserable trek back to the village, with the trio navigating muddy bogs and stumbling through watery ditches to get to their grandmother's house.

Rossner is resting on a chair inside by the time a German soldier pulls up on a bicycle and, rifle at the ready, enters the house. Bertho gets the sense from him that he's disappointed that the airman isn't an enemy. A car with officers soon arrives, who take Rossner's statement on the spot.

Bertho and his cousin are waiting anxiously outside when another cousin, Emilienne Micau, comes up with an idea. The twenty-five-year-old woman is visiting from Angers, thinks it's a good idea to embellish the rescue and ask for a very specific reward. The Germans are imprisoning Belloit's uncle, Joseph Thoby, and this could be the only way to secure his release. But the story isn't strong enough to ask, Micau reckons. "You have to tell them that, without you, he would have drowned," she suggests.

Under her instruction, the cousins fill buckets of water and douse themselves before the officers come outside. She also designates herself as their spokesperson—even her cousins must admit "she's easy on the eyes."

A French-speaking officer hears her out, and eyes the two men as she points out their bedraggled condition. The German is sympathetic. "This does not depend on me," he says. To do this will require taking a train to a German base to fetch a pass that will allow them to visit the Luftwaffe air base at Vannes-Meuçon. With that, the Nazis leave, taking the limping pilot with them.

The next day, the teenagers get their pass and take a train to get close to Vannes, and then take bicycles to the base itself. After a long wait a German officer hears their plea and, right in front of them, makes a phone call. Then the door opens and Rossner himself is there, the swelling in his face already abating. The teens tense up—he's the only one who can refute their story of the rescue.

He and the officer start a conversation. After that, the officer thanks them and Rossner himself escorts them to the front guardhouse gate. The conversation is awkward: he tells them he's twenty-five, flies a Focke-Wulf, and wants them to know that he's never been shot down before. "The contact we had showed us [his] character," Bertho says. "Far from the arrogant behavior of some young Nazis."

Rossner quickly recovers from his wounds and goes back into action. He's shot down and killed just weeks later, on May 29. Five months later, Joseph Thoby is released from his prison camp in Germany. The others captured with him will languish another twenty months. Bertho sums up the adventure as "a bluff that ended well."

CHAPTER 6

"FIZZLE UP"

Maynard Smith gladly takes off his oxygen mask and exercises his cold fingers as the temperature rises inside the ball turret. Johnson is bringing the B-17 down to a very comfortable cruising altitude below 6,000 feet; no oxygen required and no risk of frostbite. His relief is a physical thing, passing through his body in shuddering waves as adrenaline recedes.

But he knows that as long as they're in the air, they're in danger.

His brain is still processing what he's just witnessed. From the ball turret Smith had a good view of the action: the flak bursting directly behind their formation, the damaged bombers falling out of formation, the fighters' relentless attacks, the midair explosion of the *Black Swan*, the sad disappearance of the *Joe Btfsplk II* losing altitude with a smear of black smoke from one destroyed engine marking its final course.

The 306th has mostly missed the worst of the violence. Sure, the Messerschmitts dropped bombs on them, but they didn't hurt anyone.

Indeed, this bomber group has been spared the worst. No planes are lost and none are crippled.

So it would be easy for Smith to use the perspective from inside the turret to distance himself from the violence, to treat it like a high-end movie production. Something unreal. But he's been at the base long enough to see the empty beds, the raided footlockers, the signs that the dead and missing are indeed no different than he is. The relief is now mixed with dread of the next bombing run—he knows what he should be afraid of and has vivid images of several ways a bomber crew can die.

Smith's also desperate to get back to base. Dying in a midair collision or some botched landing would be worse than being shot. Maybe. The good thing is that, from now on, the mission is simply to get back alive. For the first time today, he shares this goal with the 8th Air Force.

L. P. Johnson is feeling good. His twenty-fifth mission is behind him. He wishes the run went better, but it's enough to return alive. Now the biggest risk is the bombers around him, especially considering the formation's unexpected members from the other groups.

But after an hour of uneventful flight, the mood in the cockpit is lightening up. The lead bomber, containing Putnam and navigator John Dexter of Little Rock, are making a turn toward land. This means they've reached England, and safety. The 306th follows the group as they turn and start to descend, hoping to bring the formations across the coastline at around 1,000 feet.

McCallum leers at Johnson from the co-pilot seat, suggesting they "fizzle up" the lead pilot's final mission to make it a better story. "Let's be dramatic and ditch ourselves off the English coast," he says. The pair chuckle, but Johnson will later say, morbidly, "I nearly had the last laugh."

LOST IN NAVIGATION

Robert Morgan, flying in the *Memphis Belle,* is not feeling chipper. His bomber has lost an engine, the 303rd Bomb Group has lost men, and the errant bombing casts a pall on the return home.

He's miles behind the 306th and their ad hoc formation. As he watches, the group ahead turns as one. A voice comes over his intercom: Captain Charles Leighton, his navigator from Flint, Michigan. "Don't follow them," he says. "They're going back over France."

Morgan sits in frustration as dozens of B-17s curve away and vanish in the overcast to the west. "We could not help them," he later writes in his memoirs. "The prohibitions against breaking radio silence, and thus risking a massive, minutely focused attack, were cruelly rigid—but ironclad. Another day at the office."

Leighton is correct. Navigator John Dexter is convinced the 306th is approaching English air bases at Land's End, where the lost and wounded bombers can set down. But they're actually flying straight into the teeth of one of the most heavily fortified locations in France. The formation turned east two hundred miles too soon.

There is no official sanction for the mistake, but Dexter certainly feels responsible for the error. In 1981, when Smith sells signed pamphlets showing photos from the day and a re-created map of the route, Dexter sends a letter with a check for $32.50 so he can buy one. "I want to get a copy of the maps showing the SNAFU," he writes. "I am the one who caused the SNAFU and I want to make sure the map is correct." (An official track chart from 1943 isn't retrieved from the National Archives and shared publicly until the 1990s. The 303rd's track map shows the mission as planned, and the 306th shows the wrong turn into Brest.)

What the hell happened? There is blame to go around, but the main culprit is the weather. The formation is beset by heavy overcast to the west, robbing Dexter of vital visual references. The featureless, gray surroundings also make it hard to gauge the influence of wind on the route. Navigation is mostly based on a time equation—turns are plotted after x minutes of flight at a particular speed and altitude.

Putnam later lays some blame on the 91st and other groups who blew past the IP and (even more disruptive to the navigator) left crews behind, necessitating a 360-degree turn to collect them. "The leadership and navigation displayed by the lead group of the 102nd Combat Wing was hardly exceptional," he writes in his BG mission report.

The compasses themselves are a source of anger for the frontline aircrews. Putnam also writes in his report of the day:

As usual, the navigation problem was made extremely difficult by having poor compass equipment. After the French Coast was crossed, all radio aids, with the exception of the J Beams, are useless, due to the fact that the enemy has beacons and stations set up to jam and mimic them. It is therefore necessary to rely wholly on the compass, when flying under such poor conditions as those encountered on this mission, and the compass installations at present are far too unreliable to put that much faith in them.

Putnam then offers a solution: "a heavy gyro compass of the remote reading type, which should be made immediately available to the operational groups." These use prongs that change voltage patterns when they interact with the earth's magnetic field. The effect of this hoodoo is that the compass autocorrects any discrepancies in the gyro compass, giving a true magnetic heading.

Others reference the error in reports but ascribe other blame. The 91st report cites unexpectedly strong headwinds that slow the formation's progress and throw off the navigation. In the 303rd's mission report, Robert Morgan briefly notes that the group has been lured to the French coast with a false German signal. This is unlikely, but speaks to the paranoia and overall lack of faith in the navigation.

It's a well-earned skepticism. Roger Connor, of the aeronautics department of the Smithsonian National Air and Space Museum, describes the early years of the war as treacherous. "Navigators were not particularly well trained in those early years for operational conditions," he says. "Right at the beginning of 1941, so about a year before the U.S. enters the war, there's only about 50 formally trained navigators in the Air Force."

One problem is that the airplane, mission, and enemies are all new, and there's no experienced personnel to train the crews. "The trainers themselves in the U.S. that are teaching these classes are themselves quite inexperienced. They don't have a strong operational background to instruct," says Connor, who curated an NASM exhibit on World War II navigation in 2019. "And of course what's happening in the training classes in the U.S., they're spending a lot of time on things like celestial navigation, which is not really used for these types of operations."

The combination of bad equipment, inadequate training, and just plain bad luck has created a perfect condition for a disaster. The formation is flying as if they are approaching friendly terrain, easing below 1,000 feet. The clouds part and reveal patches of terrain, and that's when some of the crews realize they're not in England.

They're flying into Nazi-occupied Brest, France.

There may be no worse place to stumble into. The heavily fortified German naval base at Brest is protected by scores of flak batteries on land, supplemented by antiaircraft ships bobbing off the coast. The base also teems with smaller cannon and machine gun nests meant for use against large ships, landing craft, and ground troops. Preparations are taken seriously; the British staged amphibious sabotage raids on naval bases before. Fearing more, the German coastal defenders are well armed and alert for intrusions.

Most of the weapons at Brest are meant to ward off attacks at sea level and are usually no consequence for high-flying bombers. But the lower the airplanes fly, the more German defenders will be able to take shots at them. And some of the B-17 formations entering the Brest harbor are now below 1,000 feet and still descending.

Al Platt expects to feel relief when the formation passes below the cloud cover. Instead, the waist gunner of the *Vertigo* is horrified. "When land was sighted, it was thought to be Land's End, England, but when I got a glimpse of it, I recognized it immediately as Brest," he says. "There are several peninsulas that resemble the fingers on a man's hand. Once you have seen Brest from the air, you will never forget it."

He triggers the intercom and reports to his pilot, Bob Rand, and his still-new commanding officer, Major Maurice Rosener, that they're flying directly into occupied France. "It might be a good idea to get into better formation," he tells the cockpit.

That's when all hell breaks loose.

"SON OF A BITCH"

L. P. Johnson's unnamed bomber is tucked into the clouds as they close in on the coast. The airplane's two wingmen are at their sides, in good order for such a cocked-up mission. But in the cockpit, there's a moment of worry. "It seems odd to be going northeast," Johnson says to McCallum.

Then they break through the clouds, coming in to land around 1,000 feet—and straight into an ambush. The vista below is of an unfamiliar harbor and strange-looking military ships. The area is a hive of gun positions, mounted on top of towers, sitting squat on rooftops, perched on cliffs. And these all seem to be tracking the B-17s, slewing barrels in their direction. And then they open fire.

To get a sense of how thick the defenses are, consider just one emplacement that's aiming at the formation from a coastal position near Pointe Saint-Mathieu. It's a small base located outside the city limits that is home to the Marine Küstenbatterie *Graf Spee*.

Naturally, there are eleven kinds of machine guns that are specifically designed to kill airplanes. There are also four 105mm cannons mounted at MKB *Graf Spee*, trained to attack ships or airplanes as needed. They have high explosive rounds that use time fuses for high-flying aircraft, but today is different since they have bombers under direct fire. Just like shooting at a tank or landing craft, they'll use point-detonating fuses.

The "Marine Battery" namesake here comes with the big guns: four 28cm SK L/40, which weigh more than forty tons. Targeted from a remote fire control post, they fire massive, 11-inch shells. Not the ideal weapon to shoot at bombers, but B-17 crews claim in reports that "when the coastal guns fired, concussions rocked planes."

Brest also has vessels dedicated to air defense, "flak ships" that protect the harbor and serve as escorts to submarines and convoys. Some of these are now behind the bombers, having held fire as the bombers passed overhead. There are also submarines, minesweepers, and even ferries at Brest that have 37mm deck guns.

Everything at Brest that can shoot is shooting at the B-17s.

Inside the ball turret, Smith's view of the formation is a sudden nightmare as parts of the nearby bombers disintegrate before his eyes. Sections of tails are shot away, shells burst inside fuselages, wings are suddenly chewed with networks of fresh holes.

"There are three distinct impressions you get from flak if you are in the bottom turret," according to Smith. "First you hear a tremendous whoosh, then the bits of shrapnel patter against the sides of the turret, and then you see the smoke."

Above the turret, Smith's B-17 is taking direct hits. Bullets and shrapnel riddle the fuselage, seeking that lucky shot that penetrates a fuel tank, oxygen line, or a human being. A machine-gun bullet punches through the airplane's aluminum skin and embeds in Kisseberth's thigh. The navigator cries out in his nook and flails around in pain.

It's clearly time to leave. "We pulled into a tight turn and got out of there," Johnson says. The rest of the 306th don't need a flare to come to the same decision. The battered B-17s wheel in 180-degree turns to retreat from the flak-infested harbor.

What follows is one of the rarest forms of combat in World War II—a two-way gunfight between flak batteries and the bombers they target. In Raymond Check's plane, leading the Grim Reapers squadron, Staff Sergeant J. A. Bobbett sees one of the German flak installations cross into the right waist window's frame and promptly riddles it with .50-cal bullets.

Maybe that air-to-ground gunnery training back in the States wasn't such a waste of time after all.

Smith doesn't have to imagine what's happening to the airplane above him; he can see the devastation being wrought on his wingmen. A B-17 piloted by Edwin Pipp (42-5422) suddenly lurches from view in an unsteady dive. Only four men—Pipp and three others—will survive the crash five miles from the coast, but it's the end for James Lear, the pilot who flew with Maynard Smith and the other replacements from the States in April and who was serving as Pipp's navigator.

The close-up ground fire doesn't slack off as the B-17s retreat over water. The flak ships in the harbor below have shockingly clean shots at the still low-flying bombers. The bizarre gunfight gets more unconventional as the German ships and American bombers now blast away at each other.

Inside a B-17 named *Geezil* (42-5404), ball turret gunner Victor Rose "rakes a big flak ship from stem to stern, swept the guys manning the weapons." The vessels below give as good as they get, with the 306th reporting "accurate fire" from them. Rose's B-17 is whipped with machine-gun fire, and a bullet smashes through his turret, wounding him in the face.

Even for jaded crews, the experience with the AA cannons at Brest stands out as a nightmare. Seldom do bombers face such an array of withering fire, and every one suffers some sort of damage. Comments in the mission reports offer emphasis: One simply scrawls in the area reserved for comments about flak: "Brest—son of a bitch!"[9]

For Maynard Smith, the mission has gone from routine to catastrophic in moments. One second he's looking at a placid if industrialized coastline, the next he's surrounded by bursting cannon fire, the streaks of passing tracers, and the sound of bits of low-velocity metal from flak airbursts scraping across his turret. The airplane shakes and slews, then makes a wheeling turn away from land that makes the horizon tilt nauseatingly.

The B-17s' only strategy is to slip out of the trap. So, as McCallum puts it, "We turned north and stepped on the gas."

And then the urgent call comes from the cockpit: fighters at 3 o'clock high. An Fw 190 rips through the haze and makes a beeline for Johnson's B-17. Ignoring the .50 cals now spewing from all the nearby B-17s, the fighter fires a burst at Johnson's cockpit and peels

---

9   Frank Clemons, the pilot of 42-29744, wrote those words. He'll be shot down and killed on May 15, 1943, the last to bail from this airplane as his crew bailed out. Four survive.

away, not able to go much lower but eager to escape the return fire. Now Smith is shooting at the Luftwaffe for the first time.

DUELS TO THE DEATH

The fighters make a head-on attack with their first pass. The *Vertigo* cockpit is smashed with 20mm cannons. When Rosener recovers from the shock, he sees through the growing smoke that the pilot, Rand, is dead. That fighter also chewed one engine apart, which is even now producing orange flames but no thrust. *Vertigo* falls out of formation, wounded and clearly out of control, and thus immediately becomes a popular target as the fighters return, making slashing attacks from both sides.

"The right waist gunner took a direct hit and was blown against the bulkhead between the waist and the radio room. I'm sure he was killed instantly," says Platt. "I thought maybe I ought to put my parachute on, and when I bent over to pick it up, it was blown right out of my hand." He plops onto an ammunition box and prepares for a hard landing.

The B-17 crashes into the water, breaking in half somewhere near the radio room and coming to rest with one snapped wing folded over the fuselage. Platt is thrown into an unexpected cushion of cold water. Now his immediate worry is drowning. There's a shaft of light coming from the waist gun window, but when he tries to worm through it he finds the bent wing blocks it. "I could always hold my breath a long time," he says. "But I was starting to wonder where I'd get my next one."

A fortunate swell passes over the sinking B-17, pushing the wing away from the window and saving Platt's life. He makes his way to the surface, where four survivors are struggling with a life raft. It's riddled with shrapnel holes; only constant attention with a pump will keep it afloat.

The five survivors keep the raft viable long enough to be picked up by a passing boat and become prisoners of war. But the interaction with the German fighter pilots is not over, Platt recalls in a postwar chronicle:

> One of the German pilots that had been in the group that shot us down came to visit us. Before he left he asked if there was anything he could get for us. I said I would sure like some water to drink, and he went out and got me two bottles. I didn't know until years later that he visited Major Rosener in another part of the camp and he told him that if he would promise not to try to escape, he would take him out to dinner. Which he did.

Inside his Fw 190, Walter Ebert is skimming the water to set up for an attack. He's below the B-17s, which is a pretty tight fit since his targets are flying at around 1,000 feet. Ebert increases speed to cut the distance, angling the fighter to attack the bottom of the bomber. Such approaches against bombers don't happen at such low altitudes, and the crews of the 306th duly call it "a new reported attack."

Ebert roars up from behind 42-5784 flown by First Lieutenant Bart Wigginton, a Texan who reported to the 306th in December. The fighter pilot opens up with all his guns when he gets into range, aiming for a crippling shot to the fuel tanks. The B-17 bursts into flame, making a short but violent meteoric path into the water. All ten men are killed on the cusp of the port of Brest.

Inside *Geezil*'s tail, John Roller is also battling an Fw 190 coming up from behind. The pair of airplanes are hammering away at each other in controlled bursts as the fighter closes. Rounds impact the tail section, clipping the right trigger and taking a piece of Roller's hand with it. Another round hits his oxygen supply, sparking a fire.

He uses only his left hand to peel off another burst, and the Fw 190 emits a belch of oily smoke and pitches toward the water. The waist gunner claims to see it hit the water.

The bomber could suffer the same fatal end if the fire can't be controlled. It's a bad situation with only desperate solutions: Roller grips the oxygen line and bends it, stemming the flow but scalding his hands. He emerges from the tail to see the rest of the B-17 in bloody confusion. The radio operator, R. L. Newport, is wounded badly enough to be knocked out of action. He also sees Rose, freshly escaped from his ruined turret, standing bloodily in the fuselage, ready to help douse the tail fire with an extinguisher.

The fighters are still swarming, harassing the ailing formation as it makes its way away from France. Rose mans the left waist gun and Roller climbs into the radio room to man the .50 cal stationed there. (This addition came with the B-17F model, another acknowledgment that the Flying Fortress arrived without enough teeth to defend itself.) He winces as he grips the gun with one blistered hand and scans for a target. The shock is wearing off and he's realizing that he's suffering from seven distinct wounds. He shoots until he passes out from the pain, but it's long enough to ward off the fighters.

Marcel St. Louis and the other gunners onboard Mann's B-17 are also fighting for their lives. The airplane is living up to the squadron's "Clay Pigeon" moniker. By the time the formation is leaving Brest harbor, its gunners have taken hits from flak bursts and 20mm cannons. St. Louis is wounded, badly enough to knock him off his gun position. The plane appears to be falling apart.

There's another solid impact, like someone dropped a jeep on top of the airplane, and Staff Sergeant Charles Vondrachek suddenly drops from the top turret into the fuselage along with a shower of debris. A 20mm shell has blown his position apart. A stunned Vondrachek takes a look at the back of the airplane, seeing the waist gunners down and bleeding. The tail and ball turret gunners have not been responding to interphone calls; he's the last defender standing. He climbs back into the ruined, wind-whipped turret, mans the .50s, and keeps shooting.

The running gunfight has now left the harbor and reaches the Channel. The altitude of the encounters rises, and so do the casualties. First Lieutenant Owen Luby is a former clerk from Massachusetts, who at age twenty-seven now pilots B-17 42-29620. He arrived in England in December and he just received an Air Medal on April 10.

But today, Friedrich May is directly behind Luby's B-17. The fighter pilot opens up and the shattered aircraft falls a thousand feet, hitting the water just 2.5 miles from the French coast at Pointe Saint-Mathieu. All ten men are killed.

The wrong turn into Brest is becoming a massacre.

CHAPTER 7

RISE OF SNUFFY

The wingmen around L. P. Johnson's airplane—Pipp and Wigginton—have fallen from the sky. Their squadron is in danger of being exterminated wholesale. But they're not going to go without a fight. "We broke away, went right down on the deck and hedge-hopped to shake the Jerries off," McCallum says.

The fighters press their attacks. In the top turret, Fahrenhold spots an Fw 190 approaching from 7 o'clock high. (The bulk of the attacks are now coming from the rear.) The fighter gets into range at 800 yards, and the gunner rips 100 rounds at it. "He smoked and went straight down, the pilot bailing out," Johnson's report says.

But the fighter does its damage as well. As Fahrenhold fires, the German pilot does the same, marching a stream of cannon shells and bullets across the length of the bomber. A 20mm shell bursts inside the tail gunner's position, and Gibson feels the hammer blows of jagged metal punching through his chest. An incendiary round embeds itself into the tail wheel well. The radio room also takes a direct hit.

Toward the nose of the airplane, shrapnel from an exploding shell strikes the hand of bombardier Melaun, but the injury is minor.

Smith has felt the bomber suffer previous direct hits, but this is different. "I was watching the tracers from a Jerry fighter coming puffing by our tail when, suddenly, there was a terrific explosion," he'll tell a reporter. "Whoomp! Just like that. Boy, it was a pip."

There's little likelihood he feels such whimsy and bravado in the immediate aftermath of the fighter attack. After the explosion the interphone immediately goes out. For all he knows everyone above him could be dead and the airplane is already crashing, but has too much heart to stop flying yet.

Whether the bomber is doomed or not, there's only one immediate step for Smith to take. He's got to get out of this goddamned ball turret. There's no way to bail out from here; the only way out is up. That means facing one of the Sperry ball turret's least appealing design features: the access hatch.

The ball is made so that the gunner can only exit when it's facing one direction, 180 degrees azimuth and 90 degrees elevation. But when Smith tries to maneuver the turret, he finds it's dead. Either the hydraulic pump or speed electric motor, or both, have been destroyed. He may be in a race against time and gravity, and now he's got to rotate the turret using a hand crank.

As he does, he notices that the bomber seems to be falling away from the remaining members of the squadron. This is a death sentence with the fighters thick around them, and another reason to hurry up and get into the fuselage.

After an eternity that probably took less than a minute, Smith wriggles through the open hatch and into the fuselage. Or what's left of it. It appears he's in one of those classic "out of the frying pan" situations, except more literally than anyone would ever want.

The ball turret access hatch opens near the radio room, except instead of a metal-walled closet filled with radio compass controls and VHF sets, Smith instead sees a raging crematorium. A ruptured oxygen tank is feeding the flames gluttonously. Even worse, the radio room fire is blowing back into the airplane, driven by the ever-present draft in the fuselage. The airplane is already filling with cloying smoke, swirling crazily in the rushing air but collecting on the ceiling.

Behind him, at the rear of the plane, he can see more trouble. From there he can see dark smoke coming from the obtrusive hump where the tail wheel nests when it retracts. The airplane is being consumed by at least two spreading fires.

That's when Bean bursts from the radio room, lurching unsteadily from the flames. "He made a beeline for the gun hatch and dived out," Smith says. "I glanced out and watched him hit the horizontal stabilizer." Smith will tell reporters that the flier's chute opened and he's listed as MIA. But in private Smith later says that the radio operator's body "broke apart" on contact with the airplane's tail. This is the fatal end of Bean's twenty-first mission over Europe.

The death of this veteran crewman is a powerful reminder of the risks of bailing out. It's bad enough to contend with hypothermia, Nazi soldiers, Vichy French collaborators, and military prison camps. But the jump itself can be immediately fatal—as Smith has just witnessed in awful detail.

There's a very orderly procedure on the books for emergency exits, based on calmly delivered orders and effective teamwork. Of course, all of this is abandoned onboard Smith's airplane, where there's no communication with the cockpit. A raging radio room fire physically blocks the forward and rear of the plane. So the men in back are functionally alone in a seemingly mortally wounded airplane.

Crewmembers are not supposed to leap from the gun windows

(called hatches) during a bailout unless they absolutely have to. The
windows slide open to accommodate the airman and bulky parachute. The gunners are in a rush to leave. Bukacek, at the right waist
window, leaps out over his gun and into the air.

Smith sees Folliard following suit on the left waist gun, but appears stuck there. His legs writhe in the air. Smith hauls him back
into the airplane and leans in close with a leer. "This heat too much
for you?" he cracks.

Folliard stares at him numbly and simply says, "I'm getting out
of here." Smith will later remark that the man, who joined the 306th
with his crew on the same day in April, "didn't get the joke."

Instead, Folliard and Smith stumble their way toward the rear,
the location of an escape hatch where the gunners should bail from,
if time allows. Folliard sits on the lip of the hatch, the Channel sliding
below him and the raging fire from nearby the tail wheel well at his
back, and leans forward into the slipstream.

No one who bails from Johnson's bomber is ever heard from
again. In the sea of casualties, they are just three more MIAs in a
very crowded ledger of them. But each loss leaves heartache and reeling families behind.

James Bukacek hears about his brother's loss while in his fighting position in the Pacific. "I know his brother, my father, was in the
Philippines then," says Roxanne Bukacek. "And when that happened,
they let daddy come back because he was the only surviving son."[10]

The loss lingers and families of the crewmen reach out to each
other for solace. Two years nearly to the day after their sons are lost
over the English Channel, Joe Bukacek Sr. writes to Thomas Bean:

10 Since the islands were in Japanese hands during 1943, "the Philippines"
is standing in for military operations in the area, including the run-up to the
invasion of New Georgia and manning defenses against Japanese attacks toward the Solomon Islands.

"We had built our existence around our children. Now what do we have? I do not want anything else."

FIRE OR WATER

Now Smith has a choice to make—face the flames or leap into the 50-degree Fahrenheit English Channel.

The urge to abandon ship is pronounced. He's wearing a parachute and stands before a welcoming escape hatch. The fires are spreading and the toxic smoke is getting thicker. Smith notes that the most experienced man in the B-17's rear, Bean, already voted with his feet.

But with a moment's consideration Smith realizes that the airplane, although unsteady from damage, is still under control. In public he will cite his "implicit faith" in Johnson's ability to bring the bomber back home as a reason why he doesn't leap. He also believes in the airplane's legendary capacity for taking punishment. And even if it doesn't make it to England, there are better odds of surviving if Johnson can splash down in one piece, since there are deployable rafts that will keep the hypothermia at bay and guide rescuers.

"My father said that they were taught that as long as your plane is flying and it's not going down, stay in the plane because it's safer," Smith's son recalls. "At least you've got a chance that it might make it."

Smith also privately tells his son that age is a factor in his choice to stay when the others bail: "They had a little less life experience. There's no sense in panicking. You just do what you're supposed to do."

Researchers have done little empirical work trying to trace the psychological origin of heroic actions. A study published in the *Journal of Personality and Social Psychology* suggested that heroes have twelve central traits, which read like the qualifications for a knight of the Round Table: moral integrity, courage, self-sacrifice, honesty, empathy among them. However, it also lists self-confidence as a common component of many heroes, something Smith has in abundance.

A closer read on Smith's decision to stay with the airplane can be found in a 2008 study that focuses on World War II medal-winners. In it, the authors note: "Perhaps the most common characteristic anecdotally associated with acts of heroism is that of taking a risk. This is consistent across the board regardless of whether the situation involved a lone individual saving a drowning person or a captain fighting alongside his company of soldiers. While characteristics of risk-taking among heroes have not specifically been studied, studies among the general population have suggested that this trait is related to spontaneity, adaptability to change, and adventurousness."

The traits of Smith's upbringing certainly prove his pedigree as a risk-taker and self-identification as an adventurer. "Hokie" may have been a notorious hell-raiser with poor impulse control in Caro, but in the skies over Europe his impetuousness will make "Snuffy" a legend.

There's plenty to get done if the airplane—and Smith—is to survive the afternoon. And there's no one around to do it except him. The immediate threat is the radio room inferno, since it's washing flame back through the rest of the airplane. He turns his back on the beckoning escape hatch and staggers toward the nose, choking on the gathering fumes. "I wrapped a sweater around my face so I could breathe, grabbed a fire extinguisher, went back into the radio room, and went after the fire."

The damage there is horrifying. Behind the curtain of flames he sees the fire is consuming everything: the radio, gun mount, and camera are ablaze or melting. And the fire is even eating away at the airplane's skin, leaving a melted, widening hole in the aluminum. The extinguisher is a little longer than a foot and weighs about ten pounds. Smith aims the hard, wide nozzle and sprays the base of the flames with carbon dioxide. It smothers the flames but CO_2 gas dissipates quickly, leaving hot spots that tend to reignite.

And he can see that the molten aluminum is dripping, widening an already gaping hole in the fuselage and spewing hot globules into other parts of the radio room. If one falls on the floor, it eats away at the metal like glowing acid. If a glob lands on anything flammable, fresh fire sparks to life.

This is not the only potentially murderous conflagration—the tail wheel well flames are reaching into the fuselage. The canvas cover there has already burned away, and the flames persist. As he looks at this new threat, Smith sees a dark outline on the floor, down where there's a stratum of clean air. In fact, the floor is fast becoming the only place on the airplane that is not contaminated by the acrid smoke.

The figure on the ground is rear gunner Hoot Gibson, crawling away from the shot-up tail. You don't need a medical degree to know he's wounded and in a lot of pain. Smith pushes through the haze and as he gets close he sees Gibson's face is pale and his torso is soaked with blood. From the way the man is hacking up blood, whatever tore through his body collapsed a lung on its way through.

Smith squats and draws in welcome fresh air as he drags the wounded man past the blazing wheel well. "He had been shot on the left side of the back. I remembered very distinctly from my classes on how to handle a situation like this," Smith recalls. He nabs a wall-mounted first aid kit, plucks a single-shot dose of morphine from it, and jabs the syrette into Hoot. Smith then turns the wounded man on his left side, preventing the blood from pooling into Gibson's right lung and drowning him.

With that immediate problem addressed, Smith grabs the extinguisher and turns to the blazing tail wheel fire, bathing it in bursts of extinguisher fluid. That's when he sees the Fw 190s through a gunner's window.

There are four Luftwaffe pilots positioning close to the crippled airplane, each poised and eager to deliver a killing stroke. They must be convinced the damaged bomber has been defanged. Time to teach them that 42-29649 is not defenseless.

Smith steps to the right waist gun and fires a burst at an approaching Fw 190, shocking the German pilot into breaking off the attack. The Fw 190 sweeps past the bomber. Smith careens across the fuselage to the left waist gun and shoots from there, too, giving the enemy pilots something else to consider before trying another pass.

There are sudden, barking gunshots and something whistles through the fuselage. It's not a fighter; the onboard fire is cooking off .50-cal rounds. Now the airplane itself is trying to kill him. Sudden awareness dawns on Smith—since the B-17's center of gravity is close to the radio room, it's a popular place to stow extra bullets. He races forward and confirms the worst: the fire has regained its strength and there are fresh, molten blobs of melted aluminum falling on the ammunition cans.

FLYING WRECK

Johnson and McCallum are counting the unsettling number of ways they can die right now.

"Momentarily we expected one of three things to happen: the ship would explode, it would break in half, or the Focke-Wulfs would get us," McCallum later remarks to reporters. "There was not a snowball's chance in hell of us getting back."

The rudder is not responding, and they fear the worst in terms of damage. This is bad but Johnson can steer the airplane using only the ailerons. But there are other connections between the cockpit and the rest of the plane that are being lost. There's a network of metal cables stretching from the cockpit to the flight control surfaces, marionette strings that enable the two men in the cockpit to fly the airplane.

If one is to strip everything else away except these cables and what they control, what would be left would look like a crude nervous system, with the thin wire ropes running from the cockpit's control stick and pedals all the way out to the ailerons on the wings, and the elevators and rudders at the tail. Other connections relay cockpit commands to the engines.

In other words, without these cables, the plane can't fly. There are some contingencies for this crafted into the airplane. They're built tough—for example, each tail elevator is controlled by two cables, each one made of seven separate strands of metal wire. Also, as described in the B-17 pilot's manual, if the cabling to the engines is severed the engine will fall into a default setting: throttles wide open, superchargers at 65 percent power, and propellers at 1,850 rpm.

Johnson and McCallum can tell by the lack of response controls that some of the crucial bundles of wires have been shot away or the heat from onboard fires are snapping them. Either way, it's taking a lot of physical exertion to keep the airplane steady. And they could lose more controls—they have to assume that everyone in back has bailed out or is dead, leaving any flames unchecked.

Fahrenhold leaves his position in the top turret to investigate, and grabs an extinguisher from a wall mount on the way. On a B-17, the engineer has the job of damage control. He's the go-to guy to fight fires and to rig any damaged cabling so the pilots can steer the airplane to a controlled landing.

The engineer crosses the bomb bay catwalk, opens the radio room door, and is greeted by a sheet of flame. He fires the extinguisher through the doorway, sees the dismal results, drains it anyway. The flames, still being fed by the oxygen tank and bursting ammunition, just won't quit. He has no idea Smith and Gibson are in the waist. Fahrenhold connects the interphone jack and tells the pilot, "I can't go back there."

As if this isn't enough, the Fw 190s haven't given up. They're still prowling within eyesight, but for some reason have retreated from the B-17. Maybe they're waiting for the bomber to fall even farther away from the remainder of its formation. Despite the pilots' efforts, the nameless B-17 is losing altitude and airspeed. Soon Johnson and his crew will be entirely alone.

But Raymond Check has seen enough.

Everyone calls Check by his nickname, "Pappy." He's a twenty-five-year-old from North Dakota who enlisted in the Army Air Forces in June 1941. Check speaks German even though his mother was born in Russia and his father, a railroad road master, was born in Poland. This linguistic twist is a result of the shifting and violent nature of European cartography. Check's brother is also a combat pilot, but he's flying in the Pacific theater, which is a shame because he will miss the impending wedding between Raymond Check and an Army nurse in England.

Check's B-17 has been through a lot today. A German fighter took shots at his airplane at Saint-Nazaire, his group was the target of aerial bombs, they've been on the receiving end of naval cannon fire and the victim of machine guns. His gunners have claimed an enemy fighter during the nightmare at Brest harbor and traded shots with flak ships.

There are only half of his squadron left of the six airplanes that took off from Thurleigh, with one aborted for mechanical reasons and Pipp and Wigginton shot down. Twenty men under his command have been lost in the last ten minutes. He's not about to watch another get chewed to pieces.

So Check slows the squadron's remaining pair of planes so they can provide Johnson at least some covering fire. On the one hand, pilots are ordered *not* to do this in order to preserve a squadron's cohesion. On the other, formations are based on elements of a minimum of three. There is no such thing as a two-bomber formation.

Still, the choice is courageous and earns them the attention of the Fw 190s. Check's B-17 and the other airplane are both attacked by the fighters. The combat records show two rear attacks within the next five minutes.

Check watches Johnson's struggling bomber closely. It's not flying properly, the tail crooking downward and starting to drag. Smoke is pouring from ragged tears, several feet thick, in the fuselage. He grimly surmises that the pilot is losing the ability to steer and that the airplane's too heavy to make it to England.

Then he spies something moving inside, a glimpse of a figure seen through that awful wound near the radio room. Then something falls from the hole, a familiar canister trailing smoke. Check sees the figure again, hoisting another can of burning ammunition and heaving it from the B-17.[11]

Maybe those guys will make it after all, Check thinks.

PISS AND BULLETS

It's nearly impossible for Maynard Smith to breathe inside the radio room. The exhaustion of tossing the heavy ammunition crates is making him gasp, but the haze of toxic smoke of the still-burning fire is too thick to inhale. The rank fumes from burning extinguisher residue don't help.

The flames here are lower, the oxygen tank finally spent, but the glowing hot metal from the airplane's skin is still dripping and causing secondary fires. Smith aims an extinguisher and shoots, but soon tosses

11   Primary sources indicate that Check witnessed Smith's heroism. "Saw crew of Johnson's ship do distinguished service in fighting fire," Raymond Check writes in his mission report from the day. "Pilot to be commended, too."

the sputtering bottle aside in frustration. He spies an ammunition can, repurposed to be a latrine. He grabs it and dumps the urine on the hot spots. Inspired and desperate, he opens the overalls and flap on his heated suit. "I was so mad that I pissed on the fire," he says. "Finally I beat on it with my hands and feet until my clothes began to smolder."

He falls to the floor to find clean air, inhales deeply, and rises to scurry back toward the waist. With a gunner's instinct, Smith squints through the hole to see if there are fighters in view. And there they are, careening past the other two nearby B-17s. And another is setting up to attack.

Smith forces himself back into action and mans the left waist gun, just in time to rip a stream of bullets at the fighter, and then steps to the other side and does it again as the fighter breaks off.

The Luftwaffe fighters have chased the formation away from Brest over the Channel. Now they retreat back to their air bases in France, out of fuel and thinking that Spitfire escorts may be nearby. (They're not and neither is anyone else; the earlier and unrelated P-47 fighter sweep off the coast of Brest has already concluded.)

Smith is exhausted. He shrugs off his parachute and sees two 7.9mm machine gun bullets, fired from Fw 190s, embedded in the pack. This likely happened before he picked it up—the ball turret is too cramped to wear a parachute, so the gunner grabbed it after he climbed out.

The damage to the airplane is surreal. The flames have gutted the interior; seemingly everything that could catch fire is charred or burned away. The flames have eaten away enough sections of skin that the B-17 looks skeletal, like a fish on the beach after the gulls have stripped away all the meat save the head and tail. The intact sections of fuselage are perforated with bullet and shrapnel holes.

One thing Smith knows—the pilots need all the help they can get to get this bomber back to England. And once it gets there, the bomber may be too damaged to land. There's one cure for both these impending worries: make the airplane lighter. With the fighters gone, there's no need for the waist guns. He tosses them through the windows, and scans for more stuff to jettison. Anything not bolted in place goes out the burn holes in the fuselage.

Smith will one day tell his son that his performance on the bomber was "almost robotic. He said, 'I learned it in boot camp; I learned it in training. I just did what I learned.'"

The fires are "under control, more or less" when he creeps unsteadily back to the waist, where Gibson is half awake and in clear agony. Smith squats close and whispers a lie: "We're in sight of England now, just hang in there, just a few minutes more."

It will be forty-five minutes before this becomes true.

LIZARD POINT

In the cockpit, Johnson and McCallum are reaching the limits of their endurance. With the control wires damaged, keeping the airplane aloft requires the pair to push the yoke as far forward as it'll go and hold it there, achingly. It's a race to landfall—what will quit first, the pilot's arms, the structural integrity of the plane, or the engines when they run out of fuel?

The Channel seems endless, but 42-29649 is living up to the B-17's reputation as a survivor.

Somehow the airplane hasn't broken apart; maybe that radio room fire wasn't as bad as they thought. The officers agree: she's handling well enough to try a landing instead of bailing out over land, if they can set down the struggling bomber soon enough.

The men in the cockpit and nose feel indescribable relief as the English coast appears. They're near Lizard Point, on the coast of England, a little more than 100 miles directly north of Brest. There are small airfields where the RAF stations fighters, and these have been reliable locations for emergency landings. To the battered 306th, it looks like home.

An unusual day at Predannack would feature the arrival of one or two distressed heavy bombers. But on May 1, an unheard-of eleven B-17s cue up for emergency landings. All of them are riddled with holes and many have wounded onboard. All are low on fuel, courtesy of the unexpected trip to Brest.

Johnson takes a deep breath and prepares to land. The B-17 is in terrible shape. It's not clear from the records what exactly is broken; the mission reports don't specify damages beyond the rudders. But there are ways to land a damaged airplane, although they'd take a pilot of Johnson's experience to pull off. For example, if the flaps don't work, a pilot is taught to adopt a specific glide path and speed. "Don't make the common mistake of dragging it in with a deliberately flatter than normal approach, this will greatly increase the touchdown distance," the B-17 Operator's Manual advises under the chapter called "Emergency Instructions."

One of the reasons why the B-17 is so tough is that its designers believed in redundancy, and that includes the landing gear. If the electronic wheel controls don't work when they need to be lowered, Johnson can order Fahrenhold to manually drop the landing gear There are hand cranks located in the bomb bay area for that very task. But the hand controls for those are in the rear of the airplane, and there's no account of the mission that puts him past the bomb bay. If he did, he would have been the first to see that Smith and Gibson are alive, huddled together in the waist.

If he did visit the waist, he'd also see what little remains of the midsection of the scorched B-17, the exposed ribs and gaping holes. He'd probably share with the pilots what Smith is thinking: it's "a miracle the airplane hasn't snapped in half."

There's no doubt Johnson makes a skillful, gentle landing at

Predannack. He has to. The entire process would be an exercise in paranoia, waiting for just one more thing to go wrong, one more control cable to snap, one structural part to give way, McCallum calling out information from the gauges, vigilant for anomalies. The battle torn B-17 bounces and slows, becoming an immediate marvel to the British ground crews and medics chasing it down the airfield. All the men onboard, including the badly wounded Gibson, survive the harrowing flight. The men who bailed are still listed as MIA, with roughly seventy-five thousand other American troops.

When the bomber rolls to a halt, Johnson finally relaxes his stiff arms from the controls. It's the end of his twenty-fifth mission, just the second man in the 306th to reach that milestone. It's been a mission that missed the target and got tragically lost on the way back. On the bottom of the day's report, Johnson scrawls his coda: "This is a hell of a way to finish."

For Maynard Smith it's all just getting started.

PART 3

MISSIONS AND MEDAL

CHAPTER 8

"GREAT AND UNUSUAL BRAVERY"

May 2, 1943. Captain Bill Van Norman knows a good story when he hears one. As public affairs officer of the 306th Bomb Group, it's his job to find morale boosting tales and pass them along to a hungry and acquiescent press corps. And reading the reports from the May 1 mission to France, he sees the chance to create heroes. Even better, *living* heroes.

The media is nearly an arm of the U.S. military in 1943, as it will be through the war. The press corps is part of the Allied war effort. The Office of War Information (the OWI, to which Van Norman is attached) is the chief liaison that feeds the press the information that the government wants the public to know. Access to combat areas and tips to good stories are the carrots; the stick is the Espionage Act and prison time. And the Office of Censorship has to clear everything.

There's a thin and sometimes shifting line on the boundary between patriotism and journalism. Some of the nation's most popular columnists, like Drew Pearson, on occasion defy the censors without sanction. But most reporters tend to self-censor for the greater good. "There was a huge and gassy thing called the War Effort," says John Steinbeck, then a frontline war reporter. "Anything which interfered with or ran counter to the War Effort was automatically bad."

At the same time, Eisenhower and Roosevelt understand that the American people will expect a steady stream of actual news from the front. It can't be pure propaganda. As a result, the censors allow some very morbid coverage to be released. There are articles that the OWI itself produces that include raw and jarring battlefield descriptions.

One of the best ways to put a positive face on the reality of the war is to highlight the people who have persevered in the face of the worst. There are plenty of candidates to choose from—each day, across the globe, U.S. servicemen are enduring and overcoming impossible odds, sacrificing themselves for their comrades, going above and beyond the call of duty.[12]

But L. P. Johnson's mission report has caught the OWI's attention. There's a recommendation from the group intelligence officer (S-2) on it that says: "This crew should be re-interrogated as there is evidence of many incidents of great and unusual bravery and skill." No other S-2 has requested this extra look, which helps explain why Van Norman focuses on 42-29649.

So Van Norman has a tale of a heroic crew on a tough mission. What to do with it? On the one hand, the mission itself is an embarrassing mess. But editing out the misstep over Brest will be easy. The reports about it are all secret, so if the crews don't mention how lost and confused the formation became after Saint-Nazaire, no one else will either.

A good tale needs one person to focus on. There are three bona fide heroes on the bomber: the two pilots, whom the group com-

---

12   Group commanders and B-17 pilots are recommending medals for other heroes of the May Day, including Roller, Vondrachek, Johnson, and McCallum.

mander has recommended for the Silver Star, and the ball turret gunner, Maynard Smith. When interrogated, Johnson credits him with saving the airplane by fighting the fires and lightening the airplane. His formal statement states Smith's acts "by the will of God alone did not cost him his life, performed in complete self-sacrifice and utmost efficiency and which were solely responsible for the return of the airplane and the lives of everyone onboard."

Van Norman instinctively knows that the story is better when the hero is an everyday enlisted man, not an officer. So the pilots are relegated to side players, despite their Silver Stars. That leaves Smith, the gunner on his first mission who stayed to save the day, to be the front man. That story has legs, as long as the man is awarded dramatically.

Some *Stars and Stripes* reporters in England at the time also surmise that Washington, D.C., wants to grant a significant award to coincide with an impending visit by Secretary of War Henry Stimson. And there's no greater recognition than the Congressional Medal of Honor.

It's the highest award the U.S. military bestows. First introduced in the early 1860s, by World War II it's already the oldest, continuously issued combat decoration of the United States armed forces. The U.S. president presides over its formal presentation, and it's not mandatory but recommended that even top generals salute the recipients.

Whether pushed by the Army or pulled by the civilian government or some confluence of interests of both, the decision is made to award Maynard H. Smith the Medal of Honor. The identification of the gunner as a hero worthy of the honor comes from the public relations people, not L. P. Johnson. It will be decades before the pilot admits this. For the OWI, the story is a slam dunk. No enlisted man in the 8th Air Force has received the MOH, which will give the story even more play. For the Roosevelt administration, it's equally appealing as an award worthy of the secretary of war's stature.

Van Norman starts the process of making Maynard Smith famous. And he knows just who to tip off first: the Writing 69th.

That's the self-given name of a group of eight print reporters the Army Air Forces groomed to accompany heavy bombers on missions over Europe. Members include contemporary and future luminaries of journalism such as Robert Post of the *New York Times,* Walter Cronkite for United Press, Andy Rooney for *Stars and Stripes,* and Homer Bigart of the *New York Herald Tribune.* The eight men (and a handful of newsreel videographers) receive a week's worth of training, learning how to survive the altitude and how to bail out under a parachute. They also are taught how to recognize aircraft and shoot the guns, which is highly unusual for noncombatant media even at the time. Van Norman is a part of the public affairs team helping them prepare.

On February 26, 1943, six of the Writing 69th fly on a raid of B-17s and B-24s over Germany. Courtesy of the weather, bombers hit the secondary target of Wilhelmshaven, which is home to still more U-boat bases. The flak punctures Rooney's B-17 and the fighters swarm. Post's B-24 is targeted by a fighter and his plane explodes. Bigart's formation of Flying Fortresses suffers heavy losses. Post's death ends the program—the Writing 69th will never fly again after their first missions.

Now there's a cadre of writers who are personally invested in the bomber war, but have no access to the front lines. They need to be fed the best tips, and they have the knowledge to help tell the airmen's stories correctly. So Van Norman reaches out to Rooney and Bigart to spread the Maynard Smith story to the world.

The two writers are both at the start of storied careers, but they are very different men who write for very different publications. Bigart is a meticulous writer who came up through the lowest ranks of daily newspapers as a general interest reporter who didn't mind traveling to chase stories for the *Herald*. He's a notoriously slow writer with a bad stutter, one that gets worse under stress. Calling the rewrite desk is a torture on both ends. He's got a sharp wit, but it doesn't come out in large groups. After his flight over Germany, he writes a piece that gently chastises the others' coverage, as well as his own, a frank assessment of the tendency of embedded journalists to infuse their copy with personal aggrandizement.

Rooney is quick, clever, and iconoclastic. He's a pacifist covering history's biggest war, and has a keen eye for absurdity and oddball characters. And although he works for the Army's official newspaper, Rooney is writing for a publication that consistently pushes the boundaries of the censors. *Stars and Stripes* grows more popular as the war continues, graduating from a three-times-a-week sheet to a daily with an eventual staff of more than 150. The paper has two in-house censors, but *Stars and Stripes* delivers enough news for GIs to make it a must read. Plus, there are sports updates and photos of Hollywood starlets.

For the early crop of reporters, 1943 is a high-water mark of their fight to release news despite the censors. "*The Stars and Stripes* . . . was probably the last refuge of the itinerant American newspaperman whom big business has driven from his desk," Rooney writes later. "It moved with the battlefront and in moving took along its own peculiar atmosphere of laissez-faire-as-long-as-you-get-the-job-done. It was a collection of privates and corporals and sergeants who took on the whole blasted Army, at one time or another, and came close to winning."

Johnson, Smith, and the rest don't land at Thurleigh, so Van Norman arranges a limited press conference for when they do on May 2. It's not hard to corral reporters, and a couple from the Writing 69th are on hand. Bigart is tipped off from his desk in London. Rooney routinely haunts the air bases in England to scrounge stories for *Stars and Stripes*. After raids, the newspaper tries to have a correspondent on hand to interview crews in the briefing rooms. The radio people in London are always interested in a story of danger and heroism from the front lines.

The aircrew is surprised that, after their requisite debriefing upon return to the base, they're put on display. Maynard Smith is humble and complimentary, but also carefully chronicles his own actions in comparison to those who bailed out. "I didn't jump," he tells them. "I figured I'd ride her down." He includes his quip about the heat to Folliard before the man jumped to his death and the moment he urinated on the fire.

"Snuffy Smith was enough of an eccentric to have been a *Stars and Stripes* man," Rooney will write in a book, a backhanded compliment that says a lot about his opinion of the newspaper and Maynard Smith.

There is plenty about the mission that is omitted. For security reasons the name of the air base and bomber groups are never used. The name "Brest" is never mentioned, and any hint of a wrong turn is not mentioned, either. The bombing mission is called a success. And the full number of men lost that day is not acknowledged.

Johnson sees a chance to strike a blow for his family's business. In Kentucky, the United Mine Workers of America is calling to strike, war effort or no. It's a politically charged issue. "I wish we had that old moose, John L. Lewis, along," Johnson says, invoking the name of the union leader to shame the workers into going back to work.

It seems Van Norman is backing the right guy for the Medal of Honor—Smith says all the right things, and with a little panache. Van Norman sets him up to appear on Armed Forces Radio, on a segment called "Soldier of the Week." It's broadcast globally. The old, odd man out on base is now on center stage. And he enjoys it.

"Combat crews here are hardened to heroism, but the story of

'Snuffy' Smith on his first raid May 1 over Flak City (St. Nazaire) is still talked over in Nissen huts at night," Rooney writes in *Stars and Stripes*.

Smith's shtick plays well for most, but Rooney doesn't like him. He privately finds Smith a "moderately pompous little fellow" and thinks the gunner's short stature is the key to his personality.

The selection of writers ensures that several wire services pick up the story. By May 3, versions of Bigart's and Rooney's coverage of Smith are in daily newspapers across the country. Johnson's comments also prompt a separate Bigart article titled "HARLAN COUNTY FLIER HAS STORY TO TELL MINERS" that appears (among other places) in the *Washington Post*.

The tale spreads to rural areas more slowly. On May 12, Maynard Smith's mother checks the mail and finds a newspaper sent from New York City. In it is Bigart's story of her son's exploits over Europe. She notifies the *Tuscola County Advertiser* weekly newspaper and they lay the story out on the front page: "CARO MAN GOES ON FIRST BOMB RAID."

It will run on Friday. Before it does, Maynard Smith flies his second combat mission.

FLYING WITH THE JUGS

May 13, 1943. Maynard Smith is looking out the waist gun window in the B-17 flown by Lieutenant Maurice Salada. The crew is entirely new to Smith, except for William Fahrenhold, who is again manning the top turret. The B-17, part of a composite formation cobbled together with airplanes from the 91st BG, has begun its bomb run.

Now, Smith thinks, we'll see what the Germans have in store for them.

This mission is going as well as his first went poorly. The weather is good and the flak has been absent. Even better, the P-47s are on the scene. The fighters have started escort missions on May 4, the first mission since the raid on Saint-Nazaire that became Smith's trial by fire. They don't have the range to go deep into Germany, but the "Jugs" (beefy "juggernauts" compared to other warplanes) have arrived to handle the Luftwaffe threat over parts of France.

Today's mission to the Potez aircraft factory at Méaulte is short enough, at just three hours, for the fighters to join them. So Smith is staring at a crowded sky of eighty-eight B-17s at a comfortably high altitude of 24,000 feet, plus a formation of friendly fighters positioned below them to optimize their performance. The hefty P-47 isn't much of a climber.

It's an ideal bomb run for the composite group, straight and level and with no threats tempting them to take evasive action. Then the flak starts, just as they go over the target, a sudden thick barrage of exploding shells. These cause a frightful display but the gunners below don't have a good bead on Smith's formation, and the flak explodes low and to the left. The bombers drop their loads unscathed, ten 500-pound bombs per airplane sprinkling the facilities below. It's a picture-perfect run.

Following formations fare worse. Salada's crew reports seeing B-17s falling from the sky. One explodes in midair just after the target; three men escape, except each parachute is on fire. Three B-17s are lost during the run, all from flak.

The fighters don't seem happy to see the escorts in the air. The Germans will usually withhold their fighters until the escorts turn back, leaving the bombers on their own. But this mission is short, and the friendly fighters stick with them the whole time. That keeps the Fw 190s at bay—for the most part.

There are a few heart-stopping moments for Smith's composite group, however. After they release on the target and the flak eases, ten Fw 190s start to stalk the formation. One starts to make head-on attacks, and then pulls up steeply when it's three hundred yards from the formation's lead airplane, jettisoning a bomb on a shallow angle. It's a "skip bombing"—style attack that fighters make on ships and ground targets, but done at 20,000 feet. The bomb sails into the formation and explodes, lightly damaging a B-17. A second Fw 190 repeats the attack, and then another, with the same result. Then they leave.

Smith's group hardly even fires any ammunition. When the bombers return to Thurleigh, Smith finds that none of the 306th have lost a bomber or even a single man. The mission reports described it as "easy" and "picture perfect . . . Crews want more missions with escorts."

GERMANY FOR BREAKFAST

May 14, 1943. Any relief Smith feels about the previous day's mission evaporates when he's woken up and assigned to join Salada's crew for another mission, this time over Germany itself.

Somehow the ground support people have screwed up breakfast, and the 306th board the trucks to their airplanes without a good meal. It's just the first morale killer of the morning. The mission briefing is terrifying: this is the biggest raid yet, what the Army Air Forces calls a "maximum force" effort meant to prove just how much damage daylight bombing can bring. There will be 154 B-17s, 21 B-24s, and 12 B-26s dispatched against targets across Europe.

The 306th will be part of the main attack against the naval facilities in Kiel, Germany. Salada's bomber will be one of the B-17s joining the B-24s on the raid. There will be no fighter escorts for their run. Raymond Check, witness to Smith's May 1 heroism, leads the group.

For Smith, it's a different B-17 but nearly the exact same crew as the day before. They take off at 9 A.M. After the usual mechanical aborts, there are 126 B-17s and 17 B-24s flying over the Channel, heading dead east. As the newsboys are delivering the *Tuscola*

County Advertiser with Smith's front-page story, he's inside a ball turret again watching for the coast.

When the formation makes landfall, they're over the Nazi home-land. The fighters swarm immediately. There are around 150 of them: Fw 190s, Bf 109s and 110s, and Ju 88s. The mission becomes a fifty-mile, running gun battle across the state of Schleswig-Holstein.

The 306th faces this onslaught in a tight formation. The fighters make a few passes as the B-17s start their bombing run at 25,000 feet. The Germans have lit a smoke screen to conceal the target but the wind blows it the wrong way and it actually helps the navigators and bombardiers locate Kiel.

There's little flak, so the fighters continue to harass the formations as they near the target. An Fw 109 makes an attack on Smith's airplane from 1 o'clock high, and is chased away with rattling gunfire. Two minutes later a Bf 109 tears past their nose on the way to shooting at their wingman. But they aren't giving the 306th much attention, and the bombardier has a long, smooth flight over the target.

The 423rd squadron's combat diary speaks well of the mission: "This was our first raid on Kiel and we caught the Nazis with their pants down, for opposition from both flak and fighters was nowhere as intense as we had expected it to be. Our uninterrupted bomb run ensured good results, later proved by photos."

The 306th alone drops 61.5 tons of bombs, in 500-pound packages, on the docks, rail yards, and naval facilities. Explosions sprout across the ground, detonating inside buildings, capsizing work boats, shattering rail lines, and damaging a bridge. A few errant bombs hit residential areas, blasting apart houses, but most of the ordnance drops on military infrastructure. The attack is one of the most successful to date.

But it comes at a cost. Smith has a great view of the fighters as they focus on the B-24s. He watches as one Liberator explodes in midair, and two others are sent spiraling toward the ground in flames. The fighters plague the other formations until they're back over the water. The final butcher's bill at Kiel: Five B-24s and three B-17s lost and dozens damaged. There are three men confirmed killed, seventeen wounded, and eighty-one missing.

Smith is seeing the escalation of the air war develop in front of his eyes. From here on out the missions will be larger, the damage they do will be more devastating, and the number of crews lost will be higher. His reaction is emotional retreat.

OF PUBS AND FLAK FARMS

May 15, 1943. Maynard Smith is at the Silver Grill public house in Bedford. This building has been some sort of beer house since the 1860s, and it's a refuge for him. The beer here is weak—the nation hasn't recovered from a reduction in its strength during World War I. But he likes the company here better than on base.

Smith doesn't have much in common with the twenty-somethings at Thurleigh, besides their common jobs and shared dangers. And while intense stress creates bonds between the younger men, Smith finds little comfort spending his free time with them. Other crews stay together on trips to London, play on the same baseball teams, gather to shoot pool, and stay together everywhere, all the time. The strange environment, abundance of masculine preening, and the ever-present proximity of death make this a natural response, one shared on battlefields across the world.

But Smith isn't a young man, and he's not wired that way anyway. He's a contrarian who pushes against officialdom and peer pressure alike. He asks "why?" too much and hates that the Army requires he do things he feels are stupid. "I hated military discipline," he will one day admit.

As a juvenile, his response to the pressure of small-town

expectations was to rebel, energetically. As an adult, living on his own in Detroit, he refused to let career, marriage, or fatherhood define his life. But this military life is a step back into an academy he never wanted to attend and a fishbowl society that he never liked.

Smith's response is to escape. He spends a lot of time in the base library, chiefly reading about mechanics and aerodynamics. He bikes or takes the shuttle into town—a lot. One of his favorite things to do is holding court with English locals in bars, men closer to his age who either tolerate or enjoy his probing conversations.

He's got a lot on his mind. England has sparked his innate curiosity and, as is his way, he's dedicated some brainpower to theories on the state of the nation. Smith tells the Thurleigh and Bedford bar regulars that the Americans' presence in their nation will spark a more pure democracy here. One of his pet peeves is the House of Lords, the branch of legislature that is awarded by heredity or direct appointment. The American "soft invasion" will surely lead to its abolition, he argues.

One OWI writer, Sam Foal, accompanies him to a pub. "Smith, in his heavy, analytical conversations, would just as soon explain the difference between an engine and a motor as between a molecule and an atom," Foal says. "'A motor,' he points out, 'propels itself, an engine propels something other than himself.'"

Smith never describes himself as lonely, but it's hard not to see it that way. Foal notes him preferring "to spend his time off strolling in the park of the town near his station and watching swans in the pond. His strolls are generally solitary, because the fellows at the station don't care much about either strolls or swans."

The Army Air Forces physicians see such escapism as a sign of a morale problem. The group flight surgeons are compiling insightful studies on the emotional toll that the air war is having on the crews. Doctors chart the symptoms in revealing reports at the time that show that "abnormal behavior is becoming more common." Among the problem signs they report are insomnia, temper tantrums, nausea, weight loss, blurred vision, and uncontrollable tremors. And one common symptom of emotional exhaustion is "introverted withdrawal."

Over just three missions Smith has seen more than 150 Allied airmen die in the air around him. The images of the B-17s breaking apart in midair linger, as does the hard-won knowledge that his airplane isn't immune from a similar fate. "He said he watched the tail section break off a plane, and it just glided to one side, and then to the other side, and then to the other side, back and forth and back and forth until it finally landed," his son recalls. "He said, 'Can you imagine what it was like for the men inside?'"

The repeat trips to high altitude, the impossible cold, the frozen oxygen lines and malfunctioning heat suits, the way his fingers stick to cold metal, it's all getting to him. And he has twenty-two missions left.

There's another source of stress on Smith that no other on base could share—the Associated Press has written a story from Army Air Forces headquarters in London saying that Smith is slated to receive the Medal of Honor. The attention already put him under a different level of scrutiny among the men, but the military's highest honor will certainly widen the already considerable gap.

The men at Thurleigh have not had much of a chance to meet Smith before the "hero" moniker is hung around his neck. A scant few, like St. Louis, know him from training. The rest hear of him in context of the biggest award possible, and he doesn't measure up. He's odd, has a strange attitude and a checkered background. Why would they give this Snuffy guy the Medal of Honor? He just got here, after all. And what does it mean? Can he go home? Get extra pay? Meet the president, or some members of royalty? No one knows.

The wire service story runs in the newspapers on May 16. That's also the day Maynard Smith is ordered to report at a place called Moulsford Manor. He's being sent to a "Flak Farm" for seven days.

For all the seeming callousness of the 8th Air Force, putting tens of thousands of men at risk in the name of daylight precision bombing, there is a steady effort underway to ease their emotional burdens. The group doctors abandoned the idea that a two-day pass, spent drinking in London or Thurleigh, is enough of a tonic for the men's combat stress. They may blow off some steam that way, but they're certainly not coming back refreshed. So in late 1942 the first "rest home" opens in England. These are quiet places where aircrews can shed their uniforms, unplug from the war, and decompress in rural tranquility. The crews call them "Flak Farms."

Moulsford Manor is just the third such rest home opened in England. It opens just three days before Smith gets there, making him and the eight other men from the 306th among the first to ever use it. It oozes legitimate English charm. There's a carefully manicured hedge standing in front of a quintessential, two-story country estate. A dozen cheerful windows face the neatly trimmed front yard. Smith spies the banks of the Thames beckoning nearby.

This tract of land is tied to the very marrow of English history. It was owned by the Crown until Henry I granted the Manor of Moulsford to Gerald Fitzwalter, one of his barons, in 1130 AD or so. The manor changed hands innumerable times until A. B. Marks took control of the place in 1929 and made it into a hotel. Now it's a rest home for up to thirty-five war-weary men.

There, like a vision, stands a young woman to greet them in the doorway. She's one of two Red Cross recreation workers who staff the rest home. They may dress like nurses but they are trained to boogie—literally. Dancing and games are some of the specialties of these recruits, "women of virtue" shipped from the United States to keep the men company. They are each college-educated, at least twenty-five years old, and committed to serve at the rest home for at least a year. English people own the property and tend to the grounds, but Americans run the recreation and dining.

The men are shown to their rooms. Smith feels enormous relief to have his own room. He shucks off his uniform and hangs it up. Except for evening dinner, it won't be needed. There are civilian clothes in the room, waiting for him.

The nurses fill them in on the options. There's any number of outdoor activities to choose from: golf, basketball, horseback riding, baseball, archery, bicycles. If it rains, there's always the pool table, playing cards, and darts. And the nurses play music and dance with the men, who tend to be equally enamored and respectful of the Red Cross women. The men consider them to be like family, and tend to enjoy their company on that level.

The Army Air Forces continues to monitor the flak home residents. Medical officers and psychologists visit on a schedule, interviewing the men and offering evaluations. They can extend a man's stay, if they deem it prudent. But space here is at a premium; it's understood that every crewman will get to visit a Flak Farm once during his tour.

Assignments to a rest home usually come when someone shows signs of fatigue, loses a friend, or survives a particularly tough mission. Smith is withdrawn and certainly has endured a traumatic mission, even by 8th Air Force standards. He doesn't need the news of an impending Medal of Honor to fast-track him to a rest home.

It also may be a matter of safety. Not the safety of this impending MOH recipient—he'll fly more dangerous missions in the weeks to come—but for the safety of the men he'll fly with. News of the impending medal could shake his focus and distract the other men. If this is a factor in assigning him to a rest house, it's the first sign that the effort to boost the men's morale by granting Smith the MOH could backfire.

The reprieve is all too brief. Maynard Smith spends May 19, his thirty-second birthday, at the Moulsford. On May 23 he leaves the manor and heads back to base. Famous or not, exhausted or rested, pending Medal of Honor or not, Smith is going back into action.

ROCKETS OVER GERMANY

June 11, 1943. Maynard Smith doesn't like the way this mission is shaping up. By now he's seen tight formations and loose ones, ad hoc constructions and days when it all goes according to plan. But he's never seen a mess like the one developing outside his turret.

In the cockpit of his bomber, Check is fuming. He's the squadron leader of six planes from the 306th, attached to a composite group filled out by the 92nd BG. This group is new to Europe, just arrived in May, and it shows.

Robert Williams, the 306th operations officer, offers this scathing review of the navigation of the mission: "The 92nd Bombardment Group again proved itself a disgrace to the Air Force and a menace to the rest of the Wing by their display of so-called formation flying. At no time during the flight did they resemble anything more than a casual gathering of aircraft, and at times they were scattered so as to be a menace to the squadron that flew with them."

Check is the leader of that unfortunate squadron. Check's too far along into his tour, with more than twenty missions under his belt, to have any patience for the pilots now around him. The leader seems to know his stuff, but none of the others are keeping in their positions. And this is a mission deep into Germany—out of the reach of escorts, so the B-17s only have each other to ward off fighter attacks. And these idiots are all over the sky, either too far away to offer protection or drifting close enough to risk collision. One mission report makes a point to say, "Captain Check complained vehemently about the formation flown by the 92nd in the composite group."

This is the biggest raid the 8th Air Force has yet mustered—252 B-17s take off, with about 34 turning around for various aborts. The weather is awful, with clouds that make the rendezvous even more nerve-wracking than usual. Most of the crews are annoyed that the mission is even proceeding at all, since the primary target is expected to be likewise socked in with clouds and thereby immune from daylight bombing. By the time the bombers close in on Germany, the weather is as bad as expected and they head for their secondary target: the naval facilities at Wilhelmshaven.

The flight route is a mess. For starters, the planners have them flying too far south, close to the East Frisian Islands. This enables the German radar to pick up the bombers' numbers, heading, and altitude, plenty of data to deduce the target and prepare the Luftwaffe to give a warm welcome. The lead bomber also flies farther south than the mission plan calls for, close enough for the antiaircraft guns on the islands to take potshots at the formations as they cruise overhead.

The waves of fighters meet them well before they reach land, launching their first attacks several miles south of the North Sea island of Heligoland. There are about eighty fighters, mostly Fw 190s, swarming the formations. The clash is ferocious and unrelenting, steady attacks that plague the bombers as they cross the coast and begin their bombing run. Without fighter escorts, the Fw 190s can press their attacks home. The bomb run is a nightmare of attacks from every direction, and the fighting makes getting any kind of aim through the Norden nearly impossible.

The 306th, attacking the Wilhelmshaven docks as other formations head to other nearby airfields and naval installations, isn't harried as badly as the rest. Their bombs drop on target, detonating at least one oil storage tank, shattering some barracks, and damaging the railroad tracks stretched across a pier.

Most of the others flying that day fare much worse, and their ordnance falls thousands of feet off target. The lack of escorts exposes bombers to disruptive attacks during their bombing runs, ruining the accuracy that Eaker has promised.

Smith is hammering away at the Fw 190s with the twin .50 cals, listening intently to the directional calls being offered over the interphone. The airplane is at 26,000 feet and into its bombing run. His breath is rasping heavy inside the oxygen mask. Not for the first time, he marvels at the almost science-fiction battlefront around him—fighting for his life at altitudes where humans clearly don't belong, wrapped in gadgets but always vulnerable to brutal injury.

Again, the Germans are using a new weapon against them. The B-17 crews see strange streaks of white smoke, followed by a black, flak-like airburst. These come in bunches of three to five. They are rockets fired by Bf 109Gs and Fw 190s from the *Erprobungskommando* 25 test and evaluation detachment embedded within I/JG 1. The squadron is putting 210mm *Werfer* launchers through some real-world paces and introducing the world to a crude, early look at what will become the missile-dominated future of air-to-air combat.

The rockets explode a few hundred yards in front of the 306th, doing no significant damage but promising a whole new way to die in the weeks ahead. This battlefield test doesn't need to shoot down bombers to be a success; the lessons learned today will ensure that next time rockets are used, the scorecard will read differently.

Smith's composite group drops on their specific target, the Bauhafen ship berths. Up until now the flak has been moderate, but the many gun crews directly around the Kriegsmarine facilities open up at the right altitude, covering the sky with black bursts and dangerous shards of metal. Smith sees a nearby B-17 vanish in a flash and transform into fragments of tumbling, burning debris.

The attacks from below disrupt the formations enough that there are only about ten seconds of steady flight in which Check's bombardier can aim the bombs. His squadron drops dozens of 500-pound bombs on the corner of the docks, where they explode in majestic but harmless geysers of frothing water.

The fighters return to harass the bombers after they clear the flak-cluttered airspace over the target. About fifteen minutes after dropping their bombs, Smith spies an Fw 190 creeping alongside his B-17. It's drifting nearly parallel to the bomber, low, its pilot seemingly oblivious to the risk of getting too close. Smith takes a precious extra second to line up the shot and then opens up at about 650 yards.

The Fw 190 drops immediately, leaving a dark trail of smoke behind it. Smith and the tail gunner, Sergeant W. B. Edwards, watch the airplane's 26,000-foot dive as long as they can. Edwards sees a fighter on the water's surface, on fire but afloat, and thereby corroborates the shootdown.

The Army Air Forces claims eighty-five Luftwaffe fighters that day. This, as usual, is impossibly high. The Germans record just seven fighters lost in action there on June 11. The typical reason for such inflated numbers is multiple claims on the same aircraft, with as many as four gunners taking credit for any single plane downed. There are not too many other gunners making claims in that location and time, but a nearby tail gunner named E. S. Mason shoots an Fw 190 moving in from the rear at about the same time. He claims the Fw 190 is hit with about thirty rounds and goes into a spin, a very different description than that given by Smith and Edwards. The ball turret gunner, then, likely earns his kill honestly.

The Germans are no better at estimates. They claim twenty-one B-17s shot down on June 11; the actual tally is eight lost and sixty-two damaged. The real numbers are bad enough: eighty missing airmen, plus the three killed and twenty wounded onboard the bombers. "This mission should never have been flown, with the weather conditions prevailing," Williams says in the mission report, which serves as good as any other coda to the June 11 raid.

ONCE MORE OVER GERMANY

On the morning of June 13 Maynard Smith is selected to man the ball turret on a mission to Bremen. This time, he's part of an all-star crew of senior officers inside B-17 42-3172, *Chennault's Pappy*.

Major John L. Lambert, commanding officer of the 423rd squadron since February, is piloting the lead aircraft on the mission. He plucks the crewmen he trusts, which includes Maynard Smith in the ball turret. This is one raid that will not get lost; there are two navigators onboard to make sure of it.

In the tail gunner's position is none other than Colonel Claude Putnam, head of the entire 306th. He's soon to give up command of the group and head to headquarters, part of his grooming to take command of the entire 91st BG. But today he's just a crewman on the front lines, looking for targets from the B-17's tail.

There may be an element of celebrity at work here. Flying in combat with a Medal of Honor recipient is the sort of thing that would appeal to some military men. But there's no way that anyone with a shaky combat reputation would be invited to join this crew; even Clark Gable himself, in England at this time to make a documentary about the 351st group, had to receive his wings before he could film onboard. Experienced fliers do not take chances on anyone they don't trust. Smith has come from the rest home to the ball turret of the lead bomber of an entire mission, flying with top officers.

The mission has a similar route but diverges toward two targets: two prongs of 150 B-17s will attack Bremen and Kiel at the same time.

The mission planners figure that the move will split the response of the fighters, making both missions easier. The Germans don't oblige this plan, and focus the defense on the attackers heading to Kiel. They get hammered while Lambert, Smith, and the rest of the formation hit Bremen without much fighter opposition.

Even the weather is cooperating. There are no clouds obscuring the view; no natural ones, anyway. The Germans have a solid smoke screen covering the naval facilities. The formations start what looks like a smooth bomb run at 26,000 feet. The flak thus far has been inaccurate and sporadic.

But the gun batteries below have been tracking the lead group, and the Germans open fire just before the first of the bombers is ready to drop. A heavy barrage fills the sky over Bremen, peppering nearly every airplane in the formation with shrapnel. The target is so obscured by flak explosions that the results of the bombing can't even be seen.

In the cockpit a whirling piece of shrapnel cuts harmlessly through the lower part of the cockpit. Other flak shells rip into the right waist position. Smith hears the metal rattling against the turret and feels the shudders as the flak impacts his bomber. But after they clear the barrage, he finds *Chennault's Pappy* is sporting some new, ragged holes but the crew is untouched. Smith can see an antiaircraft shell has punctured the wing between the engines, perfect placement to damage the fuel tank there. The airplane soldiers on.

But another B-17 is mortally wounded. Flown by Lieutenant William Marcotte, it is under control but clearly can't keep up with the formation. Marcotte's plane is last seen going down but still under control, with eight men exiting under parachutes.

That's the only B-17 lost during the mission over Bremen. However, in nearby Kiel the aerial battle is vicious. The force of sixty B-17s dispatched there—the second, smaller prong of the two-headed attack—meet a hundred Luftwaffe interceptors, "the heaviest fighter attacks to date," which dog the formations during the entire mission. The results are staggering: twenty-two B-17s lost and twenty-four damaged, one beyond repair. There are 3 men killed, 20 wounded, and 213 listed as missing.

Check selects Smith one more time for a June 22 mission to various industrial sites in the Ruhr. This is to be Check's second-to-last mission, and he tries mightily to make it happen. But after the 6:45 A.M. takeoff he realizes the cockpit isn't heated. (This puts it on par with the rest of the airplane.) He lands and takes off again, this time with heavier clothing, but he can't find the formation and the airplane returns to Thurleigh. Such aborts don't count toward an airman's tally of completed missions. But maybe it's for the best: by the day's end, twenty B-17s are shot down and eighty-two damaged.

Smith is drawing good crews but he's also getting lucky. Ever since his first disastrous mission, he's largely missing the worst of the violence as it swirls around him. Death has struck those close by, and like all the airmen there, he figures his time will come sooner or later. He only has five missions on his ledger—his luck can't possibly hold out for twenty more.

It seems that Smith has seen enough of the air war. He's introverted, awkward, and brash with the younger men. He smugly likes the attention paid to him, but it comes from men who are also eying him warily, like a specimen. And there's that jealousy that the strange "old man" is to be glorified with the Medal of Honor despite his short (but lively) combat record.

At some point in early July, Smith's life outside the base becomes more important than the one in the Nissen hut. He skips a briefing and earns Kitchen Patrol duty. *The Story of Stars and Stripes*, a book co-written by Andy Rooney and Bud Hutton, describes the infraction: "Snuffy Smith was on KP because he and his first sergeant couldn't agree on how many hours away from the post Smith could stay with a pass that was good for twenty-four hours for anyone else."

This jibes with Rooney's coverage at the time, which says "he came in a little late from a pass" two times. He goes further in his memoirs, called *My War*, saying that Smith "fucked up," then goes on to say that he's "been in some form of trouble or another since he joined the Army."

Rooney never gives any examples or proof; it seems to be an extension of the base rumor mill, a reputation likely fed by Smith's initial jail-or-military choice to serve. Sam Boal, with the Office of War Information, writes a four-page piece about Smith for *The New Yorker* that provides contradictory details. "Smith had been put on K.P. because he had been late for briefing, a serious misdemeanor and *the only mark against him in his Army career*," he writes (italics added). "He was late because he was talking philosophy with his friends in some pub."

It follows that Smith would be in no hurry to return to the base, which is cloying and unfriendly at best, and an unparalleled source of stress and trauma at worst. But Boal's account also makes Smith's infraction more damning, since missing a briefing is so disruptive to your crewmates. "By the time he returned to the station," Boal says, "his crew had been briefed and a substitute gunner had been given Smith's waist spot."

As a replacement gunner, Smith goes from being selected for flights in the lead bomber to entirely absent from the combat rolls. He never flies in combat after the June 22 abort with Raymond Check.

KP duty always needs to be done, and isn't always a punishment. In this case, it is. The kitchen work is humiliating, but at least it's quiet and safe. And he doesn't know it, but Smith's rule-breaking has set the stage for him to graduate from hero to legend.

CHAPTER 9

CHECK'S 25TH

June 26, 1943. Raymond Check is at the controls of *Chennault's Pappy*. It's not a tough target, as far as it goes, and he's with an old friend. Lieutenant Colonel James Wilson, a former squadron leader volunteering to be with Check today, is his co-pilot. He'll be ready for tonight's party celebrating the final mission and stick around for Check's wedding to the American nurse, planned the next day.

Today's mission is comparatively simple: about two hundred bombers take to the air and strike a handful of German air bases in France. The bulk heads to an air depot near Villacoublay, but thirty-nine are tasked with striking the German air base at Tricqueville. The 306th supplies twenty-one B-17s for the attack. There's a new group commander in the sky, Lack Robinson, who is replacing Putnam. The trip is short, enough so that a dozen Spitfires will be joining the 306th in France as escorts. So everything is set up to go smoothly.

But Tricqueville is now the home of JG 2. It's the end of an era for the *Jagdgeschwader* "Richthofen" as their commander, Walter "Gulle" Oesau, is promoted to *Jagdfliegerführer* Bretagne, the flight leader for Brittany. On July 1, 1943, he'll hand the reigns of JG 2 to Egon Mayer. That's still weeks away: today his men are busy defending against the raids on their own airfields.

The Allied raid on Tricqueville seems uneventful. The flak is negligible and even the few shells at their altitude are well behind the formation. The bomb run begins but the sun is bathing the front of the airplane and making the bombardier's job even harder. The bright light is also masking a larger threat—a dozen Fw 190s from JG 2 ready to attack.

They strike during the final seconds of the bomb run, after the flare's been fired and the bomb bay doors open. They come in pairs, making frontal strikes on the lead bombers in the squadrons. That includes *Chennault's Pappy*. One of the fighters dives, unloads on the nose of the bomber, and peels away. A 20mm shell punches through the windscreen and explodes, tearing into Check's neck. Another shell sparks a fire that sweeps over Wilson's hands and melts his oxygen mask.

The Spitfires react, chasing after the fighters, but the damage is done. Wilson's wounds make it impossible to fly the bomber; he's steering with his elbows. There's more pandemonium as another fighter attack detonates a box of flares behind the pilot's seat. The fighters withdraw as the escorts engage them.

Things would have been even more tragic if Lieutenant William Cassedy wasn't onboard. He's Check's normal co-pilot and refuses to sit out the captain's last mission, instead serving as a waist gunner. He dashes to the ruined cockpit, replaces Wilson, and takes control. The rest of the crew put out the fires and the plane continues west. Cassedy, seated next to the corpse of his friend, guides the plane home to England. Check is the only man killed onboard a bomber that day, but five B-17s are downed over the various airfields, leaving fifty men MIA.

The hardest part is the landing. Cassedy swings the bomber downwind from Thurleigh, the exact opposite of the way B-17s normally land. But there's a reception waiting for Check on one end of the flight line, a celebration of his final mission. His fiancée will be among those gathered, and his co-pilot doesn't want her to be anywhere near when the medics pull Check's body from the cockpit.

NECK ORDER AWARD

July 16, 1943. The C-47 Skytrain, with one of the world's most important men sitting inside, rolls to a stop at Thurleigh airfield. Right now, the Army Air Force needs a living hero, and Secretary of War Harry Stimson is here to anoint one.

Stimson, the famously stern seventy-five-year-old secretary of war, is on a tour of Britain to shore up the Allied war effort on multiple levels. Delivering a Congressional Medal of Honor to Maynard Smith at his air base is one of the most public of the trip.

Gusts of wind whip across the airfield. The Skytrain's door opens and the secretary of war emerges, ass first and gripping a handrail as he finds the metal steps and backs out of the airplane's door. He's pretty spry for his age. His long coat is buttoned up, his tie tightly knotted if a little askew. The wind bends the brim of his hat as he strides away from the airplane, surrounded by eager military brass.

There is a throng of people waiting on the tarmac for Stimson. Officers stand three columns deep, each in pressed uniforms and white gloves. There is also a cluster of high-ranking brass standing nearby, forming a who's who of World War II leadership in the European theater. And they each have an ax to grind with the secretary.

General Ira Eaker, the commanding general of the 8th Air Force, is there to greet the secretary—and to continue his lobbing for daylight precision bombing. Stimson is arriving at the air base at a grim time. People on both sides of the Atlantic are doubting the effectiveness of the bombing campaign against Germany. Casualties are appalling, with thousands of American lives being lost every month. And Eaker is the man most responsible.

General Jacob Devers is also here. He's just become the commander of the European Theater of Operations. His job is to prepare for the invasion of Europe, both by building up ground forces and making sure the right targets across the Channel are being bombed. As such, he's eager to lobby in person against the demands for more bomber support of the ongoing ground war in Africa. There are only so many bombers to go around.

World War II exists in overlapping layers. Stimson is one of the few at the time who sees the entire picture. One central reason for Stimson's journey to England is entirely top secret—Stimson is one of the few people on the earth who knows the scope of what is being called the Manhattan Project. It's his job to fill in Winston Churchill on the progress, and to tell the British that while their allies will share information, all nuclear material will be kept in American hands.

Stimson has other secrets on his mind, some of which have a direct bearing on the men who are flying and dying from the airfield. The cryptographic war is setting the conditions for the Battle of the Atlantic, which in turn is driving targeting for the bombing campaign over France.

He's all too aware of the threat of German U-boats, which continue to strangle shipping across the Atlantic. He has a personal interest in the military side of the Battle of the Atlantic; at the start of the war he lobbied to use radar-equipped planes to locate marauding German submarines, but the Navy rejected the plan.

The secretary of war is one of the few that knows that the

Germans had changed their codes and adapted their Enigma machines to secure their submarine communications. He knows the extent of the bloodbath at sea, and he knows it will not abate soon. And that means the bombers will have to continue to attack well-defended submarine pens in France.

The medal ceremony is the public face of the trip, and a blatant play for a U.S. heavy bomber morale boost. It's calculated to make news. It will be the first Medal of Honor for combat heroism in the air to be presented to a living airman since the award to Jimmy Doolittle, the first awarded to an airman in Europe, and the first MOH in history to be awarded to an enlisted airman.

There's a fairly large contingent of press there, much to the annoyance of Andy Rooney. True to his contrarian self, the propaganda machine puts him off. He chafes at the canned ceremony, the pomp, and the mere presence of reporters from London who usually don't show their faces here. And he certainly sides with those who don't see Smith as hero material.

"I wasn't enthusiastic about the ceremonial medal-awarding story but there were no bombing missions scheduled and it seemed worth a few paragraphs," he holds forth in his memoirs. "Snuffy was unpopular with most of the crews on the base and their attitude was that there were probably thirty or forty other crewmen just as worthy of the Medal of Honor and a lot more likeable."

A camera operator hunches over a tripod to capture the scene, not for posterity but for newsreel propaganda. The eventual newsreel chronicles Stimson's trip—from the landing at Thurleigh to meeting the sheep mascot of a naval gun station at Dover—in the brightest possible light. But the newsreel lies at least once, when the camera lingers over a shattered piece of a bomber and identifies it as the one Smith flew on. The tail number and its very presence at Thurleigh makes this impossible; the unnamed bomber is too damaged to ever fly again after May 1 and could not have returned to Thurleigh.

The entire 306th is on hand, except for the B-17 pilots who are doing racetrack circles on the outskirts of the base in preparation for a dramatic eighteen-plane fly-by. All leave is canceled, and attendance is mandatory, even for flight officers. There's a good number of the 367th Clay Pigeons who are hungover since, as they note in their combat diary, "a very successful stag party was held in the Enlisted Men's Lounge" the night before. This day's ceremony, in contrast, is not even mentioned.

The wind is whipping so hard that the flag bearers have a hard time holding them upright. A mic stands at the ready beneath the nose of a looming B-17, ready to transmit the ceremony live on radio.

The secretary's eight-car convoy arrives at the ad hoc ceremony grounds, and the brass files out with him. A band plays and the B-17s roar overhead. There's only one problem. A question circulates— "Where is Sergeant Maynard Harrison Smith?"

While Stimson is arriving, Smith is in the base's kitchen, cleaning stainless steel trays. No one has told him of the ceremony and none have thought to get him ready.

His dull, oblivious day changes when the base commander's men rush in to hustle him back to his Nissen hut. His best uniform is still wrinkled, and he never really knew how to achieve a tightly knotted tie. The base command underlings have zero sympathy and race him to the ceremony. So much for a trip to the White House.

Smith's floored to see what looks like the entire base turned out for him. There are seven generals and about twenty-five senior Air Force officers in attendance. A band is blaring and the daunting figure that is Harry Stimson stands front and center.

The secretary has two Medals of Honor in his pockets. One is for a bombardier, First Lieutenant Jack Mathis, whose final act in this world was dropping a load of bombs on target. Stimson intones his citation:

> For conspicuous gallantry and intrepidity above and beyond the call of duty in action with the enemy over Vegesack, Germany, on March 18, 1943. 1st Lt. Mathis, as leading bombardier of his squadron, flying through intense and accurate antiaircraft fire, was just starting his bomb run, upon which the entire squadron depended for accurate bombing, when he was hit by the enemy antiaircraft fire. His right arm was shattered above the elbow, a large wound was torn in his side and abdomen, and he was knocked from his bombsight to the rear of the bombardier's compartment. Realizing that the success of the mission depended upon him, 1st Lt. Mathis, by sheer determination and willpower, though mortally wounded, dragged himself back to his sights, released his bombs, then died at his post of duty. As the result of this action the airplanes of his bombardment squadron placed their bombs directly upon the assigned target for a perfect attack against the enemy.

No matter how inspiring the valor, there's something just plain maudlin about a posthumous medal ceremony. The assembled men don't enjoy the grotesque details. So on a happier note, the ceremony moves on to the exploits of a rumpled and very dazed Maynard Smith.

Eaker takes the mic. While establishing Smith's actions "above and beyond the call of duty," he takes a dig at the men on Smith's bomber who died on May 1. "Sgt. Smith not only performed his duty, he carried on after others—more experienced than he—had given up," Eaker says. "Through his presence of mind, determination, and bravery, he saved the lives of six of his crewmates and the Fortress in which he flew."

A few newspaper reports note that Smith tips a wink to some NCOs in the audience during the ceremony. Stimson himself takes the microphone and reads Smith's citation for conspicuous gallantry and intrepidity in action:

The aircraft of which Sgt. Smith was a gunner was subjected to intense enemy antiaircraft fire and determined fighter aircraft attacks while returning from a mission over enemy-occupied continental Europe on 1 May 1943. The aircraft was hit several times by antiaircraft fire and cannon shells of the fighter aircraft, two of the crew were seriously wounded, the aircraft's oxygen system shot out, and several vital control cables severed when intense fires were ignited simultaneously in the radio compartment and waist sections. The situation became so acute that three of the crew bailed out into the comparative safety of the sea. Sgt. Smith, then on his first combat mission, elected to fight the fire by himself, administered first aid to the wounded tail gunner, manned the waist guns, and fought the intense flames alternately. The escaping oxygen fanned the fire to such intense heat that the ammunition in the radio compartment began to explode, the radio, gun mount, and camera were melted, and the compartment completely gutted. Sgt. Smith threw the exploding ammunition overboard, fought the fire until all the firefighting aids were exhausted, manned the workable guns until the enemy fighters were driven away, further administered first aid to his wounded comrade, and then by wrapping himself in protecting cloth, completely extinguished the fire by hand. This soldier's gallantry in action, undaunted bravery, and loyalty

to his aircraft and fellow crewmembers, without regard for
his own personal safety, is an inspiration to the U.S. Armed
Forces.

Stimson drapes the Medal of Honor around Smith's neck. It's the
only Army award that is not pinned to the recipient. A metal, five-
pointed star is affixed to a strip of light blue ribbon with thirteen
white stars. This is the highest honor a military member can receive
in the United States. It's a form of immortality.

The medal was first authorized in 1861 for sailors and Marines,
but the following year it expanded to include soldiers as well. Medals
had been regarded as European conceits until the Civil War returned
into vogue the notion of recognizing individual gallantry. It's considered inappropriate to say someone "was given" the Medal of Honor.
They are always called "recipients."

After the ceremony, a group of 306th men carry Smith on their
shoulders in a rousing display. In the official photos, Smith is beaming smugly. The rest of the men in the photo seem pretty happy,
too. It's a big day for the group, even if it comes with a fair share of
cynicism and irony. There's plenty of that to go around in the air war
over Europe, and not as many reasons to celebrate.

Reporters ask Smith postceremony questions. How are you going
to celebrate, someone wants to know. He says he wants to go into
town but doesn't have a pass. The press people ask his superiors
about this, and the officers arrange for one. It's a ballsy comment,
given his trouble over this and subsequent KP duty. It's also a sign of
his behavior to come.

His reaction to the ceremony prompts a softball question: "Isn't
facing Stimson and the generals worse than the experience you had
putting out that fire?" one asks. Smith stares back for a moment. "No,"

he says. Everyone laughs. Any pain behind the one-liner is happily ignored.

It won't take Smith very long to publicly express some disappointment in the secretary of war's visit. He says he'd rather have an audience with President Roosevelt. Smith adds that he would have settled for King George or Queen Elizabeth, since he has some suggestions on reforming the House of Lords to lay on them.

Rooney is delighted when he hears the explanation of why Smith is late to his own Medal of Honor ceremony. It's quintessential *Stars and Stripes* material in his eyes: sardonic, unapologetically focused on the enlisted man and just slightly anti-authority. "It was a better story than I ever dreamed of getting," he reminisces in *My War*.

Rooney's gleeful, iconoclastic take on the event sets the tone for all subsequent coverage. His portrait of Smith also endures. He calls him "the dour little gunner," following his judgment that Smith has a classic Napoleon complex. Rooney notes in his article that the men on base haven't figured out Smith, but "they talk about Snuffy, himself. He is a character—not the typical American hero folks picture."

His article puts the ceremony snafu at the front of the story, tabloid style, and details Smith's day from the kitchen to the ceremonial field. The headline that runs in London is "SNUFFY QUITS KP TO GET CMH." It runs across the wire services to publications across the entire planet.

The newspaper biography co-written by Rooney describes Smith's reaction to the full-disclosure approach: "Snuffy objected when he read the story in the paper, but the Desk had felt that the news value outweighed the consequences of any possible effect on morale that Snuffy's un-Congressional Medal of Honor job on KP might have had."

Various Medal of Honor stories are printed prominently in

newspapers across the country. Cartoon panels illustrate the May 1 flight. Smith is called the "second most famous man in the 8th Air Force" after Clark Gable. He appears on live radio shows that are broadcast at home and on multiple front lines.

Smith is not quite equipped to cope with the strange forces that work on a man who is labeled the "Number One Hero in the European Theater of Operations." The role of know-it-all goofball suits him better. For all the pushback that Rooney describes, Smith seems to embrace his iconoclastic image. He poses for photos in kitchens, spuds at his feet in piles; the *New York Times* runs it and dubs him the "Potato Peeler Bomber."

He's an enlisted man's hero, the bane of commissioned officers. Sam Boal's *New Yorker* piece specifically mentions that "Smith is a triumphant answer to the junior officers, especially the shavetails." This tickles the remnants of his juvenile delinquent heart. "Shavetails" is slang for newly commissioned officers, including the irksome lieutenants who have tried to restrain him since he started his military career. His enmity doesn't extend to officers he has flown with; he'll always claim that he "always got along well with the crews" and the coming resentment is never focused on L. P. Johnson and the rest.

Money is never far from Smith's mind, and the medal comes with a pay raise. The rumors place this amount as high as $150 extra monthly, and he's been actively asking questions up the chain to get an actual figure. The reality is a disappointing $2 monthly bump, bringing his monthly salary to $174.80. "He sends $100 home to buy war bonds and spends the balance, mostly on the weak beer he drinks at the pubs," Boal writes in *The New Yorker*.

Rooney notes a change in him since the ceremony: "From that day on Snuffy gloried in living the life of a hero. If you've heard of modest heroes who didn't want to talk about their exploits, Snuffy wasn't one of those. In town he handed out autographs, and at the pub he held forth almost nightly and his monologues on such matters as relativity, theocracy, and pragmatism, about which he'd recently read in the base library, got the rapt attention of his British audience."

Shortly after the ceremony, Smith gets an official cable from home:

NO CARO MAN EVER HONORED AS YOU WERE TODAY. HOME FOLKS THRILLED BY NEWS AND BY YOUR GLORIOUS EXPLOIT. CARO IS PROUD OF YOUR MAGNIFICENT RECORD. CHAMBER OF COMMERCE SEND HEARTIEST CONGRATULATIONS ON BEHALF OF PEOPLE OF CARO.
-W. R. GILDHART SECRETARY

It seems Hokie Smith is redeemed in Michigan, at least on the surface. News of a Caro boy becoming a hero puts the town on the map, for a split second. It inspires a well-known (in Michigan, anyway) poet named Edgar Guest to write a verse:

In the little town of Caro in the thumb of Michigan,
The members of the Rotary Club are cheering to a man.
There's a local church elated, and a school that's very proud,
And a druggist telling stories to a happy youthful crowd.
They've a hero now to boast of in a boy they've grown up with,
For the little town of Caro is the home of Maynard Smith.

The poem goes on like this for a while, citing the splendor of the deed and the pedigree of the young Maynard. Even though he's in his thirties, Smith's described in the poem as a child soldier. His father, the judge, makes an appearance. In the end, Guest spares no hyperbole by declaring, "Now the town is made immortal by a brave boy's deeds alone, and the little town of Caro shares his glory as its own."

Local newspapers are the only ones to even mention the legend of Peck's Bad Boy. The *Detroit Times* assigns a down-on-his-luck reporter named Gordon Friesen to profile what the paper terms Smith's past of "boyish pranks."

Friesen is a failed musician who, along with his wife Sis Cunningham, fled Oklahoma during a crackdown on Communists. (It's a witch hunt but in this case the "witches" are active and acknowledged members of the Party.) Moving to New York to pursue music and stay out of jail, the pair fall in with Pete Seeger and his "People's Songs" union support organization. Struggling to make ends meet, the couple decamp to Detroit, where their music careers suffer years of stagnation. Friesen finds work as a reporter at the *Detroit Times*. The pair will later publish the influential music magazine *Broadside*, with Sis as its stalwart editor, which becomes the bible of the folk revival movement of the 1960s.

But Friesen's work today is far from revolutionary, in any sense of the word. It's canned patriotism painted in the glib tone of a personal interest newspaper feature. It should be tepid stuff—the mother of the hero speaks—but Smith's delinquent past adds interesting wrinkles to the narrative. His two wives and child are not mentioned; it's become patriotic to ignore Smith's previous entanglements and outstanding legal obligations in Caro.

"He was the town's Tom Sawyer, getting into one boyish scrape after the other," Friesen mythologizes in the *Times*. "And he always thought up a good way out. His life as a boy was one mischievous, daring adventure. Everybody got to know him. Perhaps no one is as widely known as 'Hokie' Smith."

Friesen visits the Smith home on State Street, where Mary tends to her victory garden and passes the time with visiting neighbors like

Asher Cummings. "She still lives in the same two-story house on the quiet, shaded State street where Maynard was born 32 years ago, the house that Judge Henry H. Smith built for his family," Friesen notes. "It was Mrs. Cummings who told the story of the time Hokie, then around 10, rode his new pony into Carl Palmer's drug store, turned the horse around and rode right back into the street as though it was something he did every day."

Mary Smith lives alone and awaits the frequent dispatches from her son in England. "From his letters I have an almost complete diary of his life since he enlisted in the air force last September," she tells the reporter. The nights of drinking, the sexual liaisons, and the internal struggles with officers are seemingly omitted—the few letters to her that he later stores as keepsakes are long but are also uniformly tame and relate to his training, travel, and work duties. One is a postcard from a church, a clear signal of his virtuous living while away at war.

A newspaper article quote makes clear Maynard Smith's mother knows less about her son's war service than she thinks. "When you hear about big raids like that one on Schweinfurt when 60 bombers and more than 500 men were lost, it's pretty hard not to worry," she tells Friesen. By that time, Smith is not flying combat missions.

The reporter asks her about the May 1 mission and the great honor that followed. "His widowed mother was not surprised," Friesen writes. "Years ago, she had got over being surprised what Maynard might do. But she is bewildered by the fame that has come to her son."

CHAPTER 10

EXHAUSTION AND ROMANCE

July 28, 1943. The 8th Air Force is mounting the deepest raid into Germany ever attempted from England. There are 202 B-17s heading toward targets more than four hundred miles away, a major attack on Nazi aircraft production. Marcel St. Louis is flying inside this mass of airplanes, at a waist gun within the nameless 42-3076, along with the other sixteen B-17 bombers of the Clay Pigeon squadron.

The ambitious targets of the raid are just one sign of the way the air war over Europe is changing. One new and welcome sight is the 105 P-47 fighters joining them on the way in. For the first time ever (and about damn time) all of the fighters have drop tanks, extra fuel that enables them to protect the formations for thirty extra miles as they fly into Europe. They have to turn back before the bomb run, unfortunately, but the Jugs have a few tricks to play on the Luftwaffe later that day.

The target selection is an early sign of the Allied command's shifting priorities. Instead of submarine pens, the priorities are the industry supporting the Luftwaffe. There will be an invasion of Europe—no one believes airpower alone will end the Nazi regime anymore—and this won't be possible unless the Allies own the sky. The day's effort is meant to slow German fighter production, taking the battle for aerial dominance into the supply chain. This focus will eventually become sharper.

There are 120 B-17s dispatched to the airplane factory at Oschersleben. More than four thousand workers assemble fighters within the factory, which made airplane parts through World War I. The company fails in the 1920s, but the Nazi government resurrects it in the mid-1930s. Now it churns out Fw 190s faster than pilots can be trained to fly them.

Terrible weather hampers the bomb run, and only thirty-seven airplanes drop on the target. The trade-off isn't worth it: fifteen B-17s are shot down by flak and fighter attacks. The tactics are changing: Germans have improved air-to-air rocket attacks, using them today for the first time to successfully damage B-17s.

Marcel St. Louis is inside one of the 182 Flying Fortresses that take off to attack another Luftwaffe aviary, the Fieseler Works, at Kassel. Named for a World War I ace and legendary aerobatic flier, the firm won its spot in German military aviation in 1936 when a Gerhard Fieseler–designed observation aircraft beat Messerschmitt and Siebel to a Luftwaffe contract.

These days the place manufactures Fw 190s and Bf 109s, but there's another weapon quietly being crafted here: an unpiloted flying bomb. Inside the factory they call it the *Flakzielgerät*-76 (FZG 76), meaning "anti-aircraft targeting device 76." This helps throw off the British spies who are constantly trying to glean information about Germany's next high-tech weapon. But the craft will gain infamy as the V-1 buzz bomb, built to deliver 100kg of unguided explosives in a balletic arc across the Channel and into England.

As happens in both raids, a vast majority of the bombers turn back after they cross the coast, citing the bad weather and inability to discriminate targets. Most dump their bombs in the sea and head home. Entire groups quit the scene. But the 306th dutifully proceeds to the aircraft factory, although sapped of many of its planes due to mechanical failures. Across the whole raid, only 56 of the 182 bombers that take off make the bomb run.

Along with bombs, the Allied airplanes also carry tens of thousands of leaflets, dubbed nickels. The Clay Pigeons note in their combat diary that this is the first time "nickels were carried, and 84,500 were dropped on the target area." An example of this weapon of psychological warfare from in 1943 is USG 8, a brightly colored rendering of a B-17 with its bomb bay doors open. "Now the American Flying Fortresses are in action," it says in German. The text on the back says, "This leaflet was dropped by an American bomber" and "Adolf Hitler declared war on the United States on December 11, 1941."

During the mission, St. Louis's squadron endures the worst of the air war: furious flak, slashing cannon and machine gun attacks from fighters, and barrages of air-launched rockets. Two bombers are shot down outright, and many others including 42-3076, are badly damaged. St. Louis is knocked down from his waist gunner station during the bomb run by an exploding flak shell, alive but wounded.

Across both raids of the day, twenty-two B-17s are lost. But the P-47s spring a trap of their own as the bombers return. The Germans are not expecting escorts to be appearing so far from England and are taken by surprise as the Allied fighters swoop in on the attack. The Jugs claim nine enemies downed during the ensuing dogfights, versus one P-47 lost.

St. Louis is deep in a morphine haze as the damaged bomber limps back home. It's just as well; the battle has left it in terrible shape, burning and crippled. 42-3076 is one of three airplanes in St. Louis's squadron that make emergency landings at forward English airfields that day. St. Louis's airplane crashes during landing at RAF Hawkinge near Kent. Just after all ten men evacuate, the B-17 catches fire and burns. They're lucky. Across all groups, 205 airmen are listed as missing in action over Germany.

As the B-17s land, 8th Air Force planners are finalizing details of the next day's mission: yet another attack on the submarine pens at Kiel.

THE MEDICAL BOARD

May 27, 1979. Jimmy Carter is sitting in the White House and Peaches & Herb is singing on the radio. Air Force veteran and historian Wayland Mayo is attending a service honoring six Floridian recipients of the Medal of Honor. It's held at the Royal Palm Memorial Gardens in West Palm Beach. There, he runs into Maynard Smith.

The chance meeting, which Mayo eventually writes about online, delves into the events of 1943. "I was somewhat perplexed when Smith told me of his experience after his first mission. He said he flew four more missions, and was ordered before a medical board that found him to be suffering from operational exhaustion."

Smith later tells a reporter that he suffered a breakdown of sorts a couple months after receiving the medal. He says that he's walking down a street in Bedford when "his mind went blank" and "I just forgot where I was." After that, he never flew; the abort on June 13 is his last combat mission.

Rooney and Hutton say in their newspaper history: "What *The Stars and Stripes* didn't print about the gunner [that] they took off KP to receive a Congressional Medal of Honor was that, after he managed to get in four more missions thus qualifying for the Air Medal, an award infinitely inferior to the CMH, he was taken off flying status and went no more to the war as a gunner because all concerned felt that his experiences that day over France had taken too much out of Smith to make him an efficient member of an air crew."

The chronology of this rather uncharitable account is slightly at odds with the records. If Maynard Smith was considered burned out after just one mission, why did experienced pilots choose to fly with him, repeatedly? He's certainly not assigned to any milk runs; the blood-soaked records of his five missions prove he earned the Air Medal honestly. This theory also disregards Smith's attempted sixth mission, which aborted over faulty cockpit heaters.

Studies that examine the 8th Air Force survey of aircrews show that almost every airman suffers some form of emotional fatigue, marked by irritability, bad sleep, nightmares, and excessive drinking. The service has classifications to delineate different conditions. "Operational fatigue" is a physical condition, a result of repeatedly waking up early after poor sleep in order to fight for your life during long flights at freezing temperatures. "Operational exhaustion" connotes a psychological barrier to flying in combat. On base they call it being "flak happy" or having the "Focke-Wulf jitters."

There is some sympathy among the Army Air Forces brass for what these men are going through, although the sentiment comes from the need to keep experienced crewmembers flying. The high casualty rates are a logical first place to look for a cause of bad morale. Dr. Douglas Bond, assigned to the 8th's Central Medical Establishment, is tasked with correlating the combat losses with the psychological damage. Using a year's worth of data between May '43 and '44, he determines there is one emotional casualty for every two aircraft lost. With missions primed to grow larger, commanders fear the numbers of emotional casualties will also rise. The men fall under scrutiny.

In 1943 those undergoing evaluation for exhaustion stay with their units, so it's possible that the medical evaluators had an eye on Maynard Smith for a while and kept him flying. But he's not just stashed inside the group; Smith's assigned to experienced crews taking important positions within formations. Putting a potentially unstable replacement gunner onboard a lead aircraft not only puts that bomber and nearby planes in danger, but it could foul an entire bomb run. It's more likely that his evaluation began after he missed the briefing, but that he went before the board for an official determination after he received the Medal of Honor.

It's usually pretty easy to chart Maynard Smith's life through media coverage: his biggest triumphs and failures were often public. But those few who pay attention to him after the ceremony are not doing follow-ups. Rooney and Hutton explain: "The self-censoring staff of the army paper felt that other air gunners, who might read that Snuffy Smith, the Congressional Medal of Honor winner, was through flying after only five missions, might find their morale lowered in that knowledge, and that such a reaction was worth far less than the story's value in a purely newsworthy sense."

The presence of the Medal of Honor warped the narrative. The Medal of Honor Society will tell you that recipients in World War II were usually taken off combat duty, not as a matter of policy but of common sense. Living heroes were meant to build morale, not create real-time tragedies. Some lobbied to get back into combat, like Marine John Basilone, but it took a long time and a particular zeal. Basilone's desire to get back into combat cost him his life: he was killed on Iwo Jima.

For the USAAF, Smith's MOH was a celebration of survivability as much as bravery. Awarding a living gunner with the nation's highest honor only to have him killed or captured would be counterproductive. Despite this, his direct superiors ordered him into combat well after they knew he was going to be awarded the medal. Had he been killed, the 8th Air Force would have had two dead heroes for Stimson to laud—a pretty depressing sign that performing these bombing missions is nearly suicidal.

The imperative that the group commanders care about to the exclusion of all else is to fly good missions, hit the targets they are told to hit, and one day there will be no targets left and they can go home. Keeping men out of harm's way is not really an 8th Air Force priority; exactly the opposite.

So let's say the War Department et al. want Smith, soon to receive the MOH, to fly just enough missions to earn an Air Medal, as Rooney cynically insinuates. How would the group comply after he gets back from the Flak Farm? Placing him with experienced crews would be a good way to keep him alive. But again, the deadly nature of the missions he flew on, some of the biggest raids on Germany to that time, make this theory less likely.

Rene Gracida, who later becomes a Catholic bishop, served as a tail gunner on a B-17 over Europe during World War II. Ask him if a pilot would chose to fly with someone who was unsteady, even if they were famous award-winners, and he'll make a disgusted face. "I don't see that would happen," he says. "You have to trust those men with your life."

Smith's breakdown in Bedford changes the dynamic; he's no longer trustworthy on a crew. But he's an outlier in another way—stats from the time show most men treated for emotional exhaustion return to combat duty. Any airman who is out of action for more than fifteen days is considered a permanent loss, even though some of these fliers will return to combat after months spent in hospitals. Even considering that, the official tally at the end of the war of 8th Air Force fliers diagnosed with emotional exhaustion who never return to combat is only 2,100 out of more than 100,000 airmen who served between 1942 and 1945.

Smith is one of the ones who never again flies in combat. Whether to preserve him as a symbol or to protect the other men, or a mix of both, the end result is the same. And if he seems complacent about this when he discusses it with people later in life, it may be that he didn't mind being taken out of harm's way because he had other things to do with his time besides dying. Like being famous.

"A NOTE FROM MY GIRLFRIEND AT BBC"
(Typed letter found in the steamer trunk of Maynard Smith.)

August 19 1943

My dear Smithy,

Did you listen in to your broadcast on Tuesday after the 9 pm news? I discovered you were on the air quite by chance, and though I was at work I managed to sneak into the Telediphone room[13] and listen to you all by myself. It was quite hopeless trying to listen in the news room. But I must say that the voice that was you didn't sound at all like the voice you use when you talk to me. However, I can quite understand that Ed Morrow thought you would make a good announcer.

I've just heard that two more Congressional Medals are to be awarded; this time to a couple of Colonels for their part in the Ploesti raid a short time ago. Not at all like 'our' medal though—what are a couple of Colonels compared to my little air gunner!

I'm very tired this week—this is the third night of finishing at midnight and still have another to do and then for a

---

13   The Telediphone Unit was the transcribing department of the BBC that used these recording machines to produce transcripts.

blessed three day break at the weekend. And whilst on that subject—when am I going to see you again? Don't keep me waiting too long, will you.

Maynard Smith certainly had the appetite to pursue the many women available to Americans in England. As this letter demonstrates, his celebrity became a springboard to launch himself at an entirely new strata of potential mates, ones that would be off-limits to most airmen. The official line on sex in the Army Air Forces is, ignore it whenever possible. It was as though, John Steinbeck wrote, "five million perfectly normal, young, energetic, and concupiscent men and boys had for the period of the War Effort put aside their habitual preoccupation with girls. The fact that they carried pictures of nude girls, called pin-ups, did not occur to anyone as a paradox. The convention was the law. When Army Supply ordered X millions of rubber contraceptives, it had to be explained that they were used to keep moisture out of machine-gun barrels—and perhaps they did."

For airmen in England, and to the bitter chagrin of servicemen everywhere else, there is no shortage of women around. You don't even have to leave the base to meet them. There are nurses, for those brave enough to approach. Smith, an older man with two wives in his background and a Medal of Honor on his neck, seems to have that confidence. Says Boal: "He is visibly popular with the Red Cross nurses, an important triumph when one considers the fixed, impersonal smile most soldiers get."

The odds are better when it comes to British women off the base. Not all of them are locals, strictly speaking. In order to free up British farmhands for military service, the government created a corps of women called the Land Army to work the fields. They are housed in hostels that operate more like barracks. With American airfields operating from these same rural areas, the Land Army women and Americans have a lot of social interaction, official and otherwise.

Granting the men leave to go into Bedford is critical to keeping up their morale. Bedford resident George Rayner says the men from the bases would come into his hometown in droves, and the local females knew this: "They would get transported into town from the base in trucks, and they'd just fan out and of course all the girls who were old enough would go into town and that's how they'd meet up and have a good time."

The local economy is jumpstarted by international soldiers on benders, dinners, and dates. There are movies at cinemas like the Granada, the Plaza, and the Bridge Hotel where, resident K. R. Taylor recalls to the BBC, "When you went to see a film, you had to stand and sing the [British] National Anthem and 'The Star-Spangled Banner' before the show began."

Bedford hosts plenty of dances. These are held at hotels, restaurants like Dudeney and Johnson's Shop, and a hall near the train station called the Rendezvous, which has indulgent, American items at its small snack bar including milkshakes and double-decker sandwiches.

Many of these are fun but rather chaste dances hosted by the United Service Organization. The USO started operations in 1941, and quickly became a powerhouse of logistics that brought stage shows, comics, starlets, and an unabashed display of Americana to fighting men across the world. Even more important, but less remembered, are the local volunteers who support the USO events.

The best venue in town is the Corn Exchange, and one hosted by the USO draws Smith's attention. Since 1941 the BBC Symphony Orchestra uses this stately music hall, built in 1874, for public concerts. These are open to the public and broadcast nationally. The capacity also makes the Corn Exchange a natural place to hold large dances.

Dances are good places for Smith. The men wear dress uniforms, so his Medal of Honor is prominently displayed. The USO volunteers are expected to dance with the men, as long as they are being "gentlemanly," and Smith's award and celebrity probably shield him from anyone cutting in.

It's a scene of a romance novel set in rural England during the war: at the USO dance at the famed Corn Exchange, Maynard Smith asks a young, dark-haired teen named Mary Rayner to dance.

MARY OF BEDFORD

At eighteen years old, Mary is a vision to a lonely soldier. Her dark hair frames a fair and gracefully aquiline face. Her torso is slender, but not to the absence of pleasant curves and swells. Her smiles involve her entire face, causing cavernous dimples to curve her cheeks.

The Rayner home on Kathie Road is on the extreme south end of Bedford, right off the main road leading forty miles to London. This is a long walk when the kids want to go into town, but it does have the advantage of being just a mile and a half from Cardington airfield. There, the Women's Auxiliary Air Force, wearing dark uniforms and jaunty caps, trains for their jobs of connecting barrage balloons to trucks and using winches to reel the balloons in and out. Mary Rayner and her little brother, George, sometimes sit on the front porch during thunderstorms waiting for lightning strikes to detonate the balloons.

Bedford is one place that doesn't much need barrage balloons. It's not a priority target for the Germans. It's become the place where Londoners send their children for safety, where the BBC Symphony relocates when the Blitz begins. Bedford is close enough to London that the sky glows red-orange when the Germans launch fire raids, but in some ways it's a world away from the ravages of the Blitz.

Since there have been very few attacks on Bedford, the ones that do occur are memorable. Especially to the Rayner children. "Most of the time, when that happened, it seemed to be a single plane that somehow got lost," says George Rayner. "But, there was one particular time, we had an Allen Engineering Works on the other side of Bedford, and they think that that was the target this time. Only it wasn't regular bombs, it was land mines. They come down by parachute. I mean it was maybe two miles from where I lived, but they were the loudest explosions you'd ever want to hear. Windows get broken and everything." One nighttime raid kills nine people, the only bombing fatalities in Bedford during the war.

The war is not just something on the horizon. Indeed, the war is throwing the Rayner family into chaos. There are six Rayner children, with Mary the eldest at eighteen. Their father, Archibald, left his job as a construction worker to serve in the Royal Army Ordinance Corps. It keeps him at various bases inside England, but he's still gone from their lives. His absence leaves Mary with lots of responsibilities—and a fierce independence.

In some ways the burden suits her. Mary's always enjoyed being an older sibling, protective and lovingly bossy. Her mind-set was cemented at age eleven when three-year-old George falls into a river. Mary leapt in and pulled the flailing child from the water, earning an award from her Girl Guides company.

The war has inflated this sense of responsibility. "If I was to go out sometimes and play with my friends in the blackout, and all of the sudden, if I didn't go home when I was supposed to, there'd be one hand on each shoulder," George says. "One was Mary's and the other was my other sister, June."

Mary has a job working at the Igranic Electrical Switchgear Company in town, which manufactured parts for the de Havilland Mosquito. The ration books define day-to-day life. The family eats a lot of fish, which are not rationed, but Mary never loses the taste for it.

The family had to be fit for gas masks. Mary Rayner, who wrestles with asthma, hates them. But even Mary's one-year-old brother isn't exempt. Infants don't have the lung strength to breathe through the filter, and the Rayners receive a cardboard box with a simple hand pump that would supply the child with clean air if the Germans start bombing with poison gas. Parents would be left to fret for their children through a small window in the box.

World War II has not only taken their father away, it has brought total strangers into the Rayner home. There are always a couple of evacuee orphans staying with the family, children whose parents are compelled to stay in London as it's attacked. "They came off the train and walked through this breach; they had chaperones of course," George recalls. "People would come out of their houses and say, 'Well, I'll take one, I'll take two.' Until then, they didn't know where they were going to live."

The Rayners take in Gloria, whose father is a fireman in London who is busy venturing into the hellscape aftermath of incendiary bombings. The young girl herself has witnessed Luftwaffe bombing firsthand. "She was so nervous. It would take almost nothing and she'd start screaming," says George. "That really was frustrating and sort of scary."

Gertrude Rayner has a timid disposition that masks gritty strength. She births twelve children, four of which die before adulthood. The family has tight ties to the United States. One older brother left for America as a teenager, to return to England during World War I as a U.S. soldier.

After the war, two of her sisters move to the United States, and the Rayner children know her mother has her heart set on following.

The family get about four letters a year from America, each one saying, "Come on over."

And each time Archibald Rayner responds the same way: "I can't just pick up and go to another country. I have children."

Now America is coming to the Rayners. Throngs of U.S. airmen in khaki uniforms are appearing in town, filling the pubs and theaters. The roads are clogged with trucks and jeeps. The nearby airfields are abuzz with practice flights and, most dramatically, assembling overhead for combat missions.

Even the children knew the men in the sky are dying. "You'd look up and the sky was full of planes, and you knew what was going on. Then, off they'd go," George remembers. "When they came back in the afternoon, with the fingertip formation—you know, three-three-three—you could see vacant spots where planes hadn't made it back."

Mary Rayner is also now serving as an air raid warden. She ventures out during warnings, which sound every time London is struck, to hustle people into gas masks and bomb shelters. During slower evenings she prowls the streets and ensures people are turning out their lights.

Air raid wardens have a unique reputation at the time. On the one hand, they are vital links in the civil defense system, brave frontline responders trying to save lives. Even more important is the psychological impact of being able to do something, anything, when faced with the Nazi onslaught. No Axis or Allied bomber commander will ever truly understand the tendency for the civilian victims of bombings to stiffen their resolve in the aftermath.

The air wardens are also, frequently, women, and this brings some discomfort to stuffy British society. Downplaying the morale-sapping impact of bombing is one reason for minimizing their roles, but the fear of emasculating men is deemed another concern. The

attention they do get is reduced to comedy: often in civil defense mag-
azines in England, air wardens are depicted as "Sally Silly," wearing
a sexy outfit (think, lingerie) and on the prowl for U.S. airmen.

Even worse, they are depicted as opportunistic man-eaters.
One cartoon from 1943 is titled "At the Air Warden's Wedding" and
shows an Englishwoman in a white dress standing near an airman
who is bleeding to death on the ground. "Well, what are you waiting
for?" she asks the minister. "He's still breathing."

This stereotype is very unflattering, but it certainly establishes
the conventional view of the relationship between British women and
the American airmen at the time. Plenty of Army Air Forces personnel read the British mags and this reputation, naturally, sparks their
sexual fantasies. The cliché of Americans being "oversexed and over
here" is rooted in truth. The stats certainly indicate a warm reception
near Thurleigh: more than 150 women from Bedfordshire County will
marry American military personnel over the three years the base is
open.

"I was impressed the first time I saw Maynard," Mary will later
tell reporters. "I don't think it was the medal, although I was aware
of its honor. It was the man."

In private conversations later in life, her view of the meeting never
loses this romantic luster. "She said he walked in and they locked
eyes," says their daughter, Christine Pincince. "And that was it."

It's not permitted, on either side of the equation, for a soldier
and a USO volunteer to leave a dance together. But Smith is unfazed:
without the cycle of combat flights, he has the time and the schedule
to follow up this initial meeting with a full courtship.

He pulls out all the stops to impress her: "Maynard was older
than the boys I had been dating and he was quite the man about
town. He has that special way of doing things—a bit cocky I think,
but altogether charming."

As the months continue and the rendezvous become more frequent, it's clear that Maynard and Mary are falling in love. The family is not thrilled, and George Rayner ticks off the three strikes his parents have against Smith: "Well, she was eighteen. He was thirty-three, had been divorced, and was American."

THE HERO MACHINE

June 19, 1943. Robert Morgan should be overjoyed as he and *Memphis Belle* ease the now-famous bomber through the skies over her namesake in Tennessee. Life's been a gas since the crew finished their final mission in mid-May when Hap Arnold himself greeted them after they landed and the newspapermen swarmed them like Fw 190s, firing dumb questions.

But he's not overjoyed. He's annoyed because the P-47s that are "escorting" the bomber (the kind that were almost never available on their missions) are now showboating for the throngs assembled below. One of the people in the crowd is his fiancée, Margaret Polk. She's the belle that the crew named the airplane after, the one whose photo Morgan gazed at in the cockpit over France and Germany.

He does not want to be outdone by a couple Jug pilots, "so I cut the *Memphis Belle* loose." He spends a half hour performing steep climbs, stalls, and tilted turns before roaring over the assembly at full throttle. He makes a crisp landing, and when the crew emerges the police fail to contain the crowds surging toward them.

Margaret Polk emerges from the sea of faces and embraces Morgan. The crowd parts around them and the newspaper people snap pictures and start jockeying with each other for a good position to snag interviews. The pair will be on the cover of *Life* magazine soon.

Lost in the celebration is the fact that other bombers had completed twenty-five missions before the *Memphis Belle*. The first B-17 to complete twenty-five missions is the *Hell's Angels* (41-24577), which completed the feat six days before Morgan touched down in late May. But the *Belle* has a better name, a romantic backstory, and, most importantly, a high-profile movie coming that's produced by Paramount Pictures and is actively supported by the highest echelon of the Army Air Forces.

William Wyler's documentary will be a lynchpin in the next year's strategy to boost morale, and getting the public to know the name is the first step for a successful rollout. So aside from the immediate boost of having newly minted heroes, the intense media attention on the *Belle*'s return is also the first part of the marketing plan of a propaganda film. The media-military spin machine has lofted the *Memphis Belle* into the mainstream consciousness with great energy.

"Snuffy" Smith's celebrity has been quickly and thoroughly eclipsed. His heroism may have the nation's highest medal attached, but the ones carrying the PR torch forward in public in 1943 are the *Memphis Belle*'s crew, each of whom have twenty-five missions and therefore can tour the States with no hard feelings from the men still fighting in England. Indeed, the crew fills all the expectations that Smith does, and then some: they're a symbol of possible survival and they're the kind of handsome officers and scrappy enlisted men that people at home expect.

The War Department public relations people don't need Snuffy in 1943 because they have all they need with the *Memphis Belle*.

The Army can be hard on its heroes, in ways they can't see coming. Like Smith, the airmen of the *Memphis Belle* receive some perfunctory advice on how to speak to reporters, but there's no way to prepare them for sudden fame ginned up by the Army and compliantly patriotic media.

Robert Morgan survived a ruthless air war, but he's not done being knocked around by turbulence. His time in Memphis, between the parade and the parties, is spent with Margaret and her family, planning a wedding. The War Department is planning something else—a nationwide tour of the airplane and its crew to further whip up the populace. The description in Morgan's memoirs is powdered with dry bitterness:

The War Department, in the person of an all-business public relations officer assigned to our tour, a PR officer I remember sourly after all these years, only as Captain Tom. Captain Tom took me and Margaret aside and relayed the strong suggestion from on high. There would be no wedding in Memphis. Not just yet. Not until after the national tour of the *Memphis Belle* and her crew was completed.

The story, the officer says, works better if the pair are still apart, still longing, still in the same lonely boat as so many others. The drama of them *about* to be married, he says, sparks a better human interest angle than if they already *are* married. "The war demanded from Bob Morgan not only 25 missions, but a good storyline as well," he says in a letter to Margaret Polk, referring to himself in the third person.

As a couple, they have the perfect wartime romance—at least on the surface. The existence of Morgan's wartime girlfriend in England is steadfastly ignored by all, but frankly acknowledged in his own memoirs.

Each tour stop is built around a repeating template. Fly the *Memphis Belle* to adoring crowds and VIPs at an airfield, attend a banquet, make speeches, get a fine dinner, and drink with whoever wants to buy them. The young men of the *Memphis Belle,* still reeling from the war, have been thrust into an alien world of applause, indulgence, and pleasure.

The tour quickly descends into the rowdy style familiar to any musical artist or comedian who spends an extended time on the road. They are surrounded by temptations that they never try to resist. Morgan describes life on the road as "parades, speeches to crowds of people, me introducing the crew of the *Belle* again and again from some flag-draped podium with a microphone in the middle. The boys always being charming, humble, brief. The limousines. The hotels. The good dinners and the drinks that never stopped getting poured."

And, he adds, "The girls, girls, girls, girls. The girls in the factories, the girls along the parade routes, the girls in the hospitality suites. Those gorgeous, eager, grateful young American girls. . . . We were boys in uniform who the newspapers told them had done something special, and they treated us that way. God knows we accepted it."

Morgan's less hedonistic highlights are meeting Orville Wright and receiving his major's oak leaves in a surprise moment on stage. An unexpected high point is the reception in Wichita, home of a massive Boeing manufacturing plant. The crowds are enormous, but it's the tour that catches his attention. It's where he sees the brand-new B-29 bomber, long kept secret but soon to be unleashed on Japan.

On the road Morgan gets a surprise visit from his fiancée, father, and brothers. His father dubs him a "rascal" after he witnesses his son drop off Margaret Polk and meet up with "a voluptuous brunette" for a late-night date. Before she leaves he asks Polk to elope; she refuses because she wants a ceremony.

Captain Tom asks the crew to extend the tour, and asks again. The three-month commitment gets longer and longer. The crew calculates that they've flown more miles in the States than over Europe. The allure of easy women starts feeling crass and empty. Drinking masks the growing homesickness, helps them ignore the festering memories of combat.

Morgan loses his fiancée in the whirlwind. He keeps philandering to the point she can hear glasses touching and women giggling in the background of phone calls. Polk later says that "all that wine, women, and song" put too much strain on the relationship. Morgan also becomes fixated on the B-29, and he's pretty much decided to pursue flying the bomber against Japan, something she objects to.

A painful and emotionally charged separation ensues, conducted via letter and telephone. The communiqués are sad to read, but they cite the corrosive influence of the publicity so often that it's hard to ignore. In one letter, Morgan writes: "I come home. I am made a hero when all I want is you. The public damned near killed me and got me to the point where I wanted to tell all of them where to go. You told me I had a job to do here in the States. I did it and a damn good job. I made an awful error in blowing up, but I couldn't help it darling."

Polk is open to dialog, but is not one to wilt. "Something to tuck you in bed tonight," she responds. "Have you ever tried to reflect yourself in my place? What would you have done, or would you do now, under existing circumstances?"

Emotions are raw but the relationship is dead, and they both know it. The Army Air Forces publicity machine has killed the fairy-tale love story by being so eager to promote it. "The public," Morgan tells her, "took a tired man away from you."

When word of the breakup reaches reporters, her hometown newspaper takes Polk to task. The *Memphis Commercial Appeal* runs a story, with no byline: "The original Memphis Belle, Miss Margaret Polk, has just returned the engagement ring, together with one of those you-and-I-will-always-be-good-friends notes. So there's that."

The article harshly blames her for causing "disillusionment" in the pilot and hurting the war effort. "Twenty-five trips in a good cause, to be sure. But the next 25 will not be made with the same zip and zest. What can the girl wish for, anyway?" it reads. "Perhaps she just heard of that fellow who just dived a plane 780 miles per hour. He's a colonel, too. You never can tell!"

The tour drags on, month by month, heading west. They stop in Harlingen Airfield in Texas to meet the aspiring gunners there, heckle Lena Horne in Las Vegas, and land in Los Angeles to perform at William Wyler's studio. But they first hobnob with movie stars at a Hollywood cocktail party. One crewman, Vince Evans, meets his future wife there and auspiciously decides to get into the movie business.

The next day the crew provides voice-overs for the movie, barking urgent interphone messages while seated in a sound room and watching the combat footage. "It brought a solemn mood over us," Morgan says in his memoirs. "We watched footage of B-17s going down, airplanes that had friends of ours on them, and we felt our stomachs tighten."

As the Los Angeles trip winds down, Captain Tom asks the crew to extend the tour by a month. They refuse, but accept one last assignment: a blowout in New York City paid for by the Bulova watch company. A ball at the Waldorf Astoria, where they're staying, Cab Calloway at the Cotton Club, Broadway shows, free personalized watches engraved with the word "VALOR" on the back.

And then it's over. On August 31 they fly the *Belle* from New York to Bolling Field, near Washington, D.C. The next day they say goodbye to the *Memphis Belle,* climbing into their positions one last time. "It was like a funeral," Morgan says. "Here we were leaving the one indispensable member of our crew—the gal that took us there and brought us back, the gal that's been with us all this time across the country."

Morgan heads to his hometown and father's home in Asheville, North Carolina, for a thirty-five-day leave. He's dejected and burned out. The failed relationship is on his mind. "I felt like the two of us had earned the right to our destiny. Then something big and relent-less had taken our romance and used it for its own purposes, eaten it up and spat the two of us in separate directions. The Hero and the Sweetheart. How I came to despise that word, hero."

During the tour's stop here, he made sure to buzz the eighteenth hole of the local golf course. This made quite an impression on one of the employees there, Dorothy Johnson. He courts her with marriage in mind.

With a romantic goal established, he still has to officially decide the next step in his career. In August he receives a letter from none other than General Ira Eaker. He says that press clippings and speak-ing to officers on the scene "leads me to believe that you and your boys are carrying out perfectly the mission we charged you with and creating the most favorable impression. I know this is a very difficult assignment and it is almost, if not more hard upon you and your crew as was your assignment here."

Eaker pleads with Morgan to remember and remind his men "that they continually bear in mind the great responsibilities they bear." This is self-serving for Eaker: there's a problem with Eaker's stated idea that the men who finish twenty-five missions will never see combat again. There's a big push to remind aircrews that this is not actually the case. If the most famous pilot in the nation were to deploy to Japan, instead of staying at a desk job or training wing in the States, well that would send the signal far and wide.

Morgan is a prime example of the way the men love Eaker, and he calls him "a gallant warrior" and that "I probably would have flown a mission by myself if he asked."

Anyway, it's an easy sell: Morgan has been fixated on flying the B-29 since he's seen it. Like most Americans he harbors more ill will for the Japanese than the Germans, since they're the ones who attacked the United States to begin with. He calls his B-29 contact, a brigadier general he met on tour, and asks for his own squadron. So with his new bride by his side, he heads to Wichita to qualify to fly the new heavy bombers against the Japanese Empire.

The men are moving on, but the marketing has just begun. The *Memphis Belle* is the most reliable celebrity within the 8th Air Force, no offense to Clark Gable or Snuffy Smith. Her name will only get bigger: the movie premier is still a year away.

BLACK THURSDAY

October 14, 1943. The nadir.

Marcel St. Louis's dismay grows as he peers out from the waist window of the B-17 *Hammer of Hell* (42-30175). Outside, the P-47s are peeling away from the massive flock of 291 B-17s, heading for home just as the bombers are entering Germany.

This is his thirteenth mission since being released from the hospital, flying with pilot Lieutenant Colonel Dick Butler and co-pilot Lieutenant John Kappmeyer. The early morning mission briefing sticks with St. Louis. It unfolds like a death sentence, and even has a eulogy in the words of the 8th Air Force's commander, General Sam Anderson. He's ordered the following spoken to all crewmen: "This air operation today is the most important air operation yet conducted in this war. The target must be destroyed. It is of vital importance to the enemy. Your friends and comrades, that have been lost and that will be lost today, are depending on you. Their sacrifice must not be in vain. Good luck, good shooting, and good bombing."

The mission route deep into Germany, the poor weather reports, and the solemn words of the general make even battle-hardened men groan in their seats. Dread hangs over the briefing room, the pre-check activities, and from the takeoff all the way through to a clumsy rendezvous. The resulting formation is about twenty miles long.

All for the sake of ball bearings.

If the nail in a horse's hoof can determine the fate of an entire cavalry battle, these small metal spheres could determine the fate of Europe. Ball bearings maintain distance between moving parts, enabling contacting pieces to slide with little friction. Ball bearings are essential ingredients in the armored vehicles and warplanes that form the backbone of the Nazi war machine.

The undisputed center of German ball bearing manufacture is Schweinfurt. There are four factories there that produce almost half of Germany's supply; one, called Kugelfischer Georg Schäfer, has more than ten thousand workers, including the slave laborers imported from concentration camps. The factories are located in two parts of the city, one in the city center and the others near the train station. The raiding B-17s are splitting up to attack targets in both parts of town at the same time.

The Germans know the ball bearings are on the bomber offensive's list of critical industries; it's not the first time the place has been struck. Two months earlier, 230 bombers from twelve groups attacked the city. After the flak and fighters finished, the raid cost thirty-six bombers. Now it's time to go back, this time in greater strength. It's a major test of mass precision daylight bombing, an attempt to cripple German industry just as Eaker and Arnold always envisioned.

The 8th Air Force is encountering improved defenses. In the summer, the Germans establish a new network of early warning radar. A sequence of attacks called "Pointblank" operations didn't hamper fighter production, and Hitler is now dumping funds into more flak guns and new places to put them, like towers and fixed positions on top of buildings of likely manufacturing targets. Like ball bearing factories.

The weather is bad, and it gets the mass of bombers hopelessly mixed up during rendezvous, but the navigation is already vastly improved since May. Nineteen of the 306th group's B-17s have "Gee-boxes" installed. These are radio navigation aids that measure the delay between two radio signals to produce a position, to within 300 feet, from as far as 350 miles away.

The British have been using this technology since 1942. This makes sense given their adoption of night bombing. The RAF offered the technology to the Americans from the start, but the 8th Air Force, with its daylight strategy, doesn't recognize the worth of radio navigation. The crews quickly do, as the weather and poor performance of the onboard compass lead to lost lives, month after month. The Gee-boxes yield "good results" past Antwerp, "after which the signal faded." This is the extent of the good news this day.

The trouble starts well before the formation reaches Germany. Bf 109s from *Jagdgeschwader* 3 start attacking from bases near the Dutch border before the P-47s even leave. These dogfights kickstart a day of violence. The sky over the Netherlands is streaked with contrails, marred by dark oily trails of crippled airplanes and parachutes of downed aviators.

The gunfight extends into Belgium. Robert McCallum, the co-pilot from Smith's May 1 mission, is now a pilot with the 423rd in command of *Queen Jeannie* (42-30813). To say he's a highly decorated, seasoned airman is a vast understatement.

McCallum's time since the close call on May 1 has been filled with bravery, terror, and demolished airplanes. On May 21, three weeks after the May Day Massacre (as some crews dub the mission that day), he's co-pilot in the *Dearly Beloved* (42-29666). That B-17 loses two engines to flak over the target and, isolated, falls prey to handfuls of fighters, mostly Ju 88s. They shoot up the cockpit, lightly wounding McCallum. All the gunners' positions, except for the top turret, expend all their ammunition as the bomber fights its way to the North Sea. The airplane is on fire and seemingly harmless, so a Ju 88 coasts along, watching the airplane fail and putting a few rounds into one of the remaining engines to make sure.

As McCallum reaches the radio room to bail out, he sees a pair of Ju 88s within range, so he climbs into the top turret. He lets loose a long, indulgent stream of .50-cal bullets and the Ju 88 reels, stricken, into the water below. McCallum thus becomes the only co-pilot in Europe to down an enemy fighter. McCallum and his crew end up ditching in the North Sea, and float for more than ten hours on a raft before being rescued and returned to England. That mission earns him the Distinguished Flying Cross and a Purple Heart, on top of the Silver Star he has for May 1.

Now he's in the heart of another deadly mission. McCallum's *Queen Jeannie* is at the rear right of the 306th's formation, a famously unfortunate location that attracts fighters because of its lack of protection from other bombers.

When the Luftwaffe attacks, somewhere above the town of Dorne, they target his B-17 from behind and score mortal hits. The airplane falls out of formation and leaks five parachutes before cracking in half and plummeting to the ground in two spiraling pieces. Half the crew survives to become prisoners of war. The other half—including Robert McCallum—die on the airplane. McCallum's parents and sister hold a memorial service in Omaha at Miller Park Presbyterian Church on February 18, 1944.

Things are about to get much worse. St. Louis and the 306th are entering Germany, over the town of Aachen, and their escorts are leaving. When the P-47s turn back, St. Louis and the rest of the raid still have an hour of flight before they reach Schweinfurt. That's when, according to the Clay Pigeons' combat diary, "all hell broke loose."

No formation has ever seen this kind of reaction from the Luftwaffe.

Seven fighter divisions, from virtually every unit in Western Europe, respond on October 14. That's more than two hundred warplanes rising in waves to meet the massive formation. Fighters will come from as far as the Netherlands, Berlin, and Munich to get a piece of the biggest air battle over Europe. Even some fighter training wings get in on the action.

The 306th's formation is textbook-tight, which the men hope will be enough to ward off the staggering number of enemy fighters in the air. Not today; today it's a liability. The Germans are again adapting, and, as is the case in war, tactics have caught up with new weaponry.

Inside the *Hammer of Hell*, tail gunner Sergeant Jim Harris is watching the Fw 190s warily and calling their positions to St. Louis and the others via interphone. The sky is teeming with them, a screen of fighters attacking in waves that occupies their attention and obscures the threat lurking behind them: twin-engine Messerschmitt Bf 109s in formations of three to five aircraft, with rockets slung under their wings. These "slipped behind the defensive screen, released their rockets at ranges as close as 200 yards and slipped away," according to the 306th combat diary. "One good hit by one rocket was enough to account for a B-17."

Harris suddenly sees the twin-tails at close range, and before he can react there are a swarm of white contrails streaking toward him. One detonates on contact with the stabilizer, shredding the tail. Another hits the wing, damaging the engines.

The bomber struggles, falls away from the formation, and naturally attracts more attacks. St. Louis is fighting for his life, blazing away at any fighters that close in for the kill, when the fighters score more shots on the wings, leaving the bomber with only one engine working. A shell punctures the fuselage and St. Louis drops, wounded.

The crew's panic rises as the airplane's power falls, and with it the altitude. The call from the cockpit comes over the interphone: Bail out! St. Louis staggers to his respective bailout hatch and leaps from the airplane. All ten men make it out, and just in time; the B-17 soon after cracks in half, falling amid the hail of airplane parts, spent shells, and flak metal.

Bailing out is an immediate trauma. Eric Stephenson, a B-17 navigator, will later offer a taut, eerie description in the *Journal of Military and Veterans' Health*: "Out into the cold night air, count five, pull the rip cord, a jagging thrust in the thighs and back, and then utter silence."

Marcel St. Louis, in a state of blood-smeared shock, falls to an uncertain future into enemy territory. He's not alone. Across the sky, stricken bombers are falling like meteors. "Crews described the scene as similar to a parachute invasion, there were so many men bailing out," the 367th squadron diary notes.

The mission continues. Outside Schweinfurt, the B-17s split and head to the two ball bearing manufacturing areas. The 306th is savaged before they even start the bomb run, according to the group combat report: "Upon reaching the I.P., and having lost 12 aircraft due to abortions or enemy action, we joined the 92nd Group and flew high squadron with them, and bombed on their release."

The bombs drop between 2:40 P.M. and 3 P.M., with the fighters breaking off attacks to get out of the way of the flak. The cloud cover has broken enough to aim the bombs. "An estimated 75 percent of Schweinfurt's ball bearing industry was destroyed," one report claims. "This was a very crippling blow to Germany and will be felt by a major part of the German war industries." In reality, it's more like 30 percent and this attack equates to a two-week delay, during which the Nazis will draw on their stockpile of ball bearings from Sweden.

The bombers don't return together. The planned route out is the same as the one in, but the survivors take two different paths, one much farther south. Some crews will later credit this for preventing even more losses, as the others who return as ordered are rocketed and strafed all the way to the coast.

There are German veterans of the May 1 mission rising to meet the planes. Luftwaffe pilot Friedrich May takes off from Tricqueville, where he's now flying with 3/JG 2, to meet the bombers as they stagger home. His men fly 180 miles for a crack at the B-17s, but they'll have to do it quickly since their fuel is low. May catches one just south of Verdun, flying at 23,000 feet, and after his wingmen make several passes from the rear, he follows suit and is credited for the kill. Time is running out for him. May is killed in combat on October 22, near Rouen. He tallied twenty-five kills.

Across the 8th Air Force, the statistics of the day qualify the mission as a bloodbath. Only thirty-three bombers of the hundreds dispatched come back without damage. The cost of life is staggering: 594 men missing in action and fifty more confirmed killed. The mission is quickly given a name: Black Thursday.

Arnold and Eaker have nearly everything they need to make daylight bombing work: lots of industrial targets within bomber range, more fighter escorts to protect them, and better navigation equipment to mitigate the weather. But losing 25 percent of your forces on a single raid is no way to win a war.

The limitations of daylight precision bombing, as envisioned by Eaker and Arnold, are becoming impossible to ignore. So even as Arnold defends the strategy—"We did it in daylight with precision, aiming our explosives with the care and accuracy of a marksman firing a rifle," he's quoted saying after Black Thursday—there are plans to upend it and align it with the looming invasion of Europe.

So after October 14, things change. The bombers will still fly across the Channel, but deep penetration raids are suspended. The Luftwaffe has successfully stymied the 8th Air Force's attacks on the German homeland. Heavy bombers are not going to end the war, but they can certainly assist with the epic land invasion planned for 1944.

"HE NEVER WALKED IF HE COULD GET A CAB"

November 1943. Smith is buried inside the 306th headquarters at Thurleigh. This is not the life of travel and patriotic celebrations that he surely fantasized about.

His medical board determination and the Rooney-promoted caricature may explain why Smith was not taken from Europe and put on a war bond drive tour. People at bond drives want to see strapping, young mankillers, not short, older men with opinions about physics and Parliament. And Rooney has made sure that everyone knows Smith "is not the kind of hero people at home envision."

Besides, the role of designated hero has already been assigned. By the time Smith receives the Medal of Honor, the military-media machine has the *Memphis Belle* and her crew groomed for the limelight. So with a major celebration for the *Belle*'s last mission planned for 1943, who needs Maynard Smith, his dead crewmen, and his anti-authority vibe?

At headquarters, there are four sections he could land in, following traditional U.S. Army structure: Personnel (or S-1), Intelligence (S-2), Operations (S-3), and Support (S-4). He's assigned to Personnel.

The job is what it sounds like: managing the influx and outflow of people, their assignments, and replacements. This new job is dull but dynamic, especially as a flood of new men pour into England. There will be 3,500 Americans at the base by 1943's end. So Smith is transferred where more manpower is needed and the stress level is low.

There are clerks with the 39th Service Group to handle the mass of the Personnel paperwork. But there is a separate section that deals specifically with officers, and another for the enlisted. It makes sense that Smith would land in the Enlisted Men's section, available on the Thurleigh telephone switchboard on extension 36.

From this vantage Smith is exposed to some chilling math that reveals a ghastly perspective on the air war that he couldn't see from the ball turret. There have been about one thousand dead or missing every month since May. That's a 200 percent turnover. And they say *he* has a mental health problem because he doesn't want to fly into *that*?

Smith quickly adopts the entitlement that he enjoyed as a juvenile. It's being fed, voraciously, by his new status and manifests on the base in very public displays of special treatment. Boal lists some in *The New Yorker*: "He is allowed to remain in bed late in the morning, often until 10 o'clock; his mail is collected and delivered promptly; and on occasion an M.P. has been known to give him a lift around the base, an attention that leaves his colleagues dazed."

He uses this influence to woo Mary Rayner. "He never walked if he could get a cab, and in wartime England this was very unusual," she later remarks to a reporter. "He knew the right things to say and the right places to go. He used to take me to the Swan Hotel restaurant where the generals hung out. The maître d', a man by the name of Walter, treated him like he was Churchill himself."

Even officers act deferential. Boal's *New Yorker* piece (easily the best profile on Smith from the era) includes this anecdote: "Late one night, when he was cooking some spam in his barracks, a Major came screaming in to find out who was stinking up the place. But when he saw Snuffy, he just said, 'Oh, it's you—okay.'"

But the schism with his superiors grows as Smith tests the boundaries of his influence and embraces the media-blessed anti-authority rep. Many enlisted men pester him for autographs, but the officers roll their eyes. They sneer as he starts signing his name "SGT. MAYNARD SMITH, C. M. H.," aping the British use of decoration initials. He'll do this the rest of his life.

He saunters into the officer's club, even though he's just a sergeant. No one intervenes. Smith also discovers that he can bully many of his direct superiors. He relates this attitude during his 1966 interview with the *Detroit Free Press*: "If I wanted to do something, and some officer said I couldn't, I would just say, 'Well I'll just have to see General So-and-So about this.' It usually turned the trick."

It's an attitude geared to chafe the officers, and it is going to get worse.

Aircrews rotate out of England, but staff work at headquarters keeps him there. He's fixated on this foreign land, its politics, its traditions, and its people. "The ground personnel experienced a very different war than the aircrews," reads one issue of *Echoes*, an excellent newsletter produced for a time by the 306th BG Historical Association. "While their work continued to be tied to the air operations in each squadron, the long assignment in England provided more access to British families and recreational places such as pubs and cinemas in nearby Bedford. . . . Many of the ground personnel had close relationships with the British who lived around the base."

Maynard Smith certainly does. His new job enables him to escape the hypermasculine world at Thurleigh and instead focus on wooing young Mary Rayner.

PART 4

DEFLECTION SHOTS

CHAPTER 11

BIGGER MAN

January 1, 1944. Now Major General Ira Eaker is reading the *New York Times,* lips pursed. The article is not negative; far from it. But even sanitized, he doesn't like it.

The headline reads "GENERAL EAKER MOVES UP," and it describes his new job as commander in chief of Mediterranean Allied Air Forces. He'll be the head of two American and two British air forces, which certainly sounds impressive. The truth is that the new position will take him away from the historic liberation of Nazi-occupied France.

By the time Eaker learns of his transfer, the 8th Air Force has lost 882 heavy bombers over Europe. Deep penetration raids remain on hold. His mentor, Hap Arnold, has been very critical of the effort's obvious failures and now he's tossing Eaker to the side.

General Eisenhower has been named supreme allied commander in December 1943, and he's bringing his own team of subordinates with him. Ike chooses the British Air Chief Marshal Sir

Arthur Tedder to plan the air operations for the Normandy landings. This would have been a natural position for Eaker, but Ike instead brings Tedder in from the Mediterranean and taps Eaker to fill the vacant spot there.

Arnold doesn't protect his protégé during this reorganization. He writes to Eaker to soothe ruffled feathers: "It will increase your experience and give you a reputation along other lines than that in which you were engaged in England. In other words, you should come out of this a bigger man by far than you went into it."

There's a groundswell from his peers inside Allied command to keep him in Europe. The men of the 8th Air Force are also unhappy with the change. Usually changes end up with more casualties. But they also like Eaker himself. For all the missteps and death, the men of the 8th respect their commander. He's an experienced airman who has flown inside a lead bomber over Germany, a fierce advocate for the campaign and a steady presence at air base mess halls, eating with his men.

In mid-January Eaker is gone, sidelined just in time to miss America's most seminal moment of World War II. His replacement is someone the Supreme Allied Commander has worked with and trusts implicitly: Jimmy Doolittle.

Everyone knows Doolittle, and not just in the Army Air Forces. At age forty-eight, he's one of the most famous airmen of the time and already a legend. He had a day job at Shell before the war, where he'd been researching new mixtures of aviation fuel and indulged in a side-career as a groundbreaking pilot. He's the war's original hero: Doolittle received the Medal of Honor for his improbable mission to bomb Tokyo just three months after the attack on Pearl Harbor. He also won the Distinguished Flying Cross and Silver Star.

Since then (after a fast-track promotion from FDR that skips colonel) he's been the commanding general of the 12th Air Force in North

Africa and the 15th Air Force in Italy. This has brought him into Ike's orbit, proving he's a capable and innovative commander. When he's promoted to lieutenant general in 1944, he becomes the highest-ranking active reserve officer in modern U.S. military history.

But being the 8th Air Force commander is a daunting task, harder than anything that came before. "I'm faced with the job that any new commander has when assuming a new command," he writes his wife in late January. "Selling himself."

He's an impressive figure, and no one doubts his courage or ability as a pilot. (Hell, in 1929 he became the first to take off, fly, and land an airplane entirely by instruments.) Doolittle's command style stands on three legs: personal contact, leadership in the air, and solving persistent crew problems.

Two of three are impossible. The command is too big for him to personally inspire crews. He haunts the bases like his predecessor did, and performs some acrobatic stunts to whip up morale, but there's no substitute for flying missions with the crews and sharing their dangers. At his level of command, Doolittle is privy to secret information derived from sources like Ultra and other code-breaking efforts. He can't be captured, so he can't fly into combat.

But he can fix chronic problems. He takes aim at the lack of heated suits, and within a couple months there are enough to go around even when one set malfunctions, which still happens a lot. Frostbite casualties drop as a result. Doolittle also institutes new programs to alleviate combat stress, including shipping airmen home for a month of rest and bringing them back. (This proves to be a bad idea.)

The new commander also invites more media to see what his men are doing for themselves. He knows the men watch sanitized or even blatantly false newsreels, but still they appreciate the attention. Another hallmark of his morale offensive is to share more strategic details with the men, which reflects his innate belief that those under his command are more apt to do the proper, dangerous thing if they know why it has to be done.

Doolittle needs all the tricks in the book to earn the men's trust. He has to do more than sell himself; he has to convince jaded, ragged men to adopt a new strategy, hit new targets, and follow new policies. All of the above are morale killers.

The chief aim that Ike wants is the destruction of the Luftwaffe to ensure air superiority during the invasion of France. This will not happen by bombing the industry on the ground, but by engaging the Nazi fighter planes in the air. The new mission mandate is simple: kill the fighters. But the bomber crews do not like to hear how this will get done.

The policy until now has been to protect the bombers, to ensure the bombs drop where intended. But now the fighter escorts won't remain with the formations. Instead, the Allied fighters will fly away and ahead of the formations to attack the fighters responding to the raid. Doolittle assures them that this will help clear the skies before a bomb run, but for crews who have been begging for escorts for years, it sounds like they'll be on their own again. The change strikes at the foundational idea drilled into the 8th Air Force community since inception: the idea that striking the target is worth dying for. Now they've been reduced to bait.

The men blame Doolittle, but he's enacting a plan crafted by Eaker. He called for the creation of "bait and kill" missions in November 1943, but lacked the bombers and long-range fighters to pull it off. Now Doolittle plans an intense series of raids using that playbook, to begin in February. By then there are enough P-51D Mustangs and P-47D Thunderbolts, fitted with external fuel tanks, to escort heavy bombers through an entire mission deep into Germany.

The negative reaction to the changing fighter roles is nothing compared to the outcry when mission caps are raised from twenty-five to thirty missions. It's not his idea—in February the entire Army Air Forces extends the length of combat tours. But he's the one who has to sell the idea to the men, who are suffering more than any other comparable unit elsewhere.

Even worse, he has to end the idea that hitting the cap means the crewman will never again fly in combat. Doolittle writes a lengthy memo on the topic, and he's not above quoting Arnold in it: "It is again beyond reason that a trained fighting man, seasoned, rested, and able, should be consigned to a permanent homeland job because he has once already been in combat."

Applying this ethos to the suffering 8th Air Force is Doolittle's job. He uses a mix of statistics and big-picture perspective to support raising the cap. He cites the lowering attrition rate shown between August 1942 to February 1944, and lists the reasons why, with the very notable exception of the cessation of deep penetration missions: "This substantial decline, in great degree, is due to the present efficiency of our fighter escort, the constantly increasing size of the attacking bomber force, and a substantial falling off in the Hun fighter strength. It is anticipated that, in the near future, the loss rates will be further reduced."

Well, sure. But even a smaller percentage of losses on missions with more bombers equates to more deaths, not fewer, in the days ahead. The rate goes down as casualties actually rise.

Morale plummets in the aftermath of Doolittle's arrival. The men feel like the 8th Air Force has betrayed the pact of survival specifically established by Eaker. The feeling of unfairness runs across the entire Army Air Forces combat crews, becomes entrenched in the men's collective experience, and manifests years later as a tragic plot point of author Joseph Heller's scathing novel *Catch-22*.

Smith works within this Personnel office, the epicenter of this upheaval. He's in a uniquely strange position. The man taken from combat after just five full missions is working in the shop responsible for explaining an increase in mission limits, and for charting every-one's tally.

The Doolittle era of the 8th Air Force reveals itself on February 20. The base is humming with activity as the 306th prepares for the resumption of deep raids into Germany. The briefing makes the men grumble in their seats. It's the first "bait and kill" mission. The main 823-aircraft mission is aimed at Leipzig, home to fighter component assembly plants, a target they know will draw a response.

There are missions like this for five straight days, part of what headquarters calls Operation Argument. The 8th Air Force bomb-ers fly three thousand sorties during what the fliers later call "Big Week." That's the name that sticks. By February 25, the 8th Air Force loses 20 percent of its bombers—ninety-seven B-17s and forty B-24s are gone, with twenty airplanes damaged beyond repair.

There are two thousand U.S. airmen killed or captured. Big Week causes the operational strength of the bomber force to drop from 75 percent to just 54 percent. The 15th Air Force, out of It-aly under the command of Carl Spaatz, loses a similar percentage over its five hundred sorties. The RAF, flying at night, loses 131 bombers.

The return on this gruesome investment is measured two ways: the number of fighters knocked out of the air and the amount of dam-age to Germany's ability to replace them. According to the American records, the Germans lost as many as 800 fighters—an impossible figure. The actual figure is 262 fighters shot down and about 250 men killed or wounded over the five days. That's still a huge blow: the USAAF's manpower is depleted but can reconstitute. The Luftwaffe cannot.

In comparison, Big Week fails when it comes to its bombing re-sults. The five days of missions yield only a two-week delay in fighter production. The blitz does prompt a reorganization of the military industry, and it passes under the shrewd command of Nazi official Albert Speer. That's a net win for the Nazis.

These results are not just an indictment of Big Week; the entire bombing campaign has failed to end the Luftwaffe. By dispersing production and surging efforts in other, repurposed facilities, the number of German warplanes actually reaches new heights in 1944.

The revolutionary concept of precision bombardment is sputtering. Instead of ending conflict by steadily and humanely stripping an enemy's ability to make weapons, the concept is mutating into a brute exercise of attrition warfare.

END OF AN ACE

March 2, 1944. *Oberstleutnant* (lieutenant colonel) Egon Mayer, head of JG 2, takes off from the coastal airfield at Cormeilles with just three other Fw 190s. They aim due east, en route to bedevil a bomber formation heading into the German interior. It appears they are heading toward Frankfurt; it'll be a hundred-mile trip to the possible intercept.

He hopes other fighters will join the attack, but after that nightmarish February, there are not enough to go around to respond to every incursion, as Hitler once demanded. The Nazi doctrine of "maximum defensive effort" against every American bomber attack has been reduced to games of hit and run.

Not so long ago, Mayer hunted bombers like a predator stalking a herd. The Luftwaffe added 30mm guns to make it easier to do it. And it's almost flattering that the Americans add forward-facing machine guns to the B-17s to combat his tactic of frontal assaults. But it's not the bombers that are the problem. It's the fighter escorts that now plague JG 2.

Mayer has been at this long enough to remember the days of dogfighting with Spitfires in 1940. The war is not like that now. The days of aerial duels are replaced with terrifying run-ins with masses of familiar P-47s and the new threat, the P-51 Mustang. That airplane is faster than the Fw 190 and its performance actually improves above 20,000 feet, where the Fw 190's falls off. And those heavier 30mm guns pack a bigger punch, but the extra weight makes the Fw 190s less responsive, a dangerous flaw during dogfights when maneuverability is the key to survival.

Bastard Mustangs, he thinks. Mayer notched his 102nd victory last week, but he's never shot down a Mustang. He has, however, become especially good at killing P-47s. He's credited with having shot down four on the first day of December. His 100th victory, in February, was against a P-47. But there are more and more of them in the air. What does it matter that he can't be outflown if he's being outnumbered?

Case in point: the inbound raid is being protected by 445 P-47s and 111 P-51s, flying wide patterns ahead of the formations to flush out German fighters. They catch up with Mayer and his wingman near Montmédy, France.

Mayer is again surprised by the way they appear so far from the bombers, the shock of a predator to learn he's the one being hunted. The P-47s dive toward the pair of Luftwaffe fighters. As he's violently turning away from one, another vectors in. The odds are too great.

As he jerks the fighter in a diving left turn, a P-47 Thunderbolt takes a long range shot, leading its eight Browning .50-caliber machine guns well in front of the target. The paths of the airplane and bullets intersect, sparking an explosion in the wing where the Fw 190's ammunition is stored. Half the wing snaps and sails away. Mayer's reaction time is amazing. He actually stabilizes the airplane with a snap roll, but loses control moments later. His wingman, already bailed out of his riddled airplane, watches the Fw 190 spin out of control 15,000 feet before impacting the ground. He sees no parachute.

There's some contention as to which American pilot killed Egon

Mayer. By far the leading contender is First Lieutenant Walt Gresham of the 355th Fighter Group, whose gun camera footage is described above. Others argue that Major Robert Coffey of the 365th Fighter Group should be considered, since he claims an Fw 190 around that time, east of Montmédy. Neither man himself makes the claim that the fighter they shot down that day was Mayer's.

The shroud of war may cover the specifics, but Mayer's death at the hands of a P-47 is indicative of the destructive effect of Doolittle's fighter tactics beyond Big Week. He's doing what the heavy bombing has been unable to do: collapse the Luftwaffe.[14] With the more experienced enemy fliers dead, the Allies will easily own the sky over France when they come to reclaim it from the Nazis.

DOWN IN FLAMES

March 2, 1944. Maynard Smith takes a seat across from Archibald Rayner at the house on Kathie Road. They both know why he's here, but neither can broach it right away. Pleasantries are exchanged. It makes for a polite, tense encounter.

This is the first time Maynard Smith is meeting Mary's father, but he's been to the home before. "We knew they were going together; he came to our house and everything," says George Rayner. "He was a funny guy. He came up with all these stories, funny stories, crazy stories, all the time." Part of the charm offensive is to share tales from his time as Peck's Bad Boy: "He was quite a guy when he was young. When he was a kid, he took a donkey or something and rode it through the Five & Ten-Cent Store."

The relationship has been charging ahead faster than the family realizes. It's not until Mary comes home with an engagement ring

---

14   In a similar way, the U-boat threat has not been ended by attacks on their bases, but by sinking them at sea. While you're here, might as well add that the high casualty rates among U-boat crews is similar to airmen in B-17s.

that the Rayners know a crisis is upon them. Archibald Rayner is granted a special leave by the Army to come back to Bedfordshire to handle the situation.

It wasn't that Gertrude or Archibald Rayner disliked Smith, per se. They may suspect Mary's desire to go to America—one Gertrude shares—is outweighing her common sense. The chief problem is that they just don't know him. The Americans came in like droves of birds, from places no one ever heard of. Places like Caro, Michigan. Tethering your future to some anonymous Yank, no matter how well decorated, is not this English family's ideal choice for their daughter.

"You didn't know anything about the background, what sort of background they came from or anything," George remembers. "They didn't know whether *he* was good or bad. I think the main thing that they had against him was his age."

Archibald Rayner, the former construction worker, is a large man. It's hard to ignore his physical presence as the two men sit to discuss the future. Smith wearing his uniform, as neatly as he can make it, and Rayner in simple, ration book–approved clothes. One can imagine him rolling up the sleeves to show the American the size of his forearms, but that would be forgivable conjecture.

Smith takes the plunge and asks if he can have permission to marry Mary. Archibald Rayner politely declines, citing age and wishing the American hero the best of luck. He then hands Smith back the wedding ring he's given to Mary.

It's a sullen, angry trip back to the base for Maynard Smith. He's done it again: fallen in love and landed on his chin. He's not ready to lose Mary Rayner, but he wonders how she'll react to her family's edict. But Maynard Smith is underestimating his fiancée. She's already cooking up a plan, one he's bound to approve of and enjoy.

Before her father leaves again to do his part in the war effort, George Rayner says his sister issues a threat: "My sister told my parents, 'If you won't let me have him in the right way, I will have him in the wrong way.'"

A CABAL AT SARDI'S

April 3, 1944. It's a typical lunchtime crowd at Sardi's in New York City: press agents, columnists, critics, and Broadway moneymen. The restaurant attracts these industry types by day, theatergoers by night, and actors by late night after their shows end. It's the haunt of Walter Winchell, George Jessel, and other members of the so-called "Cheese Club."

Seated at a large table under a wall of celebrity caricatures is a cabal of seven media men.[15] They are wartime media influencers from across the array of media and government, a cabal formed to make a certain B-17 world famous.

John Vandercook, NBC radio commentator made famous by being one of the last Americans to leave Nazi Germany, sits with other NBC A-list talents W. W. Chaplin and César Saerchinger. Vandercook is also the president of the Association of Radio News Analysts. And there's Major George Fielding Eliot, the newspaper columnist and military analyst for CBS News. Major A. A. Schechter is the head of the War Department's bureau of public relations. Burt Champion, Paramount publicity department's radio honcho, and Al Moss, exploitation manager (that's an actual entertainment position), represent the studio, which is distributing the movie for free.

These heavy hitters have just come from a screening of *The Memphis Belle: A Story of a Flying Fortress* at Paramount Studios. Now, as they pretend to enjoy the food, they're also "pledging support to promote the film."

---

15 L. P. Johnson's crewmate Donald Bevan would one day draw these; he's busy putting on plays in a POW camp at the time of this meeting.

The movie is a classic of effective and engaging propaganda. There's enough truth in it to forgive the missteps. It purports to cover one mission, where in reality the footage is cobbled together from many, some not even aboard the *Memphis Belle*. But the depiction of this new, futuristic battlefront comes across with drama and purpose. FDR himself says after a White House screening, "Every American should see this."

These men are to try to achieve just that. This lunch is a visible display of the public-private partnership behind the new movie. And the *Motion Picture Daily* dutifully runs a story about it headlined "RADIO MEN WILL AID 'BELLE' PROMOTION." The movie premieres nationwide that Friday, April 14, and not surprisingly the reception is fawning. The airwaves and newspapers ensure that even people who never see the movie know the name of the bomber and its crew.

Robert Morgan and Margaret Polk do not attend the premiere in Memphis. That would be awkward. Anyway, he's busy preparing to go back to war, learning how to fly the B-29, and dragging his new wife to various training bases. It's only a matter of time before General Douglas MacArthur captures islands that bring Japan into the bomber's range, and Morgan wants to be ready.

While the world watches and learns about the *Memphis Belle* in April, they are actually seeing the air war as it used to be. The airplanes look the same from the outside and the men dress the same, but the onboard gear, tactics, and targets have changed entirely. That month, command of the 8th Air Force becomes subordinate to Eisenhower.

The campaign now is to soften the German forces in France before the impending invasion. It's an entirely tactical focus, rather than the strategic one of Hap Arnold's dreams.

Transportation hubs that could bring German reinforcements to meet the advancing troops catch hell first. The rail yards and junctures take a pounding by bombers as the fighter-bombers hunt trains. Any way across the Seine River is a priority, since they are the crossings that lead to Normandy. These critical bridges need to be attacked, but others that don't serve Normandy are targeted as well so Germans won't be tipped off to the real landing site.

Even the way the heavy bombers drop their loads has changed; the limitations of the Norden bombsight could no longer be ignored. It's too damn cloudy too often to use visual targeting. So in late 1943 the first B-17s and B-24s equipped with new radar bombing equipment arrive in England. It's called H2X but everyone calls it "Mickey." The system bathes the ground with X-band radar, creating an image clear enough to recognize landmarks. It's impossible not to notice it onboard: a large panel connected by thick electrical cables, adorned with an array of dials surrounding a wide, round scope.

Like the radio navigation tools, the RAF invented radar bombing for their night bombing campaign. Since the British don't care much where exactly the explosives fall, it's enough to use radar to coordinate the pattern of the impacts. This is especially helpful when creating indiscriminate firestorms with incendiary bombs.

The American crews call it "blind bombing" since it's not believed to be as precise as the Norden, but the statistics show the pair achieve a pretty similar accuracy rate. The bombers with the gear are called "pathfinders." They take the lead in formations and fire the flare to signal a bomb drop. The bombardiers find that Mickey works well in combat, and new pathfinders are being shipped to war as soon as they can be built.

There are a lot of new airplanes in Europe. The 9th Air Force has been created to support the invasion as it moves inland, traveling across France with the infantry to provide tactical air support. The 9th arrives with B-26 medium bombers, C-47 troop carriers, and P-51B Mustang fighters that can both escort bombers and strike ground targets.

Despite the urgent focus on the impending invasion, politics again influences the target selection. The end of April also sees the first demand for a mission that Doolittle will grow to hate: using his bombers to attack V-1 rocket launch sites in France. The timing of the April 20 mission is interesting—the rockets have not started whole-sale terror attacks on England but the British are already scared of them. Their intelligence operatives know that the Nazis are building them by the thousands. Eisenhower, juggling an inhuman number of military and diplomatic balls, agrees to mitigate the problem with some bombing attacks. It's the submarine pens, all over again.

The crews know a good target from a bad one. Doolittle tells a subordinate: "The problem within our organization is the effect on the morale of our personnel caused by our having to do a lot of things they may feel are not basically sound."

The V-1 problem gets worse as the months pass, and more B-17s will be ordered to abandon the target sets meant to help Operation Overlord and attack the rocket launch sites instead. During 1944 these V-1 attacks will take up 20 percent of the missions that the 8th Air Force flies, accounting for 10,900 tons of ordnance dropped. It will make no perceptible difference: the rockets will rise at the same rate until ground troops seize the launchpads.

TWO-FRONT WAR

May 19, 1944. Mary Rayner leaves her house bound for Bedford, her stomach fluttering like a cage of jittery birds. Today is Maynard Smith's thirty-third birthday, and the idea is to spend some of the night together. Alone.[16] Little does she know that she's being tailed by a spy.

Just after the young woman clears the front porch, Gertrude

---

16 Mea culpa: There's no evidence that Mary and Maynard met for a birthday rendezvous. But he did impregnate her sometime in mid-May, and hopefully it's a forgivably short narrative leap to place them together on this specific day.

Rayner recruits her young son George for a mission: "My mother said to me, 'Go and see if she meets *him*.'"

The Rayner family wants to keep her away from Maynard Smith, but know she has a formidable willpower, one that is now fueled by the passion of a young woman who's clearly in the throes of her first love. Her parents feel protective and nervous, especially when Archibald's leave ends and Gertrude is left to manage a house of her own children and war refugees.

If they knew the extent of the couple's plan, they would worry more. Mary and Maynard have one sure-fire way to override her father's objections: get her pregnant. With a child on the way, there's really no choice but for the couple to marry. That's just the way it is. Having a pregnant fiancée also helps pressure the Army into sanctioning the marriage.

It's a display of defiant individuality for Mary, but a rather disrespectful move for Smith. It also demonstrates the strength of the connection they feel. "Well," George says, "they were both pretty determined."

George tails his sister at a safe distance as she collects a friend at her house and the pair make their way to the bus station, bound for Bedford. He sneaks onboard, trying to become invisible. The rural landscape out of the windows gives way to a bustling town, a once quaint and quiet place now enlivened by bands of roving airmen, bubbly young British women, and frowning British seniors.

Mary peels off from her friend and walks with a purpose toward a side street lined with cottages, each door shielded by an alcove. George follows discreetly as the plot thickens, waiting for a moment as his sister turns a corner before following. But she's gone.

George hustles to find her, his mission clearly compromised. Then comes the ambush: "All of the sudden she flew out from one of these places and hit me across the head with her purse."

He's been outmaneuvered and now outdueled by his sister, who is eight years older than he is and wields a ferocious purse. "I've had enough of this," the younger brother declares, quits his job as an agent, tramps to the bus station, and goes home.

Maynard Smith's May features sensual delights off base, but the month also brings professional changes to Smith's life in England. The 306th has a new job for him inside the group's Operations Section.

This is the brain stem of the organization, housed within its own bustling building. Inside are offices for the 306th navigators and bombardiers, a large planning room to create missions, and of course a giant briefing room that can accommodate 250 people. Alerts for the next morning's missions come in the late afternoon, starting a burst of planning activity that continues all night and straight through to takeoff. There are constant meetings and decisions made with folks wielding reports on intelligence, weather, ordnance, and communications.

On top of the cadence of bombing raids, there's also something big coming through the planning system. They call the landings in France that are scheduled for late May or June Operation Overlord, with the air component dubbed Operation Neptune.

First come attacks on airfields in France, which are mostly empty and unused. This is a response to the German plan to hold back its airplanes and deploy them when they know where the Allies land. By wrecking the airfields, Ike is denying the Germans the option of reestablishing them after his men storm the nearby beaches.

There is some deception in play as well. The bombers range across France, hitting airfields all over the map. That way, no Nazi intelligence officer can pinpoint Normandy as the location of the attack. In fact, if you draw a circle around Normandy with a 350-mile radius, representing fighter range to the beaches, more targets are hit outside the circle than within. The coastal defenses will be next, again spreading the damage around to not ruin Overlord's surprise landings. And the plan for the day itself . . . that's a whole other monster.

In a sense, Smith has landed inside a planning cell of one of the most important military actions in history. But his job within Operations doesn't involve any high-level action. He's assistant to the night duty clerk, hardly a lofty title. According to a 1944 memo his duties "are transportation of duty officers on planning and set-up of missions, a small amount of typing pertinent to mission planning as well as the daily status report."[17] Russell Strong, who will one day head up the 306th BG historical association, will recall seeing Smith frequently listening to morning briefings.

The head of the Operations Section, Major Thomas Witt, seems tailor-made to conflict with Smith's personality. He's a battle-tested pilot who continues to fly missions even as he oversees the production of missions at headquarters.

Witt is a tall Texan, the twenty-three-year-old son of a hardware and tack store owner in Cookville. He's got a high hairline and wide forehead, and before the war he was pursuing an education in agriculture. He and his crew transferred to the 306th on May 1, 1944, and he worked within the group as their gunnery officer and then the operations officer.

The best example of Witt's character comes later in 1945, when he earns a Silver Star on a mission he leads, the first to use penetrating rocket-propelled bombs. The citation reads like a nightmare for fliers interested in surviving missions: "Witt's plane made three runs over the target. On the third run, an accurate sighting was obtained

---

17   From the memo "Headquarters 306th Bombardment Group Office of the Operations Officer" on December 18, 1944. "Subject: Reduction of S/Sgt. Maynard H. Smith."

only to have the bombsight mechanism fail. Ignoring the intense and accurate flak, which by now had damaged every plane in the formation, Major Witt tenaciously returned to the target and by using the emergency release switch, placed an excellent bomb pattern."

In other situations such a willingness to stay over a target in the face of such steady danger to his men could be called callous or even idiotic. Regardless, it's the action of a serious man, and not one who would enjoy having a willfully disobedient subordinate like Smith. Few would, but Witt isn't built to bend too far to accommodate a celebrity soldier. Witt is a prime example of an officer that Smith has made a point to antagonize.

Smith's attitude is well captured in his quote in *Sergeant's Magazine:* "Having been brought up in an aura of politics, I knew how to get things done. I will give you a typical example. I wanted a jeep to go into town so I asked the administrative officer, a colonel. He refused. General Doolittle told me that whenever I was at the 8th Air Force to stop in and see him. Well, this little old staff sergeant dropped in and got my jeep."

It's hard to imagine a more grating experience for officers than having Maynard Smith bully them by going over their heads for his own creature comforts. But Smith has another use for the jeeps that Witt doesn't know about: door-to-door sales.

Smith later boasts to his son about the setup:

He said that he had a deal going with one of the base mechanics that whenever they would throw a washing machine or replace a washing machine, that he would get it, bring it over to the mechanic, have the mechanic fix it all up. Then he would go on his time off through the countryside and try to find somebody to buy the washing machine. He said that he would do a whole wash cycle. I think in those days, it had the ringer bars, and all that stuff. He said it was like an hour-and-a-half, two-hour job to do a wash cycle, as opposed to scrubbing it all by hand. He said he'd do it all and then have it all hung up on their line for them. He'd say, 'Now look, wasn't that easy? Isn't that easier than scrubbing it all by hand and spending the whole day doing all this?' Inevitably, almost all of them would say this, 'But I never have had one, have I?' He could never figure that out but you know the Pink Floyd line, 'quiet desperation is the English way.' It was like that.

Thomas Witt and Maynard Smith quickly lock into a rivalry that springs from genuine mutual dislike. Reports of Smith disappearing in jeeps while he's supposed to be on duty start to trickle up to Witt from the night clerk. Witt tolerates it, but not quietly. "From the time he began his duties in the Operations Section," Witt says in a wartime report, "repeated warnings and reprimands have been a necessity to obtain even a minimum performance from Smith."

So Maynard Smith's spring of 1944 is spent fighting a two-front war: trying valiantly to knock up Mary while simultaneously locking horns with "Witt and his cohorts." By the end of May, Smith breaks through on one front. The rendezvous work as intended and Mary Rayner presents her family with a fait accompli.

"The next thing you know, she was expecting," George says. "Intentionally." The wedding is planned for July.

SEPP VERSUS JIMMY

June 6, 1944. D-Day, just after 6 A.M. A wall of heavy bombers—including 2,300 B-17s and B-24s—are sweeping across Normandy. The first landing craft will hit the beaches in a half an hour.

The Germans see the terrible weather of June 6 as a hindrance to an invasion, and that assessment included air operations. Even with better equipment, mix-ups in the air lead to numerous deadly collisions. But the navigation improvements enable the D-Day missions to proceed despite the cloud cover, helping catch the Nazis by surprise.

Virtually all the problems that made Smith's May 1 flight such a bloodbath have been addressed. The compass problem has finally been fixed. By '44 the airplanes have the gyro flex gate compasses that the crews had asked for in early 1943. Radio navigation has become a theater of electronic warfare as Nazis try to jam the signals. "The Allies have provisions, particularly in the D-Day timeframe, to switch frequencies and so forth to keep ahead of the Germans," says Roger Connor of the Smithsonian National Air and Space Museum. "So they had quite reliable radio navigation over western France."

Bomber formations are dropping tons of bombs this morning in an attempt to shatter beach defenses, coastal gun batteries, and supply lines. Ike approved the battle plan accepting 33 percent casualties, but the opposition is nothing like what they expect and the airman body count is considerably lower.

The Luftwaffe has retracted most of its fighters from France in advance of the expected invasion. This way they can surge them to where they're needed, once the landings' locations are confirmed. But not every fighter unit leaves. JG 2 *Richthofen* and JG 26 are left behind to defend France from the thousands of Allied airplanes. There are only 140 flyable Luftwaffe airplanes available to fly over northern France on June 6, facing thousands of attacking Allied airplanes.

Josef Wurmheller is 9/JG 2's *Staffelkapitän* (squadron leader) on D-Day, and as such he's in his typical place in the thick of the action. He's come a long way from the mines of Bavaria. The fighter pilot has taken part in an impressive number of critical moments in the war: the Battle of Britain, Operation Barbarossa, the Dieppe raid, and now

Operation Overlord. From this amazing vantage he's seen the German military reach their apex, teeter, and fall into disarray.

He and his men do what damage they can on June 6, which is more than can reasonably be expected. Wurmheller outduels a Mustang and shoots it down. The commander of III/JG 2, *Gruppenkommandeur* Herbert Huppertz, downs a Typhoon RAF medium-altitude fighter-bomber and a P-47. JG 2 downs eighteen Allied aircraft of twenty-four destroyed during the invasion day. It's a mere fraction of the price Ike was prepared to pay.

Any satisfaction the Luftwaffe feels from their initial resistance sours as the days go by and the Allied foothold grows. The 8th Air Force launches missions against Caen, and the German fighters rise to counter the formations. Wurmheller lands after surviving another dogfight against overwhelming odds, only to learn that three Fw 190s have been shot down. Two pilots have been killed, and one of them is Huppertz, shot down by a P-47 south of Caen.

That day, Wurmheller is promoted to the vacant position as Gruppe III's leader. The new *Gruppenkommandeur* has 103 kills—an ace in a force that has precious few left. The Luftwaffe has burned their pilots down to the filter.

The Gruppe expects reinforcements to fly into the forward bases in France, but they're disappointed. Advance units find runways cratered and communication facilities smashed. This part of the tactical bombing campaign has worked.

On June 22, 1944, pilots and soldiers in myriad uniforms across England and France awake to another day of creeping, grinding invasion. The eastern advance off the beachhead has bogged down, with American soldiers facing sharp defenses in the hedgerows. It's a clear day over France, and Ike wants those defenses cratered. The 8th Air Force launches 1,099 bombers in small strikes, hitting a variety of individual targets, all tactical.

The III/JG 2 takes off just after 1 P.M., flying north toward their turnaround spot over Cherbourg. Airplanes from JG 26 join them, trying to scrape some strength from whoever still has pilots that can fight. Wurmheller is flying with a staff sergeant (*Feldwebel*) named Kurt Franzke, who has no recorded kills, as his wingman. The plan is to have Fw 190s engage the fighters, hopefully buying time for the Bf 109s and other Fw 190s to creep in close and fire their rockets.

They are near Alençon when the P-47s appear. The Fw 190s start maneuvering to prepare to engage when the warplanes collide; it's hard to believe the experienced pilot is to blame. Both men are killed; a dejected JG 26 combat diary entry calls Wurmheller's death a "chilling loss."

The Luftwaffe ace is not shot down, but he's nevertheless a victim of Doolittle's campaign for air supremacy. By July, everyone knows the Luftwaffe is wrecked.

BACHELOR PARTY

July 14, 1944. Glenn Miller looks at the makeshift stage with a critical but amused eye. The freshly built structure is standing inside a hangar at Thurleigh, home of the 306th BG. There are still bombers parked inside. It's a humble venue for the most successful musical artist in the world; "Chattanooga Choo Choo" alone sold a million records in 1942.

But Miller is delighted to see the hangar packed with people. There are about 3,500 in attendance; crammed together on the floor, gathered on the wings of airplanes, lined up in the rafters. They're here to see the first-ever appearance in England of the Glenn Miller Army Air Forces Band, and that is a very big deal.

Miller's been in the Air Force since 1942, and the surprise is that the man renowned for his relentless pursuit of commercial appeal is such a dedicated patriot. He takes his wartime touring and composition seriously. He hosts a weekly broadcast unabashedly called "I Sustain the Wings," and he single-handedly modernizes the U.S. military's sound without putting off traditionalists. He's made his fortune as the jazz man you can enjoy with your parents, and he takes a similarly unchallenging approach to his new military standards.

But the military gig has already nearly killed him: in early 1944, a nearby explosion prompted the band to relocate their offices away from London. The day after they left, the building was bombed by the Germans, killing dozens inside.

The Army's swing band finds its new home in none other than Bedford. That's good news for the American and British men on nearby bases, but it's also an unimaginable development for the local residents. The ripples of Miller's show extend well beyond the town. The band makes Bedford ground zero of the cultural invasion that comes with U.S. troops. Americans bring new styles of music and jitterbug dance moves that are distinctly un-British. After the war the British government will feel compelled to speak out against "American dancing," but there's no way to unspill that milk.

Miller doesn't see his mission as any kind of artistic social moment. "We didn't come here to set any fashions in music," Miller writes in a 1944 letter. "We merely came to bring a much-needed touch of home to some lads who have been here a couple of years."

The band will broadcast from the Corn Exchange, located in the town square across from St. Paul's Church, and the location where Maynard Smith met Mary Rayner. The hall was built large to accommodate markets that brought people from across the area, and that size also makes it a good candidate to become a music hall. As his band awaits their first broadcast from there, Miller wastes no time and sets up tonight's show for the men of Thurleigh.

The inaugural air base show is one of the biggest social events of the war. There's no record of Maynard Smith or his fiancée attending the concert, but it's hard to believe he wouldn't have tickets. "My father loved jazz and Glenn Miller in particular," Maynard Jr. says. "I don't see any way he'd miss that."

It's a legendary house band for a bachelor party; Glenn Miller's first show comes the night before Smith is to be married to Mary. It's too tempting to imagine him, with good seats of course, swaying by himself as the band plays "American Patrol" or maybe even dancing closely with Mary Rayner, a couple months pregnant but never more beautiful, during "Moonlight Serenade."

Smith's mood is dampened by the absence of Marcel St. Louis, but at least he knows his closest American friend is alive. Prisoners held by the Germans are usually allowed one letter and two post-cards a month—these sometimes get through, sometimes not. But word spreads to his family and fellow airmen: he's been treated and released from Würzburg hospital. Each branch of the German military takes care of their corresponding enemies, so he's now on his way to a Luftwaffe prison camp. He's alive, and that's better than the alternative.

On July 15, 1944, Maynard Smith and Mary Rayner are married before the justice of the peace in Bedford. The beaming couple pose for a photo together outside the building. They have bridged oceans, braved war, and convinced both the U.S. Army and Archibald Rayner that they should be together. They have won each other.

It's one year to the day that Secretary of War Stimson hung the Medal of Honor around his neck. The date seems geared entirely for Maynard, but Mary certainly drives the events. "I would say that she was pretty strong-willed," her brother George says. "I mean, she wanted the guy, so she had him her way, you know?"

It's a choice that will certainly change the course of her life, but also the trajectory of her entire family.

THE RUN UP THE ROAD

July 19, 1944. Marcel St. Louis is slumped to the floor of a train car, pressed in among his fellow prisoners of war. He's draped in tattered and stinking Red Cross–donated clothes. His body is scarred by war and decimated by incarceration. St. Louis tries not to move his tongue, which feels like tree bark. No man in here has touched water in a full day and night.

Not so long ago, St. Louis's home was Stalag Luft 6, a long-standing prison camp near Heydekrug in what is now Lithuania. He lands there after his release from Würzburg hospital in March, just another resident among throngs of captured British, American, and Russian airmen. There's a deranged normalcy there: organized sports, music groups, a POW newspaper, various social events. But that veneer is being shredded by the Red Army; the flashes and booms on the horizon that mark their advance are getting closer.

The Germans keep a straight face. They don't even cancel the Fourth of July "gala" at the camp, with guards making sure the men focus on their choral and orchestra performances even as the front line creeps closer. The prisoners start to horde whatever food they can, posting lookouts as they pilfer and stash anything in an unopened can. They sew spare clothes into crude luggage. The artillery gets louder.

When the call comes to evacuate, the men are not close to ready. They can take only what they can carry. The British have spent years curating their nicotine collection; they leave a million cigarettes and 150 kilos of tobacco behind. The men watch in frustration as guards toss Red Cross packages of food into cesspits, leaving the Russians nothing.

Nine hundred POWs march out of the camp to the train station and pack into cattle cars. Their first stop is the port of Memel, where an old tramp steamer called the *Insterburg* awaits to take them across the Baltic Sea.

RAF airman Victor Arthur Martin is among the throngs of POWs onboard: "Climbing down vertical steel ladders and packed into the filthy holds like sardines without sanitation or fresh air, conditions were extremely and distinctively uncomfortable. The midsummer heat combined with thirst and the sweltering hold made suffering hardly bearable for several prisoners."

It's a miserable sixty-hour voyage to Swinemünde. They're packed in the coal bunkers without enough room to lie down. The latrine is a bucket raised and lowered on a rope. Men talk about the mines dropped in the Baltic, others wonder if they will be strafed or dive-bombed. It's sometimes hard to tell who is worried about Allied attacks and who is hoping for one to offer a chance of escape—or release from the misery.

After four days on the tramp steamer, anything would be an improvement. But they are again shackled and loaded, crammed and confused, into another cattle car. There are fifty manacled men in one half of the car, and a single guard with a machine gun in the other. The train trundles for a miserable day until it reaches the town of Kiefheide in the Pomerania region, located three miles from their new prison. The camp is called Stalag Luft 4 Gross Tychow.

But first, they have to get to the front gates. They've endured a rough journey of hundreds of miles, but the last three they travel on July 19 will be the most appalling.

The train-car doors slide open. St. Louis blinks his eyes as the light and harsh German commands flood the train car. A typical routine follows: a head count, the issuance of boots and belts, and pairs of handcuffed men lined up for a march. The Nazis are dressed strangely, in running shorts and singlets. These are submarine trainees, co-opted into POW management. They look absurd but their rifles have bayonets fixed.

St. Louis spots the more capable Luftwaffe guards from Heydekrug. They are spaced out along the side of the Kiefheide road, machine guns facing inward. It's clear how escape attempts will be handled.

The mood here is overtly hostile. It gets even uglier when a *Hauptmann* starts telling the guards who they are guarding. The POWs hear him use the very unwelcome phrase *terrorflieger* ("terror airman"). Hitler has declared that Allied pilots are terrorists who are not protected by the Geneva Convention. The *Hauptmann* seems to be reminding the guards of this; the POWs later hear a rumor that he lost a wife and daughter in a Berlin air raid.

The *Hauptmann* pulls a pistol and fires into the air, a starting gun to what will bitterly be known as "Kiefheide Run" or "the Run up the Road." The submarine trainees rush in, beating the men with rifle butts and gouging them with bayonets aimed at their backs and buttocks. And always screaming at them to run. According to RAF prisoner Arthur Martin: "Already exhausted and weary from the journey, many fell. With pistol shots being fired and guards running in and out with their bayonets, dogs were then sent in to add to the confusion and misery, being actively encouraged to be vicious and bite."

Homemade packs and satchels are flung away. The men figure that the German cruelty is designed to make the men do something suicidal, like making a dash for the woods. The machine gun nests positioned along the route would cut any pair of runners to pieces. So the POWs shout encouragement at each other, and reminders to stay focused on the road and not give the soldiers any excuses to kill them.

St. Louis collapses at the front gates, bloody, stunned, and wracked with pain from the exertion. He and the rest wait for water or medical attention, and get none. They will soon find that inmate satisfaction is not Luft 4's specialty.

Barbwire fences segregate the base into five parts: a main camp and POW compounds A through D. St. Louis and the rest are sent to D block, home to a mix of American and British prisoners. Those already there are not happy to see them. The place is already twice as crowded as it can handle and there's already not enough of anything—medicine, pencils, food, stoves, name it—to go around.

As unpleasant and surreal as Heydekrug was, at least it was *finished*. As St. Louis staggers inside Luft 4, he sees slapdash construction of identical huts underway. The camp is only a quarter complete, and even the finished grimy huts don't come close to being adequate. One military intelligence report from July 1944 describes the camp:

> The men are housed in forty wooden huts, each hut containing 200 men. . . . The dormitories have been prepared for 16 men in two tiered beds. But there are not sufficient beds, for some rooms contain up to 24 men each. At camps A and B, a third tier of beds has been installed, whereas beds have been removed from camp D. There is not a single bed in camp C and 1900 men sleep on the floor. 600 of them have no mattress, only a few shavings to lie on. Some have to lie right on the floor. Each prisoner has two German blankets. None of the huts can be properly heated. The delegate only saw five small iron stoves in the whole camp. Some of the huts in camp D have no chimneys. Each camp has two open air latrines and the huts have a night latrine with two seats. The latrines are not sufficient as they are not emptied often, the only lorry for this work being used elsewhere. The prisoners have no means of washing; there are no shower baths as there

is only one coal heated geyser in the camp of 100 liters for 1000 men. Fleas and lice are in abundance; no cleansing has been done.

St. Louis's luck in World War II has remained constant from the day he took off for England—all bad. He's been lost, wounded twice, part of the May Day Massacre, Black Thursday, and the Kiefheide Run. And now he's stuck inside this awful prison camp. Then again, he's alive when so many others are not. All he has to do is stay that way long enough for the Allies to finally hurt the Germans so badly that they recognize they're defeated.

CHAPTER 12

THE JUDGMENT OF WITT

December 18, 1944. Major Thomas Witt has had enough. He turns his attention back to the typewriter, grits his teeth, and begins the argument in favor of demoting a national military hero. If he's going to take a shot, it might as well be a hard one.

"The attitude of this enlisted man is insufferable," he types. "As a recipient of the Congressional Medal of Honor, apparently S/Sgt. Smith is of the opinion that he has no responsibility to his duties, or to his officers or fellow NCOs."

The 8th Air Force is approaching the apex of its power: forty heavy bomber groups, fifteen fighter groups, and four specialized support groups strong. These are the days of steady missions of more than 2,000 heavy bombers and 1,000 fighters, mostly P-51Ds. Deep penetration bombings into Germany are now the norm for heavy bomb groups like the 306th, since smaller airplanes handle the tactical bombing missions that follow the ground advance through France.

So Witt has a lot on his plate inside Operations, and on top of these weighty decisions he must handle the consistent discipline problem that is Maynard Smith. When he finally snaps and takes specific action, he pulls no punches:

> When the process of mission planning and briefing a mission is in effect, the duty NCO in charge is well occupied even with a competent assistant. With S/Sgt Smith on duty his work is not only doubled, but definitely hindered. Having no sense of responsibility, Smith on several occasions absented himself from the office when urgently needed, commandeering the available transportation to visit the Enlisted Men's Club, Red Cross Club, etc. Upon several occasions Smith has been given orders governing specific details, and has carried them out as he deemed necessary, rather than as instructed.

Witt pauses and considers how to position the next part. He's cut this guy a lot of slack, but Witt is smart enough to know that he's expected to. So he decides to spell it out as neatly and forthrightly as possible and hope the 306th commanding officer understands his difficult position.

> Due to his heroic performance as a gunner and his subsequent award of the Congressional Medal of Honor, the undersigned has overlooked many deficiencies in this enlisted man over a long period of time. He has been treated with deference and patience which would not be accorded any other subordinate officer or enlisted man. However, his inefficiency has not only affected the duty NCOs working with him, but has undermined the efficiency and lowered the morale of the whole S-3 section. It is therefore recommended that S/Sgt

Smith be removed from the Operations Section and reduced
to the grade of private for inefficiency.

It's a historically bad performance review, and it works as intended. Command concurs: Smith is demoted and will be reassigned.
He's furious and calls his demotion "the rotten deal that the lousy
outfit gave me via the judgment of Witt." In letters he references "considerable hell raised" over his treatment, and it's certain that he helps
raise some by reaching up into the 8th Air Force in indignation.

But Witt's memo is damning and Smith's complaints get little
traction. He's played the hero card once too many times and no one
is there to help him when he really needs it. All he can do is await
reassignment.

It leaves a deep bitterness in Smith. Years later he describes his
service in England in a 1947 letter to a fellow 306th veteran as "just
so much time of my life wasted" and "am now happy being completely dissociated from the Army and in particular Thurleigh." Having said that, he never stops signing his name with C.H.M.

As Witt works to expel Maynard Smith from the 306th in early
1945, the air war grinds on. The United States never says it changes the
policy to only bomb confirmed military targets. Month after month of
ghastly combat has worn down this ethos, and the line between the
British-style indiscriminate attacks and the U.S. precision bombing is
becoming blurred. The RAF asks for support for its major firebombing
raids, and thousands of civilians in cities like Nuremberg, Hamburg,
and Berlin are killed, and countless more made homeless.

By the time February starts, the idea to use the Army Air Forces
to help the RAF firebomb Dresden doesn't seem out of place, just
an extension of what has been happening. But an Associated Press
report after that attack ruffles feathers by stating that "the Allied air
commanders have made the long-awaited decision to adopt deliberate

terror bombing of the great German population centers as a ruthless expedient to hasten Hitler's doom."

Washington objects, and with a straight face. "Our policy never has been to inflict terror bombing on civilian populations," Secretary of War Henry Stimson says. But from July 1944 to January 1945, an average of 13,536 civilians are killed every month by Allied bombing. And that's before the horrific attack on Dresden, which begins in mid-February and kills at least 25,000 people. The idea of a humane air war is becoming a punch line.

The aircrews who have been around a while recognize this glumly. "I will always be proud of the restraint shown by the US-AAF in these early months of the European air war—the time of the *Memphis Belle*," Robert Morgan laments in his memoirs. "The ordnance carried by the B-17s of the Mighty 8th reflected the humanitarian hopes of our government and our strictly defined and limited mission, which was to attack only military installations, not civilian centers. It couldn't last. The genie was out of the bottle."

It's all just a backdrop for Smith. In February the word comes down: the Army Air Forces is reassigning him to Miami to work at an Army Air Forces Redistribution Center. These places evaluate returning servicemen for reassignment or to process them as they leave the military.

One letter kept in Smith's file compiled by the 306th BG Historical Society provides one view of his legacy as per Russell Strong, the organization's head: "He failed to leave the 306th as a hero because he constantly impressed everyone that he was an ass. . . . It was early in 1945 before the 306th got rid of him, much to the chagrin of the top 8th AF brass, who had wanted him left in England."[18]

---

18 There are several examples in his file of seeming effort by the 306th historical association to make sure Smith's controversies are known, including unflattering

So Maynard Smith says goodbye to his wife and newborn baby, Christine, his friends at the pubs, George and Gertrude Rayner, the maître d' at the Swan Hotel, and his remaining friends on base, and packs his things for the return to America. He catches a ride on the *Mauritania,* a luxury ocean liner that has spent the bulk of her life crisscrossing the globe as a troop carrier. Smith doesn't mind the slow trip back to New York. "I've had enough of flying," he'll quip to a reporter.

Smith has subverted authority and made a mess of discipline inside the bomb group. He's been demoted and is now scorned by a swath of officers. He's heading back to the United States alone and under a cloud, to take a dull job inside an army that has tired of him.

It's time for a parade.

BLACK MARCH

February 16, 1945. Marcel St. Louis is sitting inside a barn, huddled with fellow prisoners from Luft 4 Gross Tychow. The men are clustered together to fend off the minus 13°F temperatures with body heat. He's marveling at how his perspective changes: every time St. Louis discovers a new depth of misery, he finds himself missing the misery that came before. For example, as bad as Luft 4 was, it's better than this endless, frigid wandering.

Ten days ago, with no warning, the Germans evacuated the prison camp. Now its eight thousand residents are trekking through Europe in large ragged groups, pushed again across the war-torn continent by the Soviet advance. They grab whatever Red Cross parcels are available and march out of the gates into a blizzard.

With his string of bad luck, St. Louis regards any change as a

letters about him and collections of negative news clippings. The letter from Witt is also included in the file. http://www.306bg.us/CORRESPONDENCE/s/smith _maynard.pdf.

bad one. Today is a great example. The guards from Luft 4 have been with them on the march, but the Germans have brought in replacements. "The fresh ones are not so good," British POW Bertram Jones remarks in a diary entry later published by the BBC. "Kicking some of our lads and beating them with sticks."

The Nazi collapse is hell on prisoners. The disintegrating Reich is dedicated to moving the prisoners from the grip of the approaching Allies. It's chaos: columns of prisoners are strafed by Allies, mocked by bitter Germans, shaken down for supplies by desperate German troops, and beaten by anyone who feels like venting their frustration. And they are starving, forced to forage for food and dirty ice water along the road.

In early February the POWs reach Ludwigslust, a town in the municipality of Wöbbelin. There is a German camp four miles outside of town, but they don't tarry there. This is for the best—Wöbbelin is a concentration camp stuffed with five thousand prisoners of the SS who have been relocated from other camps. Conditions, little do St. Louis and his companions know, are so horrible that those inside have already resorted to cannibalism. There are one thousand corpses rotting inside.

The Luft 4 POWs move on to an island on the Oder river, sleeping in fields around small, desperate fires and eating any frozen potato or turnip they can dig from the hard ground. They trade the German guards food and water for cigarettes. They are moving a dozen miles a day, a torturous pace for exhausted and unequipped men in winter.

From there it's more forced marching, tobacco shakedowns, discovering friends dead of exposure and malnutrition, sharing barns with Russian and British POWs, and trying to stave off insanity while pondering when this will all end. Days later, at the ferry station at Swinemünde on the Baltic, they happily board to enjoy the shelter.

The trip is unfortunately short and that same day they disembark and start the march again.

On February 17 the men reach the outskirts of Usedom. The final bridge to town, the Parge, is cobblestone, and the roadway feels like sharp nails to St. Louis's abused feet. There's an aerodrome nearby and, gunner that he is, St. Louis can numbly recognize Fw 190s and Bf 109s in the air. The men settle down in a makeshift encampment and, as they have done for years, wait for death or liberation.

Allied command is trying to keep track of these desperate moves so they can rescue the POWs before it's too late. A February 25 telegram from the American Legation in Bern, Switzerland, to London reads: "Some prisoners from Stalag Luft IV are reported to be at Usedom near Swinemünde on the Baltic."

By February 28 the movement of the POWs has reached Parliament. That day Arthur Henderson, the war office's financial secretary, delivers a public statement on the fate of St. Louis and many, many others stuck in his precarious situation: "About 100,000 prisoners are moving along the northern German coast to the west. The great mass of prisoners are now resting in the area between New Brandenburg and Swinemünde. The rear guard is still on the roads west of Danzig. The prisoners will continue their march westward until they reach the region of Hamburg."

Hundreds of POWs from Luft 4 have died on this latest forced trek, which the men call "the Black March." And it's not even over. St. Louis prepares to leave Usedom for the trip west and, if he's lucky, freedom.

MAYNARD RETURNS

March 4 1945

Western Union

Mrs. H.H. Smith, Care Tourist Hotel

Palmetto Ave, Daytona Beach Fla

HELLO MOTHER DEAR TRIED TO CALL YOU FROM NEW YORK
LAST NIGHT BUT YOU WERE OUT WILL ARRIVE IN DAYTONA
FOR A FEW DAYS SOON WILL WIRE YOU LATER
LOVE MAYNARD

SMOKE GETS IN YOUR EYES

March 9, 1945. Major Robert Morgan sees the island of Iwo Jima from the cockpit of the B-29 *Dauntless Dotty*. The Marines are still at work down there, and he can see intermittent orange flashes of artillery light up the night sky. Like the *Memphis Belle,* this Superfortress is named after his current love interest, but he doesn't want to dwell on that connection right now. Today he read a letter from his wife Dorothy that was sharp and simmering, and he doesn't know why.[19] But it bothers him, and such distractions are dangerous when flying a mission—especially this one.

Morgan is the commander of the 869th Bomb Squadron, within the 497th Bomb Group, and his celebrity has not immunized him from hard missions. It's exactly the opposite. Morgan led the 100-plane formation that first bombed Japan, a raid on Tokyo's industrial facilities. That was a high altitude raid at 30,000 feet, and an inaccurate one courtesy of the air currents that influence the bombs' trajectories.

Today's strike on Tokyo looks much different.

For starters, the formation is three times as big. There are 334 B-29s heading for Japan from various bases in the Marianas. But the load-out and tactics are what make today such a unique gamble. The bomb run approach will be between 5,000 and 7,000 feet, six times lower than normal. The Japanese antiaircraft guns won't be set to

---

19   Her brother has been killed in the Battle of the Bulge and she's wracked with grief, and will one day cry to Morgan, "Why couldn't it have been you instead?"

such a low altitude, and with any luck most will be destroyed before they get a chance to react. Same goes for Japanese fighters.

"No formation flying. No reason for it," Morgan writes in his memoirs. "The planes would fly single file to and from the target."

So, without even telling his boss, Hap Arnold, LeMay decides to incinerate a wide swath of Tokyo and its citizens using a risky low-level approach that failed so miserably in Europe. "One thing was clear, this was Curtis LeMay's brainstorm, Curtis LeMay's show," Morgan writes. "If it failed, as many thought likely, he would be stripped of his command."

LeMay also orders all guns except those in the tails removed to make room for more ordnance. The airplanes are carrying several varieties of incendiary bombs, meant to cause a firestorm inside the city. Pathfinder airplanes equipped with radar bombing kits will guide the initial drops, and the follow-on aircraft will use the fires to guide where to release.

The idea is to shatter the Kanto ward, the twelve-square-mile heart of the city. The industries within Kanto include the factories of mainstay military suppliers like Mitsubishi and Hitachi. It's also more than 85 percent residential and averages a staggering 103,000 people per square mile.

The men flying the mission feel a cold prickle knowing the nature of the mission. Morgan recalls: "If we succeeded, the devastation would beggar anything that had gone before. In human terms, the prospects were nearly unthinkable. Civilians were going to die on this run, die by the tens of thousands. Worse, they were going to be roasted alive en masse. That's what incendiary bombs were designed to do."

Like most bomb crews simultaneously bored and frightened during the hours of flight to the target, the men inside the *Dauntless Dotty* pass the time by tuning into local Japanese radio. The

signals reach several hundred miles off the Japanese shore. By now
the 21st Air Force crews know which stations play American music:
a surprising number do, part of the curious but enduring Japanese
interest in American culture. The signal crackles and then, through
their headsets, the men on Morgan's airplane hear Benny Goodman's
version of a 1933 classic:

> Now laughing friends deride
> Tears I cannot hide
> So I smile and say,
> "When a lovely flame dies,
> Smoke gets in your eyes."

Morgan hears someone in his airplane say grimly, "Smoke will
be in a lot of people's eyes in about an hour."

By the time the *Dotty* drops to the low altitude and closes in
on the capital, it's already an inferno. Pillars of smoke are billowing
but the fire is strikingly bright and crewmen can see the buildings
disintegrating below. Searchlights stab blindly into the night, antiaircraft shells explode well above the airplanes. The B-29 bucks and
bounces from the thermal updraft; the plane fills with a burning
stench of roasting meat that makes them gag. "The universe was fire
and smoke," Morgan puts it.

The Superfortress looses its bombs over a southern section of
the city center. Some are cluster bombs that distribute bomblets of
napalm that ignite and stick to anything they touch. These submu-
nitions can punch through roofs and walls. Other bombs have time
fuses that detonate before contact with the ground to spread white-
hot magnesium. The wood-and-paper homes of Tokyo don't stand a
chance; the wind feeds firestorms that devour entire city blocks, melt
Zeros sitting in hangars, incinerate buildings, and immolate panicked

people who are running in opposite directions on bridges. The metal on one crowded train trestle grows white hot and those who leap into the water below find it's boiling.

The Strategic Bombing Survey, done after the war, gives a description of the conflagration's front: "An extended wall of fire moving to leeward, preceded by a mass of pre-heated, turbid, burning vapors. . . . An extended fire swept over 15 square miles in 6 hours. The area of the fire was nearly 100 percent burned; no structure or its contents escaped damage."

Of the bombers that took off, 282 reach the target. Twenty-seven bombers are lost to flak guns, mechanical failures, and crashes caused by the violent updrafts. These losses are less than LeMay is expecting and *far* less than he is willing to accept.

LeMay schedules another firebombing for the next night. By the end of the dual raids, an estimated one hundred thousand Japanese civilians are killed and over one million made homeless. LeMay, once the champion of precision bombing, is no longer committed to it. He's committed to whatever works, at whatever cost.

RECEPTION COMMITTEE

March 21, 1945. Floyd Clark is waiting at the Detroit City Airport for the hometown hero to deplane. There's a crowd of nearly two hundred reporters and gawkers gathering, and Clark isn't happy about it. He's the one-man delegation from Caro, where an epic celebration is planned. These Detroit reporters could produce stories that outshine the town's carefully curated festivities.

The woman next to him, a reporter from the *Detroit Times* named Vera Brown, jabs the air with a lit cigarette. She's a pioneering journalist who loves covering aviation so much that she learned how to fly. "Here he is!" Brown cries. The airplane containing Maynard Smith has landed. "The reporters and photographers," Clark later informs the *Tuscola County Advertiser,* "came rushing from all directions."

Clark joins the flood of media people flowing to the gate, where they again wait as the other passengers get clear of the circus inside the terminal. When Maynard Smith and his mother, Mary Smith, emerge, the flashbulbs flash like a Hollywood premiere. He's a private but everyone calls him a staff sergeant. He even has the bars on his lapel, purchased over the counter and affixed to his uniform for the homecoming.

It's standing room only in the waiting room, where "everybody seemed to know that Hokie was the boy with the Congressional Medal of Honor." Smith will turn thirty-four in two months, is on his third wife, and has as many children. But his homecoming is a stand-in for all those other, younger men who are still on the front lines. So he's called "the Smith boy" in most of the coverage.

Clark wades through the throng to introduce himself to the couple. He's Caro, personified. He owns the local golf course and club restaurant. Everyone remembers when the old one burned down in 1940, the one that had a teepee built into the façade. Its demise made headlines.

His mother, Mary, joined him in Daytona—the traditional Smith vacation spot—to start the trek home. The pair traveled from Florida to Chicago by luxury train, edging ever closer to the centerpiece of Smith's homecoming, his return to Caro.

It will have to wait. Smith and his mother have a night in Detroit ahead of them. Clark walks them to where his car waits, parked in an area usually reserved for taxis but the most convenient for Smith. The MOH recipient declines a police escort and Clark pulls away from the airport, heading into Detroit's glitzy theater district.

The trio pulls up to the Statler Hotel. There is nowhere in the state that has the panache of this place. The famous stay here, usually those playing at the Michigan Palace supper club or United Artists Theater, which are both in walking distance. Smith is keen to know that this is the last place that Harry Houdini stayed before he checked into a Detroit hospital with fatal appendicitis in October 1926.

Clark describes the reaction to Smith to the *Advertiser*: "At the hotel we were given one of the best suites in the place. For the first 10 minutes everything was quiet, and then the telephone began to ring announcing that several people wished to call. First to enter was Judge Frank Picard, an old friend of the late Henry H. Smith, father of S. Sgt. Smith. Then began a steady stream of businessmen, professional people, newspaper reporters, until 6 o'clock. We had to shut the doors then."

It's the Terrace Room for dinner. It's an epic, 6,840-square-foot room, dominated on the north end by a slick, black orchestra stage designed large to accommodate big band ensembles. The wide, maple dance floor is the only thing that breaks up the blue-green carpeting. It's the hottest nightspot in Detroit, capable of hosting three hundred diners to an evening of music, dance, and first-class service. A state-of-the-art automatic conveyer belt delivers 450 dirty dishes a minute to the wash staff hidden in the back.

It's Wednesday night, and an emcee is leading the house band. Clark steps over to the emcee and asks that a tune be dedicated to the Medal of Honor recipient. The man sniffs, saying that it's against the rules. But for Smith, he's willing to make an exception.

When Smith returns to his seat, the attention of the room shifts to him as he receives a salute from the stage. He rises and takes a bow; the place erupts in applause.

Smith is getting a taste of what the *Memphis Belle* crew enjoyed when they came home. But this time the celebration is tinged with the idea that victory in Europe is getting close. For the thumb of Michigan, it's a release of years of tension, upheaval, and loss. But like the men of the *Belle,* and other frontline servicemen used as publicity props, the homecoming celebration becomes hollow when the crowds recede.

Smith's jubilant evening in Detroit ends in a fine Statler bed, quietly worrying about the next day's arrival in Caro. He's a genuine hero in a war that is being won, and the biggest thing to come from Caro, but he's also left disappointed people, unsettled debts, and the families of angry ex-wives behind in Caro.

"To tell you the truth, I had some mixed feelings about it," he will later say to a magazine writer. "My coming home a hero poured salt in some old wounds. I knew it would."

CHAPTER 13

"ONLY ONE SHELL JAMMED"

March 22, 1945. The drive doesn't go straight to Caro. First there's a stop in the nearby town of Vasser, where they will meet dignitaries and have a light lunch. Clark drives Smith and his mother; the Medal of Honor recipient seems contemplative, so the golf course owner makes some small talk. "Hokie," he asks, according to his chronicle in the *Advertiser*, "are there any roads like this over there?"

The shtick comes easily for Smith, even when lost in memory. And he's still got reforming England on his mind. "Listen," he says. "I'd like to take the King and drive him right down this highway and show him how things are done over here."

The crowd at Vasser is a who's who of regional politicians and powerbrokers. The centerpiece figurehead is Michigan governor Harry Kelly, who has come with his budget director to spotlight the historic celebration. Smith meets the entourage with a smile and his usual awkward charm. The Mueller Brass Company presents his mother with a diamond broach, and Smith promises he'll visit the plant before heading back to Army service. (He does.)

Vera Brown is there as well, covering each step of the event for the *Detroit Times* but also shaping it. She volunteers her convertible so that the photographers waiting in town can get better shots of the homecoming hero. After a light lunch together, Smith, his mother, and the governor climb into the car and set out for Caro with the top down.

The VIP convoy leaves from Vasser along State Road 81. Smith watches the familiar landscape roll past, marveling at his different circumstances. But his discomfort grows as he gets closer to town. Not for the first time, Smith realizes there is a significant part of himself that does not want this day to happen. Family pride urges him on. "I went through it because it was, after all, my hometown and my mother was still living there," he'll say later.

When Route 81 reaches Caro it transforms into State Street, just as the rural landscape morphs into a small town. Smith can hardly recognize the place for all the decorations; red, white, and blue bunting drapes every light pole and American flags jut from the grass along the curbs. All for him.

The entourage comes to a halt downtown, in front of Hotel Montague. Smith is amazed to see three thousand Michiganites gathered, waiting to witness the ceremony that will start the day's parade. The Caro schools have been let out at noon; businesses are closed for an official half-day, but many in the crowd have come from nearby towns and Detroit. There's a small stage where a patriotically adorned speaker's stand shares space with loudspeakers owned by local radio stations.

A massive banner is slung in front of the building and over the podium: WELCOME HOME MAYNARD!!

The event begins awkwardly. As a MOH recipient, Smith is supposed to be accorded a seventeen-gun salute. This "baffled the local committee" because there is a lack of ceremonial rifles in Caro. The local Legionnaires offer use of their small cannon. A man named Cecil Greenfield loads the cannon with a shotgun shell, H. H. Johnson fires it, and the pair repeat the procedure sixteen more times. "Only one shell jammed," the *Tuscola County Advertiser* notes. "But the pause was only a short one."

Clarence Myers, State Savings Bank president and head of the executive committee in charge of the homecoming celebration, takes the podium first. He introduces the master of ceremonies, who in turn introduces the governor.

Kelly proceeds to deliver remarks that couldn't be further from an accurate assessment of Smith. "Michigan is proud of you and the great service you performed in the great cause of liberty," he says, but then adds: "I like to think of you as typical of the young men who have gone forth from Michigan to fight and die for the principles they believe in."

The governor keeps his remarks short and gets on with the parade. As soon as it's over he will skip the planned banquet and leave Caro. So he hands Smith a copy of a joint resolution praising the former gunner, recently passed by the state legislature. The microphone is then Smith's. "I'm certainly glad to be back home," he says. "Thank you."

Smith, his mother, and Kelly ride in the lead car. Local high school marching bands, Boy and Girl Scout troops, and American Legion Color Guard trail behind. Maynard waves from the convertible, perched on the top of a seat and waving his cap in the air for the cameras. Children chase after the convertible on foot and bicycles. Hands are extended to shake and items to sign wherever the parade stops.

Smith knows that, among the sea of faces, there are enemies

lurking. His time in Caro left angry family members, an estranged son, and an ugly courtroom drama. Being back puts him on edge. "It was a first-class celebration all right, but behind the pose there were some reservations on my part," he says later. "And I'm sure, on the part of some of the townspeople."

When the parade ends, at the Caro High School where Smith never attended, the reporters gather to get something more than he offered in his brief speech. "I've made some mistakes in my life, but this is a great day today and I want to think of this as one of the best," he tells them, and then adds enigmatically, "You know I should be at the bottom of the Bay of Biscay right now, but something brought me back to Caro."

Leaving them to chew over those comments, he and his mother, Mary, enter the auditorium together and take in the scenery. The four-man squad from the Rotary Club who make up the Decorations Committee have hung patriotic streamers from the walls and lined up flags from every Allied nation behind the speaker's table. There are white linens and floral arrangements at each table in the auditorium, courtesy of Esther Capling, the chair (and sole member) of the Table Decorations Committee.

The presence of Judge H. H. Smith looms large in the auditorium. His father's friends and business partners seem to be everywhere, including the speaker's table. There's even a large oil painting of his father mounted in the auditorium. Smith can literally feel his father's eyes on him.

The evening begins with an unwelcome jolt. After the county's school commissioner greets the crowd, the auditorium begins a sing-along of "America." But when the orchestra starts to play, Smith recognizes the bandleader: it's Fred Gunsell, the uncle of his second wife and great-uncle to his estranged son William. The child support issue is lingering, the money still unpaid.

Well, he figures, at least Helen's not on stage; she occasionally plays piano with her uncle. This is a big gig for the Fred Gunsell Band. For a sense of the level of success of this local band, here's a May 12, 1944, article in the *Pigeon's Promise*: "Pigeon High School prom was well-attended Friday night. The gym was transformed into a spring garden complete with a maypole in the center. Music was furnished by Fred Gunsell and his orchestra from Caro."

The county schools commissioner, Ben McComb, takes the stage and renders a breathless introduction of Hokie Smith. "I never thought I'd sit alongside one of the nation's heroes!" he gushes, and then "recounts exploits from Smith's boyhood days in Caro and some of his hair-raising stunts."

Then it's Prentiss Brown's turn. He's a former U.S. senator, and a current executive at Detroit Edison Co., and can hold an audience. It's his role to read newspaper accounts of Smith's May 1 mission to the crowd. The flak, the Fw 190s spewing tracers, the raging fire, the exploding ammunition cans, the hands slick with human blood, the long trip home waiting for the B-17 to snap in half.

"To you and thousands like you," Brown finishes, "we say, hail!"

Mary Smith is then made the center of attention when the Legion Auxiliary presents her with a large corsage. She mutters her thanks and retakes her seat, "apparently overcome by the gift and by all of the program given in her son's honor."

After a barber shop quartet performance, it's time for Smith's speech. He doesn't have anything written down, but the *Tuscola County Advertiser* prints his extemporaneous comments the next week: "I am glad this affair happened in Caro, Michigan. I wouldn't want it in New York or any other place. I don't feel deserving of the Medal of Honor any more than a lot of other fellows over there."

He also goes out of his way to assure the crowd that the wounded men in the Army are getting good care, "better than they could get in Caro or anywhere else; I've seen it." This is a priority Army message at the time.

Then Smith gestures to the back of the room, where his father is watching the proceedings from the canvas of the oil painting. "He's the best friend I ever had," Smith says. "He got me out of more trouble than you could ever get into."

Smith closes by saying that he'd be happy to answer some questions about the war and his service, "providing the same did not interfere with military regulations, but very few were asked."

All three Detroit dailies have reporters covering the homecoming, including the *Times'* Vera Brown, as well as the staffers from small local papers in Flint, Saginaw, Bay City, and Port Huron. The presence of the Associated Press' C. E. Marentette ensures the newspaper story will spread nationwide. The radio stations carry it live. "Seldom in the history of Caro has this village received such wide publicity," the *Advertiser* notes at the time.

Smith visits with his mother in Michigan for a few weeks. There's a bond drive appearance and, as promised, a visit to the Mueller Brass Company. "He's not medal conscious," one worker says. "That's the way I like my heroes."

To Smith's relief, he'll soon be moving on. His next stop is Miami, where he hopes to stay as the war in Europe grinds to a conclusion. After that, he's considering how many doors the medal can open for him in Washington, D.C. Staying in Caro is never an option, and this homecoming does nothing to change his mind.

"To tell the truth," Smith will later tell the *Detroit Free Press,* "I did a hell of a lot more for that town than it ever did for me."

A few weeks later, Jim Sparling receives a copy of the *Tuscola County Advertiser* at his frontline position in New Guinea. The Japanese, driven by force to pockets of resistance, continue to fight even as they desperately forage for food. That makes for a miserable war for soldiers like Sparling, who spend long hours in rain-filled foxholes watching for Japanese attacks.

The last time he saw Smith, he was sitting on a bus after being unshackled by the sheriff. Now Peck's Bad Boy is being feted as a hero and—just as he stipulated the day he left—returned to town only when the streets fill up to cheer. "On the front page was a big picture of Hokie riding in a shiny convertible down the main street of Caro, and the sidewalks lined with spectators," Sparling will later say in his newspaper column.

The bitterness lingers through the years. When he writes about Smith's homecoming for the *Tuscola County Advertiser* fifty-five years later, Sparling describes it this way: "He had to contact his ex-wife and promise to pay back his child support so he could enter Michigan. . . . As soon as possible he snuck out of town, not paying anything as he had promised."

INTERVIEW

April 1945. Torn pages of this interview script, found in Smith's personal belongings, detail the heavy messaging involved in his radio appearances. The author and appearance are unknown, but the sentiments come from the War Department.

ANNOUNCER

Snuffy, how long had you been in the Army when you won that medal?

SMITH

Just 10 months. And that was my first mission. There were plenty of times up there when I was dead certain it would be my last.

ANNOUNCER

As I recall, Snuffy, the Congressional Medal rates a salute from the lowest to the highest rank, docsn't it?

SMITH

That's correct. I've been getting salutes from colonels and generals ever since I got back to the U.S. a couple of weeks ago.

ANNOUNCER

Did you pick the Air Force when you came into the service, Snuffy, or did you just happen to land there?

SMITH

No sir, I picked it. I knew if I got into the infantry I'd march my feet off. I'm short enough now. If I'd been in the infantry, I probably would bc a foot and a half tall now.

ANNOUNCER

After two years over there, Snuffy, you ought to be able to speak with some authority on the American soldier. Tell us somc of your reactions of that subject.

SMITH

Well, the American soldier gets the best medical attention in the world. We brought back one wounded man on that ship on that mission I have been telling you about and I know how the medics operate. We lost a lot of equipment and our Flying Fortresses that day but there was another one ready to take its place and plenty of new equipment to carry on with. It seemed to me that the British looked with

amazement at our equipment and efficiency of operation.
The American soldier takes great pride in knowing he is
being supported at home and now, if I can get in a plug
for the coming war bond drive, let's keep on buying those
bonds to keep that equipment coming. Your soldier over
there is depending on you.

SONDERKOMMANDO ELBE

April 7, 1945. The 8th Air Force is deep into another massive raid,
this time meant to annihilate the remnants of the Luftwaffe inside
Nazi-controlled Germany. There are thirty-two heavy bomber groups
in the air and fourteen groups of Mustangs converging on airfields,
bombing buildings, cratering runways, and strafing grounded airplanes.

A desperate unit of young Luftwaffe pilots takes to the air in
one more gesture of waste and bravery, the twin pillars of the air
war over Europe. There are Fw 190s, stripped of most of their ammunition and flown by a specially trained corps called the *Sonder-
kommando Elbe*. Each pilot aims a Bf 109G, armed with only one
heavy machine gun and fifty rounds of ammunition, straight at the
bombers. The pilot is supposed to jettison at the last moment before
impact.

These ramming airplanes descend on B-17s of the 3rd Air Divi-
sion and B-24s of the 2nd AD. The battle unfolds over the Steinhude,
Germany's largest inland sea. Eight B-17s and B-24s are rammed and
downed; virtually none of the Luftwaffe pilots survive. The ramming
tactics are never used again. The once mighty Luftwaffe, with the
most experienced and deadliest pilots in the world, has been reduced
to junior pilots using suicide tactics.

It's another bloody, wasteful sign of the collapse of the Nazi regime. The 306th flies its last mission on April 19, 1945. As one of the oldest groups in England, ending operations at Thurleigh is a shock to the English and Americans in Bedfordshire alike.

On April 25, the 8th Air Force flies its last full-scale mission over Europe, a strike on an armaments factory in Czechoslovakia and a simultaneous B-24 raid on railroads around Berchtesgaden, Hitler's mountain retreat.

By the end of the war the 8th Air Force's men will earn 17 Medals of Honor and 220 Distinguished Service Crosses. They've dropped 697,000 tons of bombs. In the European theater, 30,099 USAAF personnel lost their lives. Two thirds of them were in the 8th and 9th Air Forces flying from England and France. For some scale, the U.S. Marines suffered 24,500 killed in action during World War II.

Maynard Smith sees the news emblazoned on the front page of the May 8 *Miami Herald*: "ALLIES WILL PROCLAIM VICTORY V-E DAY AT 9 A.M. TUESDAY." It's great news for Smith because it's a step closer to getting out of the Army. "I've done my bit," he'll say. But there's also a bittersweet detail on the same front page, above the fold on the left-hand column: "War-scarred London burst into jubilant celebration of the end of the war in Europe yesterday, its millions of happy residents unable to wait for the government's formal VE Day proclamation today."

All across England its citizens, including those of his immediate family, are celebrating tonight. And down here in Florida, even though there is jubilation in the streets, he feels far away from all of it.

HONORABLE DISCHARGE

May 26, 1945

Associated Press—Staff Sgt. Maynard H. Smith, 35, (sic) the first Michigan man to receive the Congressional Medal of Honor, today became the first man released under the War Department's new rule permitting Medal of Honor winners to obtain discharges.[20]

---

20 The original discharge papers kept by Smith in his steamer trunks prove he left the Army as a private.

PART 5

POSTWAR DREAM

CHAPTER 14

REVENGE OF THE GUNSELLS

March 28, 1946. Nighttime falls on Washington, D.C.; streetlamps in Georgetown ignite and the jazz bands begin their first sets in the clubs along U Street. Less romantically, it's also the time when countless federal employees contemplate the next day's struggle within the Bureaucracy.

Maynard Smith lights a menthol cigarette and bitterly turns over the day's events, which include his arrest. He should have it all. He's returned from war as an acknowledged hero, something even Thomas Witt can't take away. Smith has relocated to Washington, D.C., a place where the Medal of Honor should have the most influence, to live with his wife and daughter.

Earlier that year Mary and Christine arrived on the HMS *Queen Mary*, retrofitted to carry 1,500 war brides and their children. It isn't redesigned for comfort: rooms hold a dozen bunk beds. But Mary and her daughter aren't subjected to that. "We stayed in a cabin by ourselves, because of the Medal of Honor," Christine recalls.

It takes about a week to get from Southampton, England, to New York City. Most of the women onboard have children in tow. The passengers band together to assist any pregnant brides. The *Queen Mary* will make thirteen such voyages and transport twenty thousand women who had met their husbands while serving across the Atlantic.

It should be a joyous reunion. Mary (Rayner) Smith has long dreamed of coming to America, and here she is in New York City with her daughter and war hero husband. But she finds a hostile presence waiting for her.

"She and my grandmother hated each other," says daughter Christine. "A lot of people saw the war brides as stealing their men. They're waiting for them to come back from the war, and they finally come back with wives and children." The distaste reserved for prospective spouses is, instead, coming from her possessive and doting mother-in-law.

Neither woman is pleased by Smith's choice to move to Washington, D.C. But he has a job with the IRS with a salary that he seems to appreciate. "The wife is here and the baby is healthy and happy," he writes in a letter to a fellow 306th veteran. "We have a swell apartment and I have a damn good high-paying position. And things are going along well."

The Medal of Honor has not lost its luster; indeed, World War II has raised the medal to an iconic status that it hasn't enjoyed in decades. By 1940 the number of living recipients was just 279, but World War II provides an influx. More than half of the war's MOH recipients receive it postmortem, but 198 are alive—and potentially influential. These sanctified heroes can be repurposed as politicians, businessmen, and box-office draws.

Smith is involved in the creation of the Medal of Honor Society, and becomes its secretary and treasurer. "Less political than its predecessor, the organization became more concerned with perpetuating the ideals embodied in the Medal," says the website of its successor,

Maynard and his mother enjoy a trip to the beach, most likely in Florida.

(courtesy of Maynard Smith Jr.)

Maynard Smith Jr. examines a photo album in his home in Florida. He lived with his father during his father's last years.

(Joe Pappalardo)

Smith's memorabilia, stored in three steamer trunks, is a self-curated collection of his best moments.

(*Joe Pappalardo*)

The transparent nose of the B-17 Texas Raiders, operated by the Commemorative Air Force Gulf Coast Wing. *(Joe Pappalardo)*

Army and press photographers asked Smith to re-create various moments from the May 1 mission, such as manning the waist turret. The images ran worldwide. *(courtesy of the U.S. Air Force)*

The ball turret of a B-17 flown by the Commemorative Air Force in 2019.

(Joe Pappalardo)

This archival Air Force photo shows some of the damage done to Smith's airplane during the May 1 mission. The number scrawled across the bottom matches his B-17 that day, and it never flew again.

(courtesy of the U.S. Air Force)

B 17F No. 42-29649
423rd BOMB SQUADRON, 306th BOMB GROUP
1 May, 1943

Lt. BOB McCALLUM (Picture lower left) looks at the outside damage before surveying what the inside looks like (3 pictures on right).

FLIGHT CREW

Pilot:	1st Lt. LEWIS P. JOHNSON
Copilot:	2nd Lt. ROBERT McCALLUM
Navigator:	1st Lt. STANLEY M. KISSEBERTH**
Nose Gunner:	S/Sgt. J.C. MELAUN
Top Turret:	T/Sgt. WILLIAM W. FAHRENHOLD
Radio Operator:	T/Sgt. HENRY R. BEAN*
Ball Turret:	Sgt. MAYNARD H. SMITH
Waist Gunner:	S/Sgt. JOSEPH S. BUKACEK*
Waist Gunner:	S/Sgt. ROBERT V. FOLLIARD*
Tail Gunner:	Sgt. ROY H. GIBSON**

*Bailed out over English Channel, presumed dead
**Wounded

Citation

Rank and organization: Sergeant, U.S. Army Air Corps, 423rd Bombardment Squadron, 306th Bomber Group. Place and date: Over Europe, 1 May 1943. Entered service at: Cairo, Mich. Born: 1911, Cairo, Mich. G.O. No.: 38, 12 July 1943. Citation: For conspicuous gallantry and intrepidity in action above and beyond the call of duty. The aircraft of which Sgt. Smith was a gunner was subjected to intense enemy antiaircraft fire and determined fighter airplane attacks while returning from a mission over enemy-occupied continental Europe on 1 May 1943. The airplane was hit several times by antiaircraft fire and cannon shells of the fighter airplanes. 2 of the crew were seriously wounded, the aircraft's oxygen system shot out, and several vital control cables severed when intense fires were ignited simultaneously in the radio compartment and waist sections. The situation became so acute that 3 of the crew bailed out into the comparative safety of the sea. Sgt. Smith, then on his first combat mission, elected to fight the fire by himself, administered first aid to the wounded tail gunner, manned the waist guns, and fought the intense flames alternately. The escaping oxygen fanned the fire to such intense heat that the ammunition in the radio compartment began to explode, the radio, gun mount, and camera were melted, and the compartment completely gutted. Sgt. Smith threw the exploding ammunition overboard, fought the fire until the enemy fighters were driven away, further administered first aid to his wounded comrade, and then by wrapping himself in protecting cloth, completely extinguished the fire by hand. This soldier's gallantry in action, undaunted bravery, and loyalty to his aircraft and fellow crew members, without regard for his own personal safety, is an inspiration to the U.S. Armed Forces.

The Medal of Honor, sometimes called the Congressional Medal of Honor, was created in the name of the Congress of the United States of America during the Civil War of 1861-1865 to be awarded to members of our Armed Forces for extraordinary courage and conspicuous gallantry at the risk of life above and beyond the call of duty while engaged in action with an enemy of the United States. It is the highest honor our country can bestow on its greatest heroes.

Above and opposite: Maynard Smith sold signed commemorative cards with his Medal of Honor citation and a sketch of the disastrous May 1 flight route. *(courtesy of Maynard Smith Jr.)*

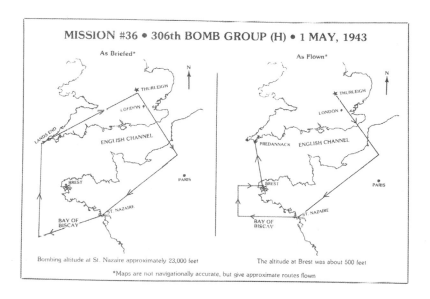

MISSION #36 • 306th BOMB GROUP (H) • 1 MAY, 1943

As Briefed*

THURLEIGH
LONDON
LANDS END
ENGLISH CHANNEL
BREST
PARIS
ST. NAZAIRE
BAY OF BISCAY

Bombing altitude at St. Nazaire approximately 23,000 feet

As Flown*

THURLEIGH
LONDON
PREDANNACK ENGLISH CHANNEL
BREST
PARIS
ST. NAZAIRE
BAY OF BISCAY

The altitude at Brest was about 500 feet

*Maps are not navigationally accurate, but give approximate routes flown

Medal of Honor

Thurleigh, Bedfordshire Eng.
15 July, 1943

Clearwater, Florida
July 15, 1983

Maynard H. Smith

Secretary of War Henry Stimson, right, presents the Medal of Honor to Maynard Smith at the Thurleigh airfield.

(courtesy of the U.S. Air Force)

A bemused Maynard Smith, pulled from punishment duty in a kitchen to receive the Medal of Honor.

(courtesy of the U.S. Air Force)

The two Marys—Smith's mother and wife—after the war. Family members recall that the two "hated each other."

(Joe Pappalardo; original photo courtesy of Maynard Smith Jr.)

Maynard H. Smith in 1943.   *(courtesy of Maynard Smith Jr.)*

Maynard Smith's homecoming parade in Caro, Michigan. The day he left for the Army, he told a future newspaper columnist that he wouldn't return until the town lined up to cheer.

(courtesy of Maynard Smith Jr.)

Maynard Smith, center, faces his mother during his homecoming tour in Michigan. They are surrounded by civic leader well-wishers who want to be seen with the local war hero. *(courtesy of Maynard Smith Jr.)*

Maynard Smith takes a drink at the Plaza Hotel, seated near aviation legend and fellow Medal of Honor recipient Jimmy Doolittle, far right, and Sen. Stuart Symington, who served as the first secretary of the Air Force.

(courtesy of Maynard Smith Jr.)

Maynard Smith shakes hands with President John F. Kennedy at the White House. Medal of Honor recipients are always invited to presidential inaugurations, and Smith attended as many as he could.

(courtesy of Maynard Smith Jr.)

Maynard Smith with his daughter Christine.

(courtesy of Maynard Smith Jr.)

The 8th Air Force unveils a plaque dedicating a corridor at headquarters to Sgt. Maynard "Snuffy" Smith. His family was not notified.

(courtesy of the U.S. Air Force)

the Congressional Medal of Honor Society. The group's goal is "promoting patriotism and fostering a love of country in the aftermath of World War II."[21]

But there has been a dark cloud forming over his postwar transition, blowing in from Michigan. Today it produces a lightning bolt when police arrest him for failure to pay his alimony. The Gunsells have an ally in county prosecutor John W. Rae, who is giving Smith his full attention, more than might be expected, to chase down a child support scofflaw.

Rae is tight with the local business owners like the Gunsells: the prosecutor is also secretary of the county planning commission and is elected to the state chamber of commerce. In 1946 he's also president of the Michigan Children's Aid Society. If all this seems like résumé building for a life in politics, that's because it is. Rae will leave office this year, to hang his lawyer's shingle and also serve as campaign manager for Republican candidates. One day he'll become an unsuccessful candidate for state representative. The prosecutor and budding politician is also an actor who regularly appears on stage at the Ann Arbor Civic Center, and his flair for the dramatic proves useful in both politics and prosecution.

The charges against Smith are the same as the ones that landed him in the Army to begin with: supporting William H. Smith. Helen Gunsell is remarried but she has sued and won the fight for support payments. The courts are enforcing this legal outcome, with vigor.

Being arrested is bad, being strong-armed for money is worse, but the next day pours salt on the wound. Rae has leaked the arrest to the *Michigan Daily* newspaper, and the wires pick up the story as well. It's the return of Snuffy the Potato Peeler Bomber, in trouble again.

---

21 The Congressional Medal of Honor Society will be created when President Eisenhower signs legislation on August 14, 1958.

Smith's strategy to fight the legal action is to demand an extradition hearing and attempt some negotiation. Weeks and months pass. The extradition hearing is delayed from its April date. Rae decides that the AAF veteran is stalling and decides to amp up the pressure. He makes sure his pursuit is publicized.

"Prosecutor John W. Rae will leave today for Washington D.C. with an extradition warrant for Maynard H. (Snuffy) Smith," reads a July 31, 1946, article in the *Michigan Daily*. "Attempts to settle the case out of court have proved unsuccessful." Governor Kelly, the same man who just the year before hailed Smith at his homecoming parade, signs the warrant.

Rae's tactic works. Smith loses the legal showdown and pays the money without having to return to Michigan. It's the first time that "Snuffy" makes negative headlines after the war. It won't be the last.

BELTWAY BLUES

January 29, 1947. Maynard Smith is composing a letter, a response to a request from a writer named Donald who wants information about Smith's wartime experience in England.[22] Smith's reply, written on Medal of Honor Society letterhead, is a mix of venom and congeniality.

He won't share his memories for any book, Smith says, because he has no interest in reliving "just a bad spot in my life" at Thurleigh, which he spells "Thurligh."

"You see, I had a few friends there, and I counted you as one of the best ones. The others were people I had no interest in, but was forced to associate with simply because I was in the Army," he writes. "I am now happy being completely DISASSOCIATED from the Army and particularly Thurligh."

---

22   The temptation to identify him as the famous Donald Bevan yields disappointment since he was shot down just after Smith arrived at Thurleigh, making the friendship that Smith cites unlikely.

But the same letter reveals the depth of his anger at his demotion and transfer, and whom he blames for it: "It has been my long awaited pleasure to run into a couple of ex-Thurligh officers since being in Washington, and I certainly let them have the works after of course they greeted me with that piss willy officer line of BS.[23] And then I had one from the Pentagon call me up and want something and I gave him the works also."

Smith is altogether unrepentant, but the contradictions in the way he's approaching his past are stark. He wants to forget the Army, but he's on the staff of a veteran's organization. He wants to put his rocky military career behind him, but he berates officers whom he feels wronged him years ago. And he really enjoys the confrontations, despite the disgust they inspire. "Brother," Smith writes, "they don't call me a second time when I get through putting them in their proper place. So much for the Army, I just want to forget the whole thing."

There is discontent brewing at home. Like many war brides, Mary Smith is finding America to be challenging and desires to be closer to her family in upstate New York. "Every night she would lay in bed and cry, 'I want to go to Albany,'" Christine recalls.

Maynard Smith is not the happy man-about-town that he was in England. "He looked down on her," their daughter says, "because she was English and she was a woman."

Smith is still a tax agent for the IRS in Washington, D.C., his "damn good high-paying position." But his restless nature and need for wealth is whipping up an entrepreneurial spirit. Being a faceless civil servant is not enough for him, and he can still feel Judge Smith's eyes on him. "My father told me you should either be so rich you

---

23 "piss willies (noun, plural): The sensation a male gets after urinating. A combination of goosebumps and slight jitters/shivers/shakes" (www.urbandictionary.com).

could go fishing all the time or be so poor you had to," he says in a later interview. "I decided to go with the former."

A SALVE FOR LOST MANHOOD

July 7, 1947. It's a big day for Maynard Smith and his company, the Continental Sales Co. This is the first day he's shipping out his product. It's the start of something big—no pun intended. This is the day Smith introduces the world to the wonders of Firmo, the male enhancement cream. Or at least introducing it to elderly customers in Virginia, where it will first be sold.

It's a scheme worthy of Ralph Kramden, nearly ten years before *The Honeymooners* even airs. Smith has no experience in creating medical products, or even cosmetics. But Smith has developed an ethos that puts marketing ahead of all else. "I know human nature, psychology, and sales," he will say later in life. "If you have that under your belt, you don't have much to worry about."

Smith creates a narrative around Firmo that he feels will attract customers when bottled at $1.50 per ounce. The product comes with a pamphlet printed under the banner of a sham company name, the Anglo-Abarac Importing Co. It claims that the cream contains a secret discovery "brought from the Orient" that can not only increase virility in aging men, but can actually increase penis size.

Firmo's key ingredient is an estrogenic hormone. These do not come from Asia and actually have been in vogue as an anti-aging cream since the late 1930s. And in the right doses on the skin—7,500 international units—it can indeed smooth wrinkles.

Smith ships the cream from his Washington, D.C., apartment. Little does he expect this interstate commerce opens the business to enforcement by the U.S. Food and Drug Administration.

The agency has not been around all that long. In 1938 Congress passed the Food, Drug, and Cosmetic Act to police the marketplace.

The FDA now has its hands full of hormone creams that cross the line between drugs and cosmetics.

One way to figure out what Firmo is is to obtain samples. So, as the *Detroit Free Press* reports at the time, "Federal agents raided Smith's apartment and seized a bushel-basket of the cream."

The FDA is interested in what's in Firmo, and just as interested in what Firmo's manufacturers are claiming it can do. An FDA filing says that the promotional material "represented that it would be efficacious to maintain sexual potency to an extreme old age; and that it would be efficacious to increase the size of the male sex organ and to increase sexual vigor."

The pamphlet specifically says that Firmo contains 7,500 IU of natural estrogenic hormones per ounce of cream. Lab analysis shows Firmo contains only 3,375 IU of hormones per ounce, less than half needed to smooth wrinkled skin.

As for male enhancement, rejuvenation, and the rest, the FDA determines "the article was not an aphrodisiac, and it would not be efficacious for the purposes represented." In other words, it's bunk and Smith's company is breaking federal law by making false claims about a product shipped over state lines.

He's arrested and charged with mislabeling, free on a $500 bond. His lawyer, Emmett Lee Sheehan, announces that he is going to try and get the government to drop the charges. They don't. On May 5, 1948, Smith pleads guilty to a federal charge of mislabeling. It seems the lawyer's maneuvering pays off, at least a little, since the court declines to impose a prison time in lieu of a year's probation. "He drew a suspended sentence when the court took cognizance of his war record," reads one United Press clip.

The Feds are also using another point of leverage to go after Smith. Postal authorities, the *Detroit Free Press* notes, declined to push the case after he "agreed to return money to users." The two-column story in that newspaper includes a photo of him in uniform, wearing his medal. Its caption serves as an epitaph: "Firmo was a dud."

Smith's postwar American dream is turning sour. The IRS is stable but dull, the Medal of Honor Society doesn't wield enough authority to punish his enemies, not to mention protect himself, and above all he needs to make more money to support his family and ease his psyche. Pressures mount when his son Maynard Harrison Smith Jr. is born in August 1947.

The American dream is unfolding much more gently in upstate New York, where the Rayner family is expecting a long-awaited arrival. Young Mary Smith has written her parents, Gertrude and Archibald, extoling the United States. "She told my mother and father, 'Yes, it's really good over here,' and of course my mother's sister was still trying to get us to go," George Rayner says. "I think that's what finally moved my father to consent to the move."

Gertrude quietly takes the reins. "Not so much my father, but my mother was quite timid," notes George. "But on the other hand my mother was the one who saved up the money to pay for us to come to America."

One thing the war didn't change in the United States: the immigration system. Limits imposed on the number of arrivals set in the 1920s remain after the war's end, at a moment when plenty of people are eager to leave their war-torn lands and start over in America. This includes British citizens who are enduring the economic disaster that waited at the conflict's end.

The Rayners are facing a regional quota and laborious registration process. "We finally had our green cards," George recalls. "We had to go to the American Embassy in London, two or three trips, the whole family, to get okayed." It takes years, but the Rayners arrive in Albany, where Gertrude's sister lives, in 1948.

Gertrude's goal of immigrating is fulfilled, but the second part of the dream is to own her own house. "We came over and they bought a house. She had a twenty-year mortgage," George says. "Every time she went to make a mortgage payment, she paid double. She paid the house off in ten years."

"A DARING TYPE OF FELLOW"

July 31, 1952. A crowd is gathering in Farragut Square, staring up at the sixth floor of the YMCA building on the corner of 17th and K streets. There's a thin, dark-haired woman standing up there on a ledge, and it's pretty clear from her body language that she's considering jumping.

This drama is unfolding in the heart of Washington, D.C., during a working Thursday, when downtown is packed with lobbyists, federal employees, reporters, organization staffers, and the multitudes of service industry workers who support these office-bound drones. The White House is a scant few blocks away. Farragut Square park is a hub of foot traffic, all under the watchful glare of a bronze statue of the naval hero.

So there are plenty of people on hand to watch the woman wrestle with the tragic choice before her. Firefighters are even now dashing to the base of the building to set up a net to catch her if she decides to leap.

The drama intensifies as a lone figure appears, climbing out a window and onto the ledge. The new arrival is a man, short and kind of skinny but apparently brave. He raises his arms to the woman, pleading as he closes the distance. She turns to meet him.

The would-be rescuer is none other than Maynard Smith, World War II hero. He makes each step on the ledge carefully; he has a family to live for. Smith lives in Greenbelt, Maryland, a low-income rental community just outside the city, until a recent move to Falls Church, Virginia. He and Mary have two more boys, Ronald George

Smith (born January 1952) and Lawrence Wayne Smith (born October 1952.) They are Ronny and Larry from the start.

Smith has left the frustrating banality of the IRS and is now working as a salesman at a radio shop in the District. He likes the human interaction and immediate gratification of sales.

From up here, he can see the flat rectangle that used to be the historic Shepherd Mansion, mercilessly razed to the ground the year prior. The National Production Authority has of yet not allowed anything to replace it, and now it's just a parking lot. The White House sits just beyond the square, and Smith can't help but wonder if President Truman is home and aware of what's happening just a few blocks away.

Smith reaches the distraught woman. The crowd oooohs satisfactorily as the two connect, and then gasps as the pair appear to grapple for a hair-raising moment. But he gets the upper hand and gently subdues the woman, and then guides her along the ledge, to the window, and inside to safety. The crowd cheers.

"HONOR MEDALIST RISKS LIFE TO BALK WOMAN'S DEATH LEAP," reads the *Washington Post* headline. The article describes the rescue, calling it "thrilling" and "heart-warming."

The woman's name is Ernestine Whomble, age twenty-one. She's described by reporters as "pretty" and indeed is very photogenic when paired with the image of the older hero, Smith. The reason for her pathos is the death of her child from pneumonia, over which she and her husband are despondent.

Whomble is trundled off to the Gallinger Municipal Hospital Psychopathic Ward in southeast D.C. for evaluation. There, her story starts to crumble. She did lose a child to pneumonia, but after that the truth is more elusive. Whomble finally says a man named Roland Bennett, who works with Maynard Smith at the radio store, approached her to take part in a publicity stunt. He wanted her to climb on a ledge downtown, fake a suicide attempt, and allow Smith to make a very public scene. She earned $500 for the stunt.

The day of the rescue doesn't go as she expected. The large crowd, firefighters, and narrow ledge are intimidating and she begins to retreat inside on her own. Smith's arrival is the furthest thing from helpful, she soon tells reporters: "What's happening is I'm trying to get back inside the building, but he's trying to block me. I was scared to death."

The investigation rattles Bennett and Smith, who deny everything. "There is not one grain of truth in what this young lady has said," Bennett tells a United Press reporter. "If this girl was making an act, she should be in Hollywood," Smith adds. "She may be suffering from hallucinations of grandeur."

On August 4 the city presses charges against the pair for filing a false police report, even though no one technically did that. The corporation counsel for the District of Columbia, a career lawyer named Clark King, says that the motive for the publicity stunt is to help Smith run for governor of Virginia.

The political usefulness of such a short-term burst of attention is dubious, since Governor John Battle is only two years into a four-year term. "I require no publicity," Smith argues to the press. "I've had a lot in my lifetime."

By the end of the week, both Smith and Bennett plead guilty. Smith has no explanation of why he was inside the downtown YMCA when Whomble stepped onto the ledge. The judge, taking Smith's war record into account, waives the ten-day jail sentence and fines him $75.

It appears to be a public display of what Sigmund Freud called a hero complex. It's not a clinical term that describes a medical condition. Instead, it refers to a person's tendency to create crisis that only they can respond to. There's nothing genetic about a hero complex; it's entirely learned behavior. A hoax is the most nefarious form of this tendency.

Modern rescue hoaxes fall into common patterns. The hoaxer is usually a public servant, most commonly a firefighter, who responds to the emergency in the role of hero. The perpetrators are typically impulsive males in their twenties, young people eager to prove their worth rather than old pros trying to stay relevant.

Smith clearly doesn't fit these trends, but his life experiences may help explain why he might resort to such a stunt. He's not a public servant, but he has public status as a Medal of Honor recipient. This inflates his importance but also cements his identity as a man-of-action. He also rediscovered his rebellious side after becoming famous in the military, and he has the inability to resist impulses that are common among younger men.

Smith may feel denied the high status he thought would await him after the war, and may want another dose of fame to capitalize on. Smith has seen firsthand what the media can do to prop up a person, if fed the right narrative. He didn't, seemingly, learn that the media attention can be just as destructive.

The initial story about the ledge gets scant coverage nationwide, but the wire service story on his arrest gets plenty of play coast to coast. It's got a strange twist that makes for compelling headlines: "WAR HERO ACCUSED OF PHONY RESCUE."

One of these articles contains perhaps the best, if inadvertent, analysis of what happened with Maynard Smith on that ledge. His wife, Mary, tells a reporter that it's "ridiculous" that her husband is considering a run for governor. After all, they just moved to the state. She also doubts that there was a hoax—but doesn't fully commit to Maynard Smith's innocence. Instead, she says: "Snuffy is a daring type of fellow who might be talked into something like that."

The family is having trouble staying within their means. The word of this financial irresponsibility reaches the Rayner family. "He'd put a down payment on something and then he wouldn't pay any more on it," says George Rayner. "There'd be a knock on the door, and of course she would be the one to answer the door, and they'd take the refrigerator out. I remember her talking about it."

Part of the problem is Maynard Smith's revulsion toward everyday jobs—i.e., ones where he reports to a boss and does what he's told. Mary has no such hesitation and works at a bank. "He was happy to lay on the couch with a book," daughter Christine says. "My mother would go out to work every day to pay the bills. She'd always say to him, you need a J-O-B. But he thought that was beneath him."

She lies about money, mostly to get him to help pay expenses. "She'd invent some fantasy just to get money to buy me shoes," Christine says. "I mean, just buy your daughter some shoes!"

OFF TO UPSTATE NY

December 25, 1957. It's a sad holiday as Mary Smith, Maynard's mother, languishes in Caro Community Hospital. The eighty-four-year-old is stricken with colon cancer and fading fast.

Her son and grandchildren never returned to Michigan. Since 1955, Maynard Smith has lived in upstate New York, in a town located on Route 5 between Albany and Schenectady called Colonie. He's working as a car salesman at an Albany Ford-Mercury dealership, where his family recalls he was rewarded for being "a top salesman." Smith drives a brand-new Mercury car home each year.

Mary Smith has been her son's steady advocate, enabler, and companion. If she sensed a change in him after the war, she never tells anyone publicly. "It isn't a penalty to be the mother of a hero like Maynard has turned out to be," she once says. "I wouldn't mind the posing if one of those pictures would just look nice."

She dies before the end of Christmas Day. Journalists will later note Maynard Smith came back to town for the funeral, the only time he set foot in Caro since his parade. The final tie to Michigan has been severed. The inheritance and proceeds of the State Street house sale are his, and he tries to better his life in upstate New York.

"I know that when his mother died, he got money," George Rayner says. "He bought a house in Albany. I guess he paid the down payment and got a mortgage, didn't make any more payments, and lost the house."

He switches car dealerships in 1959, and he brings home a pink, gas-guzzling Buick. "I remember him explaining about the really cool new type of Dynaflow transmission," his son recalls. "It was nice having a new Buick to drive around in for three years. I worked at night as a bouncer-bartender in a rock and roll club. He always let me take it out."

Eventually he works doing audits for the IRS, coming full circle from his days in Caro before the war. Every chance he has to travel out of town and be the center of attention at Medal of Honor events, he takes up. "He'd be flown, all expenses paid, and he'd love that attention," his daughter recalls. "Look at me, look at me, look at me."

His daughter (and everyone else) says that Smith "enjoyed the friendship of the opposite sex" while married. Christine says her mother knew about the infidelities, and was understandably upset.

Smith's relationship with his wife is straining to the point of breaking. Still, he comes and goes as he pleases in Albany, shooting pool over drinks and plotting his next move. Life is dealing Smith setbacks, but his stubborn will is unbroken. He's not lost his impulse to make it his own way. There are two ideas that he hopes will change his fortunes: publishing and advocating for a state lottery.

ENTER THE BULLPUP

April 3, 1965. Lieutenant Colonel Robinson Risner is screaming over the jungles of North Vietnam in the cockpit of the F-105 Thunderchief, the largest single-seat, single-engine combat aircraft ever seen.

For a man moving at high speeds, he can hardly move. Risner's laden with eighty pounds of gear, including the G-suit to stay conscious during violent flight and survival equipment in case he's shot down.

Risner, a famed ace who claimed eight enemy airplanes over Korea, is now embroiled in the effort to shut down the flow of support to North Vietnam. The commander of the 67th Tactical Fighter Squadron, the "Fighting Cocks," he's leading a formidable attack on a notoriously well-protected North Vietnamese bridge.

There are forty-six F-105s, twenty-one F-100 Super Sabres, a pair of RF-101 Voodoo photo recon jets, and ten KC-135 refueling tankers tasked with rendezvous on the way in and out. Most of the airplanes (all except the F-100s) are flying out of air bases in Thailand. The Thai and U.S. governments are denying this, but it's pretty much an open secret.

But among all the airplanes, only sixteen of the forty-six Thunderchiefs carry a new weapon that the U.S. Air Force is hoping can bring some new battlefield success—guided missiles called AGM-12 Bullpups. Risner has two of the white, fourteen-foot weapons inside the fuselage. Each one is adorned with two sets of sharp cruciform fins; the wide ones in back are fixed but another set toward the nose are controlled pneumatically.

The missile is guided, but any smarts that it has are supplied by the F-105's pilot. When it launches, Risner will watch the light of a flare mounted on the missile and adjust its flight with a radio-controlled joystick, which moves those fins.

It's the start of a new era of precision weapons. The Bullpup is the first mass-produced air-to-surface guided missile, and this strike is its debut. It's been constructed for just this kind of mission: pinpoint attacks on infrastructure.

The Air Force never really figured out how to destroy bridges during the Korean War, but it wasn't for a lack of trying. A B-29 campaign against bridges employed the new Tarzon guided bombs, which used radio controls to help steer the massive bomb as it fell. Only six of the twenty-eight, 5,200-pound warheads that dropped destroyed their targets; in 1951 the Air Force discontinued the project.

Nevertheless, this failure feeds the ambitions of those in the Air Force who still dream of efficient ways from the air to cripple an enemy's infrastructure. But the equations of air combat are changing on both sides, as Russian-made antiaircraft missiles and jet interceptors make the sky more dangerous for encroaching warplanes.

The Air Force needs fast aircraft that can dogfight a Soviet-built jet, dash fast enough to deke surface-to-air missiles, and drop guided bombs on ground targets. The F-105 wasn't built to do this. The warplane was created to penetrate Russian air space, fly extremely low to evade radar, and drop a nuclear bomb.

Tactical bombing is not on the designer's menu, but the Thunderchief is nevertheless becoming the tool of choice for Air Force bridge-busting missions in Vietnam. The Bullpup missile is meant to bring a new level of precision to these bombing runs.

In March 1965, Washington, D.C., began targeting the North Vietnamese rail system south of the 20th parallel. That set the stage for the April 3, 1965, strike against the Dragon Bridge, the best-defended target in North Vietnam.

It's the kind of mission that drives Curtis LeMay crazy. He retires as Chief of Staff of the Air Force on February 1, 1965, having lost his long, long campaign to convince the White House to embark on a sustained strategic bombing campaign against North Vietnamese cities, harbors, and other critical targets. "Flying fighters is fun," LeMay says. "Flying bombers is important."

Pinprick tactical strikes, launched solely to support a ground campaign, are insane to him. In LeMay's 1965 autobiography, he says he would demand North Vietnam "draw in their horns and stop their aggression, or we're going to bomb them back into the Stone Age. And we would shove them back into the Stone Age with air power or naval power—not with ground forces."

This has echoes of the early airpower aspirations of World War II, but LeMay is not talking about precision strikes against industrial targets. He's talking about total war from the air, of systematically laying waste to a modern society until it buckles to America's will. His thinking along these lines extends to nuclear weapons—carried by bombers, naturally. His hard-line stances produce depictions of him seen in the 1964 movie *Dr. Strangelove*: a cigar-chewing, city-incinerating madman. It's a far cry from the advocate of humane precision bombing who flew over Europe in 1942.

LeMay's advice for Vietnam ignored, the United States instead begins an incremental and ultimately ineffectual policy of bombing enemy supply lines, starting with rail networks. And that brings the Thanh Hóa Bridge squarely into the American bombsights.

The slender "Dragon Bridge" seems like a vulnerable choke point in the North Vietnamese supply chain. The 540-foot span has one ribbon of railroad track and one road down its center. At its widest, the bridge is only fifty-four feet across. This makes it a tough target to see and a hard one to hit. Making it worse, the Vietnamese have a network of radar sites bathing the surrounding airspace. The targeting data from these sites flows into antiaircraft guns and missile batteries that surround the bridge.

The attack plan, therefore, includes pasting the defenses with bombs. This task, called flak suppression (still using that old word), involves fifteen bombers attacking the gun positions and radar sites to protect the other half attacking the bridge. The F-105s not armed with Bullpups carry eight 750-pound bombs each.

The Air Force puts the mission in the hands of the best. Risner is a jet ace who, while in Korea with the 336th squadron, flew more than 100 combat missions in F-86s. Now he's back in combat, in his third shooting war, flying a fast machine armed with a new weapon.

Four flights of F-105s leave from Thai bases in Karon and Takhli. The Thunderchiefs top off their fuel tanks over the Mekong River, using their strange side-mounted refueling booms to connect to the KC-130s. The F-100s rise from bases in Vietnam and rendezvous with the others, forming a group of fighters on one mission that surpasses the number of the entire North Vietnamese air force.

The strike group streaks across Laos to the mission's IP, three minutes south of the Dragon Bridge. It won't be easy to see the bridge from 15,000 feet, but the day is bright so he's hopeful. But as he closes in on the target all he can see is the glare of the sun reflecting off the hazy air.

Steering the missile requires approaching the target on a steady, level flight. Any World War II bomber crewman would immediately assume that this makes work easy for gunners on the ground, but it seems to catch the U.S. Air Force by surprise when the flak guns chew into the fighter-bombers. It turns out the Bullpup's contrails serve as a handy pointer to where the F-105s are flying.

Risner ignores the antiaircraft fire and focuses on the missile's flight, tracking the light of a flare mounted in the back. But the flare is lost in the bright haze, reducing the guided weapon to a best guess. Even worse, the impacts of the missiles' 250-pound warheads seem to do little more than scorch the bridge's thick concrete abutments.

Risner banks the F-105—turning is not the jet's best feature—and sets up for another attack with his second Bullpup. The visual guidance system requires them to be fired one at a time and the attack plan calls for two passes per Thunderchief.

Risner witnesses the smoke bloom from the second missile's impact but any satisfaction is replaced with alarm when his airplane lurches with a violent impact. Smoke immediately seeps into the cockpit. The gunners below found their mark, but the wound is not fatal. Risner steers his flight away from the bridge as the others arrive, striking in waves. The F-105 is leaking fuel and the cockpit fills with smoke, but Risner guides the warplane to a runway in Da Nang.

The recon planes arrive last. The strike delivered 32 Bullpup missiles and 120 750-pound bombs to the structure and tracks. Not only is the bridge standing, the damage looks superficial. The fortifications are just too strong for the missiles' small warheads.

A restrike is ordered for the next day, and the Bullpups will be left at home. It's another dead end for precision bombing, a concept that can't seem to survive the realities of combat. But the Air Force techs and defense industry gurus have not given up, not by a long shot.

Trying a new tactic would be familiar to the B-17 crews of World War II, and so would its failure. Another familiar element to both wars are mission caps and grim calculations regarding survival. A Vietnam combat tour is either a year or 100 missions, whichever comes first. "The losses were appalling," writes Major Ed Rasimus in his memoir, *When Thunder Rolled*. "The class of nine that had been six weeks ahead of mine at Nellis [AFB] lost four. The first short-course class of 'universally assignable' pilots lost fifteen out of sixteen, all either killed or captured." He tabulated that three of every five pilots that started the tour would not complete it.

Risner doesn't beat the odds. He's downed in September 1965 on a mission near the Thanh Hóa Bridge and imprisoned by the North Vietnamese until 1973.

CHAPTER 15

THE VETERAN'S VOICE

June 12, 1966. The *Detroit Free Press* publishes its update on the life and times of Maynard "Snuffy" Smith. They have sent staff writer Bill Porterfield to upstate New York for an onsite report. It's headlined: "FROM B-17 TO OLD PINK BUICK: THE WAR-LORN YEARS OF SNUFFY SMITH."

The article tries for a bleak, literary tone to describe a war hero whose best days are firmly behind him. "The glory is gone and Maynard Smith knows it," Porterfield diagnoses. "You can tell that from his chewed-down-to-the-quick fingernails."

The article offers this concise update about Smith's status in upstate New York: "Maynard H. Smith once stood out from the crowd; people lifted roman candles to him; generals saluted. Now? Well, he drives the old pink Buick around the block looking for a parking place, just like everybody else. He spends the day in two dingy rooms above the Beauty Bazaar Salon on Washington Avenue in Albany, putting together a monthly newspaper called *The Veteran's*

Voice with his advertising director and ad salesman. He drives into Albany every day from Nassau, a little town where he has lived for a number of years in a rented apartment with his wife Mary, whom he married 22 years ago in England, and three husky sons. Snuffy's sons idolize him."

Maynard Jr. is old enough to accompany Smith on his nighttime excursions to bars and pool halls. The reporter, Porterfield, hears a family anecdote:

> One night last winter, in a neighborhood tavern, he beat a guy at a 50-cent game of billiards. But instead of digging into his pocket, the fellow moved to the bar and began drinking. Maynard Jr. is 18 and a muscular 220-pounder. He asked Snuffy, "Pa, doesn't that guy owe you 50 cents?" "Yeah," Snuffy said. "But what the hell? Forget it." But Maynard Jr. wrapped his fingers around the man's throat and told him he'd wring his neck if he didn't pay up. The fellow paid up.

Maynard Jr. reads this account with some skepticism. The only bar fight in upstate New York that he remembers was sparked by a bet over an arm wrestling match between Jr. and an equally larger man. "I won, but the guys didn't pay up," he remembers. "One of them went after my father. That's when Smitty hit him on the head with a pool cue."

Smith establishes *The Veteran's Voice* in March 1966. It's an unabashedly patriotic broadsheet newspaper, a mélange of useful tips about VA care, calls for political action where healthcare legislation is concerned, and editorial pushback against the antimilitary sentiments in other media.

The inaugural issue of the paper contains a statement of purpose, written of course by Maynard Smith:

It shall be the policy of *The Veteran's Voice* to be patriotic. That is to be devoted to serve one's own country. That country is the United States of America. This paper will stand behind the high office of the President of the United States, knowing full well that he is a human and is subject to human error. *The Veteran's Voice* shall take a very strong stand against any act of an individual or group that is unpatriotic in nature, such as the burning of draft cards or attempted disruption of the government armed services or any branch thereof.

Smith seems to have anointed himself the spokesperson for veterans and guardian of American patriotism. Another example of this budding role can be found in the New York State legislature records, which record him founding the "National Committee for the Protection of Patriotic Americans" in 1969. It's headquartered in the same "dingy" address on Washington Avenue.

The Veteran's Voice is balanced to be more of a vehicle for advertising than a journalistic endeavor, which is in keeping with Smith's penchant for sales. The description of the staff—three salesmen and no staff writers—is a sure sign of the paper's raison d'être. "He copped the big medal as a fighting man," the *Detroit Free Press* article reads. "But he's not likely to win a Pulitzer with *The Veteran's Voice.*"

Smith brings the reporter to Hugh Deniston's bar on Green Street and drinks a few Manhattans. "You know," he says. "I've always had a hankering for ground action. I'd like to give it a try in Vietnam. You're damned right I would." He says of Maynard Jr.: "That boy is a man's man. When he finishes high school this summer, I'm going to put him in the service. He'll make a helluva soldier."

Privately, Smith is less eager to see his sons go off to war. He uses some of his influence-peddling skills to bring Maynard Jr. into the Coast Guard, seen as the safest service. But by the next year, his son will be fighting on the rivers of Vietnam. Maynard Jr. isn't the only Smith boy in the war. In 1970 his estranged son, William Smith, will be stationed at an air base in Southern Thailand. Both will survive their experiences.

Porterfield claims that Smith has lost a "shoot from the hip desperation that used to get him into trouble." But the facts of his life in upstate New York dispute this conclusion—as does Smith's wife when interviewed. "He hasn't changed much," Mary Smith tells the reporter. "He's still a hell raiser if he gets the chance, still the adventurer. Like publishing the paper. He had no experience as a journalist, but he wanted to try it, so he did. He has mellowed though, slowed down a little, that's all."

Behind the scenes, Mary and Maynard's relationship has been buffeted by financial difficulties, his frequent job changes, and public scandals. He travels for Medal of Honor events without her and also vacations in Daytona Beach by himself, extended trips that give him ample opportunities to cheat on his wife.

But Smith also makes the right noises to the reporter when it comes to hard-earned wisdom from his setbacks. "Mary's right, I've mellowed some, a great deal I think. I used to think I knew all the answers, now I know I don't. My main concern right now is my family, and to make enough money to retire comfortably."

Smith's attempt at humility morphs into an epic display of self-unawareness. "I'm just an average guy," he goes on. "Maybe I'm more adventuresome than most. I'm of a fearless nature. I don't know why. I've just never been afraid to act, to take a leap and say the hell with the consequences. Sometimes this has been a virtue and at other times it has gotten me into trouble."

Shortly after the article appears, the marriage ends, and not by his design. His daughter, who appeared in court to discuss the separation with a judge, remembers Smith's reaction. "He was so mad, just furious," she says. "He tore up all the photographs of them." The image of the pair in Bedford during World War II, smiling outside the justice of the peace, ends up shredded in anger.

It's a tragedy, given the road they traveled and the depth of feelings they still have despite the separation. "He was the love of her life, and she was his," says Christine.

REGISTERED LEGISLATIVE REPRESENTATIVE

July 20, 1967. Joseph Murphy stands before a drum filled with tickets. It appears to be just a scaled-up version of a typical raffle, like you'd see at a church or veteran's organization event, but this is something more historic. When Murphy, the New York State tax commissioner, withdraws the name from the drum at 10:22 A.M., he chooses the first-ever New York State Lottery winner.

His name is Charles M. Huckins, a forty-one-year-old truck driver from Leominster, Massachusetts. Others follow, 1,544 winners, each one drawn by hand. It takes more than twenty-four hours to select them all. The individual prizes will be allocated with another drawing the following week, but the initial day of lottery pays out $1.8 million to winners. But you don't have to win a lottery to make money off the idea of one.

Maynard Smith watches the drawing with satisfaction. He feels this is a personal accomplishment, since he worked to create the lottery. Years before, he became a registered legislative representative—a lobbyist—devoted to the creation of a lottery in New York State. His self-appointed task was to collect signatures for a petition in support of changing the state law. Smith has no client; he's figured out a way to self-fund the operation.

"He would have a phone room with a couple of guys making phone calls, and they'd call businesses," Maynard Smith Jr. explains. "Then he would say, 'Listen, you give me a little money to help me keep going here, get more petitions printed and stuff like that. And I'll leave petitions at your store. And when people come in, you can have them sign the petitions, and then we'll send somebody by to pick them up.'"

Using the telephone as a sales tool is nothing new, even then, but it has not been industrialized yet. Smith's operation has a sophistication that presages the future emergence of telemarketing in the '70s, boiler rooms in the '80s, and robo-calls of the new millennium.

Like these future marketing manifestations, Smith and his fellow callers follow a basic script. "He would convince them to do it by telling them, 'The reason that that I want to do this is because I'm hoping to help eliminate or lower education taxes and stuff like that. You're a business. I'm sure you want your taxes lowered a little bit.' And they'd say, 'Yeah, sure. We'll give you thirty or forty bucks.' He got like 350,000 signatures on the petitions."

The lottery has wide public support, which helps Smith's petition drive. In November 1966 the state lottery is approved by a substantial majority of New York voters and, in April 1967, the legislature passes the New York State Lottery Law. The law explicitly states the net proceeds be used exclusively for educational purposes.

It's a success for Smith as an influence peddler but it also puts him out of business. There is a bigger game worth hunting: taking the lottery nationwide. He establishes what he calls the Committee for the Enactment of a National Lottery. It's headquartered in "Suite 11" of a Capitol Hill multifamily, brick-faced building at 329 8th Street NE.

As Smith pitches the idea of a national lottery, the New York State version is underperforming. The cost of education is increasing and the expected revenues are not being produced. In August 1967 Smith offers his unsolicited advice to Murphy, typed under COMMITTEE FOR THE ENACTMENT OF A NATIONAL LOTTERY letterhead.

Its chairman, Maynard H. Smith CMH, is identified as "Formerly, Registered Legislative Representative for the Enactment of a Lottery in New York State."

"As a friendly gesture to you, I set forth three basic corrections in the management of the New York State Lottery that will up the sales trend and put the entire operation on a solid footing." He then does so, changing everything from doubling price of tickets to offering a 10 percent kickback to sellers. None of these reforms appear to be heeded.

Over the years the New York State Lottery will grow to be a revenue behemoth. About $64 billion have gone to K–12 education since 1967. About 30 percent of lottery proceeds go to the education fund. The rest goes to winners, retailer commissions, operating expenses, and contractors.

But no matter; Smith's future is now clearly with touting a national lottery. He focuses attention on Alabama governor George Wallace, now a wild-card candidate for U.S. president. He writes the iconoclastic, pro-segregation governor of Alabama in 1968:

Dear Governor: Your appearance on TV announcing your campaign for the convention nomination was very impressive. I am with you all the way, and I am certain that millions of straight thinking Americans feel the same way as I do.

Mr. Wallace, I invite your support of a National Lottery Act. There are three primary reasons. 1) It will greatly relieve the fiscal condition of the U.S. Treasury. 2) The great vast majority of the public wants it and will support it, if a National Lottery Commission handles it properly. This I proved in the State of New York even though the following put on a most vigorous campaign to defeat it—this campaign was led and directed by Gov. Rockefeller. The full staff of the Governor's office, the Regent of the State of New York, the PTA with anti-lottery pamphlets distributed to parents through THE PUBLIC SCHOOL SYSTEM, and many others. Yet it was approved by the public more than two to one. It was simply a case of logic and right predominating over dictatorial tactics. 3) Mans [*sic*] nature to gamble . . .

As a Medal of Honor holder with a son in the service, I also have my feelings about Viet-nam and the fiasco of the ship Pueblo.[24] It is high time U.S. officials quit pussyfooting around. Your [*sic*] the man George and I think you can win the Democratic convention with the right strategy. And I have just the strategy for you. More about that later. Your reply indicating your support of a National Lottery would be appreciated. Respectfully yours, Maynard H. Smith-CMH

If there is a response from Wallace, Maynard Smith didn't keep it. On April 4, 1986, the Department of Justice weighed in on two congressional attempts to pass a National Lottery Act, but found it unconstitutional. The Founders, they determine, specifically wanted the states to hold this revenue exclusively and without federal competition.

OF LASERS AND FALLING BRIDGES

May 11, 1972. Captain Thomas Messett is thundering over North Vietnam in an F-4D Phantom. He's a member of the 8th Tactical Fighter Wing, the famed 'Wolf Pack' that flies from Ubon Royal Thai Air Force Base. More specifically, Messett is assigned to the 433rd Tactical Fighter Squadron, which happens to be the ones testing the new Paveway laser-guided bomb.

---

24 On January 23, 1968, the USS *Pueblo* was engaged in a surveillance mission when captured by North Korean patrol boats.

The "Easter invasion" is underway. North Vietnamese armored and infantry units cross the Demilitarized Zone. The United States is retreating from the war and calling it Vietnamization. Nearly all the ground troops are gone, and the Air Force is close behind. So naturally, North Vietnam jumps on the void left by the Americans and invades. Now the Air Force is hammering the North's supply lines in a bid to prevent the collapse of the South Vietnamese government.

Messett is at the head of a strike force of just four Phantoms, heading for the Paul Doumer Bridge. This span, like the Dragon Bridge, is a priority target when it comes to cutting rail and road traffic to the south. As such, it's defended ferociously. Messett knows this firsthand, having been riddled by antiaircraft fire and nearly shot down while on an earlier attack on the bridge.

The Phantoms carry laser-guided bombs; three jets carry two 2,000-pound Mk 84s and the last hefts a pair of 3,000-pound Mk 118s. But Captain Messett's F-4 also carries something more lethal than a bomb—a Pave Knife targeting pod. The laser inside the pod will "paint" the target with the laser. Sensors affixed to the bombs control the fins that steer the bomb to the laser-designated target. The pilot doesn't operate the pod; a weapon system officer in the rear seat of the F-4 is responsible for that part.

The brilliance (no pun intended) of the laser guidance system is that it turns dumb bombs into smart ones. It's the brainchild of Weldon Word, an engineer at Texas Instruments, and shepherded by Colonel Joseph Davis Jr., vice commander of the Air Proving Ground at Eglin Air Force Base in Florida. They developed a conversion kit that could be bolted onto gravity bombs, making them precision weapons without the massive cost of making a new one from scratch.

It's not perfect. You can forget about using these visual targeting systems at night or through clouds. But the results of converted Mk 84 bombs are better than expected and make it all worthwhile.

Average accuracy is an amazing twenty feet, with one in every four bombs scoring a direct hit.

Combat conditions are different than test ranges, as the history of guided bombs has consistently shown. That makes this sortie—the first to use laser-guided Paveways—a historic first. Whether it's a breakthrough or just another failure is up to Messett and his men.

Approaching the target means a descent to around 500 feet at fifty miles out. At the IP, the F-4s light their afterburners and shoot up to 12,000 feet, where the lead planes can see and identify the target. But instead of diving in for an attack, as usual, Messett instead adopts an oval, racetrack pattern. His plane is canted at a 40-degree angle; this way the laser beam can stay on the target as the rest of the airplanes drop their bombs. The invisible cone of laser energy remains sharp enough at five miles.

It's a long, scary thirty seconds that Messett flies level, enough time for the WSO in his back seat to keep the laser on target. But the small size of the strike group has confused the Vietnamese, who are not putting up any resistance today.

The bombs zigzag drunkenly as the fins make corrective movements, keeping the laser's reflection inside the seeker sensor's field of view. All eight bombs score direct hits on the bridge. An entire span on the Hanoi side of the bridge tips into the Red River. It will be a year before the Paul Doumer Bridge is usable; Messett receives the Silver Star for leading the mission.

The Dragon Bridge gets it next, just days later. After back-to-back missions of 2,000- and 3,000-pound laser-guided bomb drops, according to one Air Force review: "The western span of the Thanh Hóa Bridge had been knocked completely off its 40 foot thick concrete abutment and the bridge superstructure was so critically disfigured and twisted that bridge rail traffic would come to a standstill for at least several months." More attacks are planned as the repairs begin. It's estimated that 104 American pilots had been shot down over a seventy-five-square-mile area around the Thanh Hóa Bridge during the war.

Paveways prove themselves in combat and change the precision airstrike game forever. Studies tabulate that 48 percent of them dropped around Hanoi in 1972 and 1973 scored direct hits, compared to 5 percent of unguided bombs. And hewing close to the lab conditions, the average Paveway landed inside 23 feet of its target, as opposed to 447 feet for gravity bombs.

The dream of precision-guided weapons seemingly has been achieved. But Eaker and Hap Arnold's vision of air campaigns that pair accuracy with bomber-sized volume has not been realized. Vietnam proves the technology can work in tactical situations, but the larger implications remain murky. Can precision weapons ever be scaled up to inflict enough damage to humanely ruin an entire nation's ability to wage war?

"$1,300 AND AN IDEA"

March 15, 1977. There's a leprechaun cartoon on the upper left corner of the cover of the *Police Officer's Journal*. This is the Special St. Patrick's Day issue, and says so in green ink on the cover. The leprechaun has a green pipe in his mouth and is tipping a top hat, revealing a mostly bald head. There's more than a passing resemblance to this paper's founder and editor, Maynard Smith.

It's Smith's swan song edition of the weekly newspaper that he founded. Now that the newspaper is sold, Smith is moving on, from the newspaper and from a profitable stint in New York City.

He's leaving behind a healthy publication, dozens of pages long every month. That's as thick as the *Village Voice* at the time, and a testament to Smith's aggressive marketing.

By 1971, when Maynard Jr. returns from Vietnam, he joins Maynard Smith and his brother Ronnie in New York City to run the *Police Officer's Journal*. They live in a four-room apartment on Roosevelt Avenue in Queens.

Smith starts the *Police Officer's Journal* "with just $1,300 and an idea." It follows the editorial template of the *Veteran's Voice;* two parts advocacy, one part helpful service content, and one part morale-building stories of interest from the beat. The cover story of the St. Patrick's Day issue includes a feature on how mobile computers are changing the way auto-theft cops operate and another piece exploring new twists in what the editor clearly thinks is institutionalized pension fraud.

It's 100 percent an advertising vehicle. He's combined the two skills he's learned upstate—publishing and phone banks. "We always had maybe eight or ten people selling advertisement over the phone," Maynard Jr. says. "You know? 'Hi, this is Jack Savage at *Police Officer's Journal,* independent paper devoted to police and community affairs. We'd like to see your thing in the middle of our July edition, and blah, blah, blah.'"

He's not given up hawking the idea of a National Lottery and now also advocates for legalized gambling in New York State. This work attracts the attention of the *Long Island Press,* which runs a feature on the one-man Committee for the Enactment of a National Lottery in October 1975. "Smith has contacted many prominent men and influential persons to obtain backing for his ideas and has letters from Mayor Beame and Harrison J. Goldin, the city comptroller, indicating a cautious interest in his plans, among others," the article says.

It continues: "On the minus side, his committee has also attracted the attention of the State Attorney General Louis Lefkowitz and the office of the secretary of state for allegedly failing to file as a lobbying organization before the Sept. 22 deadline. Smith contends he did send in the $5 registration fee and letter detailing the filing requirements but didn't use the state forms. He says he has since obtained the proper forms and has mailed them in—plus the $400 penalty for late filing."

He has dreams of coast-to-coast phone banks and political action money. For now, the efforts are limping along. "Smith is currently financing the committee's operations out of his own pocket, he said, but will soon begin soliciting businessmen and the public to help support a major advertising and legislative campaign."

As it turns out, phone banks are starting to become a problem when it comes to the *Police Officer's Journal*. "Sometimes, the people that sold the advertisements would then flake off and go and open a fake paper themselves," says Maynard Smith Jr. "And they would call people and tell them that they were the police department, they were this, they were that."

The word starts to spread to avoid scam calls. "The regular newspaper started printing articles about fake police newspapers," he says. "It got harder and harder to sell advertisements. We decided, man, if we can sell this, we're going to sell it."

Maynard Smith unloads the *Police Officer's Journal* in 1977 and eyes his favorite getaway location, Florida, for his next move. "He made a good little wad of money on it and came down to Florida," Maynard Smith Jr. says. "He bought a house on Park Street, which I still own. It's a rental property now."

REVISIONS AND ALL

December 14, 1944. Maynard Smith is sitting in the Officer's Club on Thurleigh air base. He's not supposed to be there, since he's just a sergeant, but it's not like anyone will be kicking out a Medal of Honor holder.

He's glad he's breaking the rules tonight, since none other than Glenn Miller is sitting at a nearby table, talking about an impending trip to Paris. It seems his Army band is going to perform there, and Miller is scoping out a new rehearsal hall in advance of their trip. The breakneck pace of his tour is taxing his health, but he's relentless.

The next day, Smith tells a reporter decades later, he drives Miller in a jeep to the nearby Twinwood Farm airfield and watches the C-64 transport airplane take off. That makes him one of the last people to see Glenn Miller alive. The airplane vanishes and Miller, Lieutenant Colonel Norman Francis Baessell, and pilot John Robert Stuart Morgan are forever labeled missing in action.

There is no independent confirmation of Smith's story, which appears with his direct quotes in the *Orlando Sentinel* in November 1980. Since Miller didn't stay at or take off from Thurleigh, it's not clear why the 306th would be responsible for the star's ride. Arranging a ride for Miller *would* be the kind of thing that Smith could do, and it's hardly a stretch to imagine that he would use whatever pull he has to drive the famous bandleader. He is, after all, a huge fan.

But it doesn't take much probing to poke other holes in the tale. For starters, Miller's final ride to the airfield has been discussed before, and given the bitterly cold weather, it's no surprise he's in a car, not a jeep. Band manager Lieutenant Don Haynes is known to be the last to see Miller alive, and he makes no mention of a jeep or Smith. Given the scope of the investigation into Miller's disappearance—a very public humiliation for the military—it's not likely his involvement would escape notice. Nor would Smith hold this story back for more than thirty years.

It's just too good to be true.

Over the years many people will reference Smith's habit of inflating his World War II exploits. None will do so as nakedly as Neal Shine, publisher and columnist for the *Detroit Free Press,* who says

Smith exaggerates his May 1 flight: "Snuffy elevated his ultimate participation in this bit of military history by claiming that after he put the fire out he rushed to the cockpit, pulled the wounded pilot and co-pilot from their seats, gave them first aid and then—although he had never flown before—flew the crippled bomber back to England and landed safely."

There is not a lot of on-the-record proof to match Shine's particular accusations. But Smith's written description of the May 1 mission, given to Wayland Mayo in 1979 at the Royal Palm Memorial Gardens in Florida, does have some embellishments. "I went forward to find the pilot and co-pilot pretty well shot up," Smith writes. "I put some tourniquets on them so they could maintain control of the plane. I then went back to put the control cables together as we had no tail control. I remember I repaired the six wires."

These details are not mentioned in combat reports, the Medal of Honor citation, or by any other crew. Johnson and McCallum never receive Purple Hearts for the mission. It seems to be a prime example of the kind of aggrandizement that Shine is speaking about.

"Because the world loves a hero, we have attached certain rights and privileges to that high station," Shine holds forth. "Among them, the right to tell their stories to those who will appreciate the quality of their heroism and accept it as it is offered. Revisions and all."

The editor's blasé attitude about historical accuracy is matched by his downplaying of the significance of the Medal of Honor and a total misread of Smith's personality. "Snuffy Smith was no different from the hundreds of thousands who came out of that war with their own personal versions of what it was like," he writes. "And though they gave him a medal for his efforts, Snuffy never traded on that."

Embellishments or no, it's worth noting that Smith seems to have at least cordial relations with L. P. Johnson, who is a pilot for Pan Am flying 747s on international routes. Johnson and his former ball turret gunner exchange Christmas cards, some of which Smith saves among his prized mementos. In December 1980, L. P. Johnson sends a letter: "Hello Maynard. Thank you for your nice Christmas card and note. Yes, I do remember May 1, 1943 and I have always been thankful that you were with me. We are very fortunate—I guess God saved us for something else."

Johnson rotated back to the United States after his twenty-fifth mission, tasked with forming yet another bomber group, the 452nd. It's not combat duty but it's not exactly safe, either: on Halloween 1943 he cheats death again by landing a damaged B-17 at Pendleton Field in Oregon. The group he helped create deployed in time for D-Day and launched heavy tactical strikes to support the advance across France after the invasion.

He never returns to Kentucky to enter the family mining business, nor does he become the actor he claims as his profession at the war's start. Instead, Johnson joins Pan American as a pilot immediately after the war ends. He works closely with the airline during the war—the company possesses the world's only transoceanic transport system, after all—and the Pan Am facilities in Miami hosted thousands of pilots and navigators in training.

The veteran pilot meets a Pan Am flight attendant, Lolita Labres, and marries her on New Year's Eve 1949. The pair live in New York City. He stays in the cockpit until his retirement in 1981, when they move to Naples, Florida. Johnson still uses his initials, as always. But now he's taken to telling people that L. P. stands for "Lucky Pierre."

The taciturn gunner who disliked officers clearly makes an exception when it comes to those he's flown with. In February 1981 Smith personally delivers Johnson's request to join the 8th Air Force Historical Society to the organization's staff. These small, eager favors are hints at the regard he feels for the officer who, after all, saved *his* life in 1943 by landing the crippled B-17.

The *Orlando Sentinel* article that presents Smith's Glenn Miller story has another anecdote, presumably supplied by Smith, that's clearly wrong and with a less understandable motive. The article says in no uncertain terms that Marcel St. Louis, Smith's steady companion through training and overseas, had been shot down, attacked by cannibals in Africa, and rescued by an English submarine. "But he was worn out, wounded so many times, his reserves depleted, Marcel St. Louis died in the hospital fighting, as he always did, to stay alive," writes Michael Skinner.

The only problem with this story is that it's not true. St. Louis survives the prison camps, death marches, and the chaos of the war's end. In 1945 he travels through a safety zone that the International Red Cross suggests the Germans establish to safeguard the prisoners. The German High Command agree, and from the middle of January 1945 this evacuation begins. Around 120,000 Allied POWs use these secure lanes to move west toward freedom.

Marcel St. Louis is one of them. He's liberated in May 1945. After treatment at Percy Jones Medical Center (in Fort Custer, Michigan), he's discharged from the military. He's had as much bad luck and despair as Smith has had good luck and fame. But he has survived. St. Louis marries at age thirty and has a son, Robert St. Louis, in 1951. He moves from Detroit to Philadelphia, where he works as a police officer at the Navy yard.

Maynard Smith Jr. says that his father and St. Louis connect at some point after the war. Why he would declare his old friend dead in a local newspaper article is befuddling. But taken with the Miller story, there's a chance that he's just indulging his impulsive side by making things up. The perversion of St. Louis's inadvertent stopover in Ireland, making the scene a crash among cannibals, reads like an inside joke. For a man who has been built up and dismantled in print, it may be too great a temptation not to mess with the media. There certainly wouldn't be any respect for the profession to prevent him from hoaxing them.[25]

As for the postwar meeting between St. Louis and Smith, there's no record of where or when it may have occurred, not to mention what they said or did. The two veterans have taken any details with them to their graves.

---

25 This impulse is not that rare, maybe more so in the modern age. There is even a subset of the hacking community that relishes feeding incorrect information to the media, especially if it helps obscure someone's identity or cybercrime. Media has so much influence that the hackers (or "social engineers") enjoy bending the system to their will, in the same way they subvert a network's architecture with illicit code.

CHAPTER 16

GODDAMNED SKIM MILK

May 15, 1984. A horse-drawn carriage makes its solemn way to Section 66 at Arlington National Cemetery. The United States is putting Maynard H. Smith Sr. to rest in Grave No. 7375. As a Medal of Honor recipient, he's entitled to in-ground burial here.

But only Medal of Honor recipients who are officers rate all the pomp. Per regulations, the standard honors for in-ground burial is a casket team, firing party, a bugler to play taps, and a chaplain. Commissioned officers, warrant officers, and senior noncommissioned officers are eligible for "full honors" that add an additional escort, a marching element, a band, and the horse-drawn caisson. Smith is receiving "modified honors": the standard package but with the equine delivery.

There has been some contention over who pays for Smith's funeral. The Army doesn't want to pick up the tab, even though he served in the Army Air Forces. The Air Force initially balks but, faced with the unseemly prospect of rejecting their own hero, agrees

to see that Smith is sent off properly. "That all kind of pissed me off,"
growls Maynard Smith Jr. Still, Smith's daughter Christine Pincince
describes it as "just beautiful."

Until the stroke in the living room and subsequent fatal heart
failure one month later, Maynard Smith is living with his son,
daughter-in-law, and grandson. He travels as much as he's able to
attend reunions, conventions, and Medal of Honor events. Medal of
Honor holders get invitations to presidential inaugurals, and he travels to D.C. with his son to attend Ronald Reagan's. (Smith switches
political party loyalty several times during his life.)

Smith meets Jackie Gleason at a Medal of Honor Society show.
His son says: "He shot pool with him a few times. Gleason was a killer
pool player. He did all his own shots in *The Hustler.*"

It's a good match since Smith is also skilled. "He was a killer
pool player. People were scared to play with him, because he would
play for money," Maynard Smith Jr. says of his father. "He was the
kind of guy that could hit the ball, and it would go around one ball
and then roll over and knock the ball into the hole, that kind of shot.
Minnesota Fats kind of shots. It was unbelievable."

The money he wins is secondary to the thrill of a challenge. "He
wouldn't con anybody," his son says. "He would just say, 'You know,
if you think you're good enough to beat me, then put your money
where your mouth is.'"

Traveling to military appreciation events gives Smith a good opportunity to meet new women. Indeed, he never seems to stop chasing them around. Photos that he kept from later in his life frequently
show him with female companions. At a 1981 military reunion in
Honolulu, Smith apparently meets a woman named Jeanne who gives
him her hotel information, which he scrawls on the dinner event's
program: "WAIKIKI MARINA, ROOM 1506."

It seems to confirm what he tells an interviewer who asks him if he has advice for other Air Force retirees. Of course he does. "Live a happy life," he says. "The only way to do this is to get out and move, keep moving. Get the hell out of the house. And if you're not married, get a girlfriend, do some running around. It keeps you young, look at me."

Mary has moved from Albany to Hawaii, where her daughter and granddaughter are living. Her bold spirit is still strong. "She came to visit, turned around, quit her job right away, and moved out," Christine says. "She was just a year away from a good pension."

She works for the Bank of Hawaii and spends her free time creating an award-winning garden. In 1982 she sends Maynard a Christmas card with a neatly handwritten note: "Dear Maynard, Have a good holiday and if you cook the bird don't put so much sage in the dressing! Ha. Love, Mary." Smith does not tear this up; indeed, he holds on to it and it makes its way into his steamer trunk of prized artifacts.

There is something sad and sassy about the card. It summons an image of Mary the Air Warden, the indomitable girl who defied her family to marry an American war hero. It's a nice reminder—for Smith and for future voyeurs—of the impetuous romance that altered their lives and started their family. "He was the love of her life," Maynard Jr. says of his parents. "She always said that."

The sunset years are not without real tragedy for the Smith family. Drugs have plagued the family for years, with Ronnie falling into heroin and Larry injecting cocaine. Ronnie suffers a fatal overdose while living in upstate New York in 1980. After his father's death, Larry will succumb to complications from HIV contracted by a needle and die in 1989.

Maynard Smith seems to speak about his troubled boys obliquely in the 1979 interview with *Sergeant's Magazine,* when asked what he thinks about the current generation. "They're not too much worse off than we except for the dope problem. These kids don't realize that this dope will ruin their lives and in some cases shorten their lives. They like to have you buy that marijuana thing as being harmless. I don't. Every kid that gets into marijuana eventually gets into pills and more dope. It's the beginning of the end."

After his stroke in March 1984, Maynard Smith spends the rest of his life in the hospital. Dying is a dismal process for him, what his son calls "a hard month." There is little levity, but Smith does gripe about the sudden change in his diet. "Here I am on my deathbed," he manages to tell his son. "And they are giving me goddamned skim milk."

Maynard Harrison Smith dies on May 11, 1984. Two days later, more than a hundred people show up to the David Gross Funeral Home for a memorial service. Nearby MacDill Air Force Base sends an honor guard. After that there's what the Pentagon and airlines call a "dignified transfer" of his remains to Washington, D.C.

After the caisson ride, Smith's flag-draped coffin is carried to his grave and the man is given a seventeen-gun salute. He's laid to rest under a marker reading "MAYNARD HARRISON SMITH, MEDAL OF HONOR, SGT., US ARMY, WORLD WAR II."

His passing is dutifully noted in newspaper obits, including the *New York Times,* but none explore his story in any significant way. Even the *Tuscola County Advertiser* downplays Smith's death. For as many front-page stories as he's generated in that paper, his passing doesn't rate more than an obit on page 16, next to a recipe for East Penuche Frosting.

His death has not brought the estranged members of his family back together. William Smith refuses to speak with anyone from his father's side of the family. Barbara Morgan—Smith's daughter with Arlene McCreedy, born in Detroit—surfaces briefly in 2002 when she reaches out to the *Advertiser* for clips about him. She is living with her family in Texas.

Mary Smith retires from her bank job and moves to Florida, where her daughter Christine has relocated. In Fort Walton Beach she meets Robert O'Brien, a retired master sergeant who drives a small bus around her community. The pair marry, make it a point to travel, and spend their time at home making pies and tending another lush garden. True to her nature, Mary Smith-O'Brien volunteers at a community library. Her second husband dies in 2004.

She survives to 2015, dying at the age of ninety-one. According to her obituary: "Mary's final resting place will be Graceland Cemetery Memorial Gardens in Albany, New York, where Mary will be forever with her parents, sisters and son."

At the end of May 1984, Maynard Smith Jr. is supposed to be attending a Memorial Day observance at Bay Pines National Cemetery. There are twelve chairs set up on stage for guests of honor, but one is left empty but for a black, draped cloth. Members of a local Marine Corps ROTC from Clearwater stand at color-guard attention as a bugler sounds taps for Smith. About two thousand people stare on in silence.

On the stage is a fellow Medal of Honor holder, Navy Lieutenant Commander John Mihalowski. The pair live in Florida and crossed paths frequently, enough so for the Navy man to offer a glowing coda to Smith's life. "A man of great inner strength, of love for people in trouble and of an almost total selflessness," he says. "Maynard belonged to a vanishing breed."

KILLING WITH PRECISION

April 12, 1999. It's twelve thirty in the afternoon and Brigadier General Dan Leaf, flying in the cockpit of an F-16, is trying to stop a massacre unfolding thousands of feet below.

He's the Commander of the 315th Air Expeditionary Wing, operating from Aviano Air Base in Italy during Operation Allied Force.

The military campaign against Yugoslavia began on March 24, 1999, with British and U.S. airstrikes attempting to curb an ethnic cleansing campaign by the Yugoslavian government. The fight will be short, just seventy-eight days, but the use of airpower to influence conditions on the ground will be revolutionary.

Now Leaf and his wingman are following a convoy with a fuel truck at its center. "We could see the town they'd just burned, parts of the town, and we only had so much time," he recalls. "They were racing to get to the sanctuary of the town because they knew we wouldn't strike them when they were there. We would protect the town that they were going to burn."

The pair of F-16s is flying without any ground support, relying on their onboard cameras to identify targets and lasers that guide their weapons. One airplane designates the target for their wingman, who launches the weapons. "My wingman shot rockets and then I dropped two 500-pound jobs and he finished the job with one," says Leaf, who's now retired. "I get goosebumps thinking about it."

Leaf is a fighter jockey but he acknowledges that the big bombers shouldered a great deal of the weight. Operation Allied Force is the first to use all three of the USAF's heavy bombers in combat. B-52s, B-1s, and B-2s deliver nearly half of the twenty-three thousand air-to-ground munitions dropped during the campaign.

Bombers had finally fully graduated from being indiscriminate death dealers and nuclear-bomb carrying horses of the Apocalypse to frontline combat players. The key enabler is the use of Joint Direct Attack Munitions (JDAMs), a conversion kit that turns dumb bombs into GPS-guided smart weapons. These are the heirs to the Paveway.

It's the B-2's combat debut, one that will prove to combatant commanders that the stealth aircraft is suited for conventional "night one" missions in airspace defended by radar and antiaircraft weapons. The B-2s also use its synthetic aperture radar to take images of their targets as they approach, using those coordinates to make their JDAMs even more accurate. Working with jamming aircraft from the Navy is another trailblazing moment for the "one fight, one team" ethos that would be so vital during coming, extended wars of the new millennium.

The world got its first glimpse of precision weaponry during the Desert Storm in 1991. Press conferences in the Pentagon showed images of bombs entering chimneys and windows, dramatic presentations of the value of laser-guided weapons. But the reality is that less than 10 percent of the munitions dropped during Desert Storm were precision-guided.

During Operation Allied Force, that number triples to 29 percent. "We got to where four aircraft could drop eight bombs and have near simultaneous impacts from different airplanes at different pieces of the sky," Leaf says. "There's an art of war there."

Leaf considers the Kosovo campaign as a milestone in precision bombing. "We have mass. We've had precision. But through the first application of B-1 and B-2s with JDAMs, that is a fundamental shift."

So has the World War II dream of precision airstrikes been achieved? "They were trying to get the bombs clustered around a single center point. That's precision. With mass precision, you get a lot of bombs in somewhat close proximity against a collection of very precise points. It's related to but not the same."

Mass precision bombing is the Pentagon's response to Afghanistan after the attacks on September 11, 2001. The network of defensive positions that the Afghans depended on during earlier wars is no longer safe. "The Soviets would bomb and there might be a few casualties, but generally they'd survive and wait out the enemy," Leaf says. "Now, they found an adversary that could put a lot of large bombs in very precise places along their fighting positions, very quickly. Mass precision. I think that is, at the risk of turning to cliché, a game changer."

What is still being considered is the role of airpower and its ability to shape things on the ground, independent of ground troops. This was LeMay's dream, and Eaker's and Arnold's. After Kosovo, Leaf argues, that part of the debate is over.

"Milosevic didn't surrender to diplomats or the Kosovar militias. He surrendered to airpower. We can debate that all we want, but that is unique," he says. "The lesson that should be learned is that, in some circumstances, airpower can be the centerpiece of a successful strategic campaign. There are many who refuse to accept that because 'we've got to have boots on the ground.' Whatever. You *can* win by airpower alone."

THE HALLWAY

February 1, 2018. Members of Barksdale Air Force Base in Louisiana gather outside of 8th Air Force headquarters for a ceremony honoring Sergeant Maynard Harrison Smith. Bright blue chairs are set up on the grass, scale models of the modern bomber fleet mounted behind the podium.

Part of building a military culture is connecting personnel to the glorious past. And the best way to do that is by calling on a legacy of heroes. Today, the 8th Air Force is invoking the legacy of Maynard Harrison Smith. No one from his family has been invited, or even notified, about the declaration of the "Sgt. Maynard H. Smith Corridor" of the 8th Air Force headquarters.

Recruitment and retention is a constant struggle in the modern Air Force. And many within the service see a crisis in morale brewing: the Air Force needs 65 percent of its pilots to remain for a full twenty-year career in order for their system to work with any continuity. But internal data reveals that fighter pilot retention is 34 percent in 2017 and trending downward in 2018. Overall officer retention Air Force wide is only 49 percent.

The bomber community is especially prone to weak morale. The fleet is aging, with some airplanes flying for more than fifty years, and slated to fly fifty more. Flying old airplanes is not a large attraction for anyone. Insurgent wars in Iraq and Afghanistan shift focus to recon and one-off precision strikes, rather than mass precision bomb attacks. Scandals in the community over the years included unknowingly flying nuclear weapons over the United States (in 2007, but still discussed), sexual harassment claims, and mass groundings for maintenance crises.

U.S. Air Force Major General Thomas Bussiere, 8th Air Force commander, takes to the podium. The speech hits the high notes: selflessness, bravery, calm during a panicky situation, great feats done by small people. The ceremony ends with the unveiling of the plaque:

Maynard H. "Snuffy" Smith

First enlisted Medal of Honor recipient in the Eighth Air Force
and Army Air Forces for heroism on 1 May 1943

The crowd applauds and the USAF press photographer shoots plenty of publicly available images. It's been seventy-five years since Smith's epic flight, but the tale of the little gunner who survived a flying inferno is still a useful piece of propaganda.

ACKNOWLEDGMENTS

Any new book that covers the U.S. Army Air Forces' campaign over Europe has the advantage of reams of earlier work on the topic. This extends to more than just books. These days, authors have at our fingertips international collections of oral histories, photo research, government documents, and genealogical records, many of which have been collected and collated by private organizations or family members. This global warehousing of primary source material proved invaluable to bringing much-needed perspective to the world of Maynard Smith. A rundown of the key references and sources, matched with specific information, is in the notes. Hopefully the new information in this book about Smith and the war will be of use to writers and researchers to follow.

I'd also like to thank Maynard Smith Jr. and his wife for sharing his memorabilia and memories with me, and making me shrimp scampi. I'd also like to extend thanks to George Rayner, Christine Pincince, Roger Connor, and Roxanne Bukacek for their time and insight. Much thanks to the good baristas at the Starbucks in Portland who proved that the people, and not the logo or the bean, are what make a great local coffee shop. Thanks and love to my family; the older I get, the less I see them but the more I appreciate them.

I'd like to thank Ian Kleinert for finding and brokering the deal, and the master connector and Prototipe partner Marc Gordon for introducing me to him. I should probably thank the SPCA of Texas for my two never-"nexted" dogs, but that worthy organization should probably thank *me* for taking such troublemakers off their hands.

As for dedication, this one is for my Corpus Christi support network, especially John "Catman" Wolfshol and *most* especially Amber Rashell Barker. South Texas may never really be my home, but being around them makes me feel like I'm someone, somewhere.

NOTES

Chapter 1

10 *"And he had his watermelon"*: Gordon Friesen, "Citizens Recall Boyish Pranks of Hokey Smith," *Detroit Times*, July 17, 1943.

13 *Things change drastically in March 1934*: "Judge H.H. Smith Dies on Vacation," *Tuscola County Advertiser*, May 14, 1943, accessed via Caro Area District Library online portal.

15 *The really loud action is here*: Norman Rozeff, "A History of the Harlingen Army Airfield and Harlingen Air Force Base," Harlingen Historical and Preservation Society, January 2003, http://www.myharlingen.us/page/open/8052/0/A%20History%20of%20the%20Harlingen%20Army%20Airfield%20and%20Harlingen%20Air%20Force%20Base.pdf.

17 *"I'm a promoter, always have been"*: Michael Skinner, "Maynard Smith Remembers the Big One," *Orlando Sentinel*, November 16, 1980.

17 *Some of the considerations smack of quackery*: Mark Kendall Wells, "Aviators and Air Combat: A Study of the U.S. Eighth Air Force and R.A.F. Bomber Command," PhD diss., University of London, 1992.

18 *Bingham, at the time the chief psychologist*: Ulysses Lee, "The Employment of Negro Troops," U.S. Army Center of Military History (Library of Congress Catalog Card Number: 66–60003), 1966, https://history.army.mil/books/wwii/114/chapter9.htm. It's a fascinating read. "Global war

generated a need for service troops far greater than anyone visualized before Pearl Harbor," Lee says. "As well as a need to use all able-bodied Americans regardless of color or other distinction in military or civilian support of the war effort."

18 *Hershey, the director of the American draft system*: Hershey Papers, Box 58, U.S. Army Military History Institute, Carlisle Barracks, Pennsylvania.

21 *The men are here to learn*: 1st Motion Picture Unit, "Position Firing," AAF Official Training Film I-3366, 1944.

24 *"And I was trying a thing like this"*: Curtis LeMay and MacKinlay Kantor, *Mission with LeMay: My Story* (New York: Doubleday, 1965).

27 *"we would skim the surface until we got to the target"*: Gerald Scott, "Memphis Belle," *Chicago Tribune*, May 24, 1998, https://www.chicagotribune.com/news/ct-xpm-1998-05-24-9805240161-story.html.

31 *a highly decorated, experienced mankiller*: Petr Katcha, "Aces of the Luftwaffe: Egon Mayer," 2007 (accessed 2017) https://www.luftwaffe.cz.

32 *"German glider activity in the 1920s and 1930s had important implications"*: Jürgen Melzer, "'We Must Learn from Germany': Gliders and Model Airplanes as Tools for Japan's Mass Mobilization," *Contemporary Japan* 26, no. 1 (2014). Also includes this interesting quote: "Nazi Germany also provided the organizational blueprint for comprehensive aviation education that mobilized all aviation activities of Japanese youth in the service of national defense."

33 *"A German pilot who flew from 1941 to 1944"*: Gerd Gaiser, *The Last Squadron* (United States: Pantheon Books, 1956).

38 *Zienowicz and his crew are labeled missing in action*: This book largely focuses on the 306th BG, but any one mission involved several groups and they all have stories to share. Details about the 91st BG can be found in Marion Havelaar and William Hess, *The Ragged Irregulars of Bassingbourn—The 91st Bombardment Group in WWII* (Atglen, Pennsylvania: Schiffer Military History, 1997).

Chapter 2

48 *Parton, Eaker's aide and future 8th Air Force historian*: James Parton, *"Air Force Spoken Here": General Ira Eaker and the Command of the Air* (Maxwell Air Force Base, Alabama: Air University Press, 2000), ac-

cessed via the National Archives, https://apps.dtic.mil/dtic/tr/fulltext/u2/
a376708.pdf.

49 *"The bomber, like the snake in the grass"*: Rebecca Grant, "The Return of
the Bomber: The Future of Long-Range Strike," Air Force Association,
February 2007, https://secure.afa.org/Mitchell/reports/0207bombers.pdf.

52 *"Our bombing experience to date"*: Richard Davis, "Carl A. Spaatz and the
Air War in Europe," Center for Air Force History, 1993, accessed via Department of Defense, https://media.defense.gov/2010/Oct/12/2001330126
/-1/-1/0/AFD-101012-035.pdf.

Chapter 3

59 *sobering statistics to the gaps in formations*: Jeanne LeFlore, "McAlester Veteran, Dr. Thurman Shuller, a World War II Hero," *McAlester
News-Capital*, November 11, 2012, https://www.mcalesternews.com
/news/mcalester-veteran-dr-thurman-shuller-a-world-war-ii-hero/article
_22ce6d5e-59d1-5091-8e02-a6f36b29629f.html. This link includes a copy
of his letter and a Shuller interview.

62 *"The coordinated operations of all these gadgets"*: Samuel R. M. Reynolds,
"Human Engineering in the Army Air Forces," *Scientific Monthly* 61,
No. 4 (October 1945).

69 *Lieutenant Josef "Sepp" Wurmheller takes a deep breath*: Petr Katcha,
"Aces of the Luftwaffe: Egon Mayer," 2007 (accessed 2017) https://www
.luftwaffe.cz.

69 *despite working for years as a miner in Bavaria*: John Foreman and Jo-
hannes Matthews, *Luftwaffe Aces: Biographies and Victory Claims*, vol. 4
(Walton-on-Thames, UK: Wingleader Publishing, 2015). See also John
Weal, *Jagdgeschwader 2 "Richthofen"* (Oxford, UK: Osprey Publishing,
2000).

72 *"Luckily for us we were able to reform"*: Robert Morgan and Ron Powers,
The Man Who Flew the Memphis Belle (New York: Penguin Random
House, 2011).

Chapter 4

86 *The May 1 mission plan unfolds in front of the men*: Claude Putnam, "Operations Report to Commanding General, Headquarters, First Bombardment Wing," May 1, 1943. Includes the bombing run track chart, group
formation sketch, battle damages, and bombing flight record.

86 *As one AAF training video explains*: 1st Motion Picture Unit, "Flak," AAF Official Training Film I-3389, 1944.

88 *"Being underway is actually a relief"*: Robert Morgan and Ron Powers, *The Man Who Flew the Memphis Belle* (New York: Penguin Random House, 2011).

90 *a routine that's part ritual, part checklist*: Combat Gunner's SOP, Headquarters 303rd Combat Group, APO 557, U.S. Army, October 15, 1944.

91 *Lieutenant Kisseberth was working his way*: Jason McDonald, "Captain Mack McKay a Pilot of the 306th Bomb Group and His Crew Point to a 'Kill' Marking Painted on His B-17 Flying Fortress," For the Imperial War Museum, http://doczz.net/doc/3993365/mack-mckay-s-crew---306th-bomb-group.

Chapter 5

101 *"In contrast to German High Command during the Battle of Britain"*: David C. Isby, ed., *Fighting the Bombers: The Luftwaffe's Struggle against the Allied Bomber Offensive* (Barnsley, UK: Frontline Books, 2003).

106 *"I did feel sorry for our gunners"*: Robert Hecker, "Flak House Days," *WWII Magazine*, January 2014, accessed via National Archives, https://archive.org/stream/WorldWar2Janfeb2014/WorldWarIi2014-01-02_djvu.txt.

109 *"Rosener came back through the waist area"*: Al Platt, "Mayday on May Day," 91st Bomb Group Memorial Association, 2012, http://www.91stbombgroup.com/91st_tales/80_mayday_on_may_day.pdf.

110 *Seven of ten inside the* Joe Btfsplk II *(41-24610) are on their first mission*: 303rd Bomb Group Association, "Events of the Crash of 427BS Joe Btfsplk II," http://www.303rdbg.com/427walsh.html.

116 *Roach will be taken in by the French resistance*: For the whole story, see Harry E Roach III, *Flak City: The Life and Death of a Bomber Crew* (Details of Roach's story can be found on the "Jay Sterling Crew" page on the 303rd Bomb Group Association's website, http://www.303rdbg.com/427sterling.html. It contains details from "Flak City—The Life and Death of a Bomber Crew" by Harry E. Roach III (son of Harry Roach Jr.) and was first privately printed in 1985. See also Carol O'Neill, Pocono Record, "The Great Escape: Son had to find out how," April 4, 2007, https://www.poconorecord.com/story/lifestyle/boomers/2007/04/04/the-great-escape-son-had/52936233007. This interview with Roach III contains details of his continuing research.).

Chapter 6

126 *The area is a hive of gun positions*: Arthur van Beveren, Bunker Blog, "Demolition of Saint-Nazaire Bunker on Its Way" August 15, 2017 (accessed 2017), http://bunkerblog.eu/demolition-of-saint-nazaire-bunker -on-its-way. See also "Employment of German AAA," *Tactical and Technical Trends*, No. 35, October 7, 1943, https://archive.org/details/Tacti calAndTechnicalTrendsNos31-40. and "German Armed Forces Research 1918-1945," https://www.feldgrau.com/.

127 *consider just one emplacement*: Richard Drew, "Atlantikwall," http:// www.atlantikwall.co.uk. This UK website is an incomparable blend of historic information and archaeological photography.

Chapter 7

138 *heroes have twelve central traits*: Elaine Kinsella, Eric Igou, and Timothy Ritchie, "Zeroing In on Heroes: A Prototype Analysis of Hero Features," *Journal of Personality and Social Psychology* 108 (January 2015).

139 *A closer read on Smith's decision to stay with the airplane*: Collin Payne, Brian Wansink, and Koert van Ittersu, "Profiling the Heroic Leader: Empirical Lessons from Combat-Decorated Veterans of World War II," *Leadership Quarterly* 19, no. 5 (2008).

Chapter 8

153 *It will be decades before the pilot admits this*: Jason McDonald, "Captain Mack McKay a Pilot of the 306th Bomb Group and His Crew Point to a 'Kill' Marking Painted on His B-17 Flying Fortress," For the Imperial War Museum, http://www.306bg.us/history/crew_histories/McKay,%20Mack /McDonald%20rpt%20Mack%20McKay%20crew.pdf.

155 *"probably the last refuge of the itinerant American newspaperman"*: Bud Hutton and Andy Rooney, *The Story of Stars and Stripes* (New York: Farrar & Rinehart, 1946), accessed via the National Archives, https://archive .org/stream/storyofthestarsa032206mbp/ storyofthestarsa032206mbp_ djvu.txt.

156 *"I wish we had that old moose, John L. Lewis, along"*: Homer Bigart, "Harlan County Flier Has Story to Tell Miners," *Washington Post*, May 3, 1943.

157 *They lay the story out on the front page*: "Caro Man Goes on First Bomb

Run," *Tuscola County Advertiser*, May 14, 1943, accessed via Caro Area District library online portal.

Chapter 9

178 *"I wasn't enthusiastic about the ceremonial medal-awarding"*: Andy Rooney, *My War* (New York: Crown, 1995).

183 *Everyone laughs*: Andy Rooney, *My War* (New York: Crown, 1995).

184 *"Smith is a triumphant answer to the junior officers"*: Sam Boal, "The Deal," *The New Yorker*, September 18, 1943.

Chapter 10

194 *the official tally at the end of the war*: Mark Kendall Wells, "Aviators and Air Combat: A Study of the U.S. Eighth Air Force and R.A.F. Bomber Command," PhD diss., University of London, 1992.

197 *"you had to stand and sing"*: Rodge Dowson, "People's War," BBC, 2006, http://www.bbc.co.uk/history/ww2peopleswar/ user/77/u1685177.shtml. The BBC has collected and organized an extensive archive of oral histories that were of great help to this book.

218 *"He never walked if he could get a cab"*: Bill Porterfield, "From B-17 to Old Pink Buick: The War-Lorn Years of Snuffy Smith," *Detroit Free Press*, June 12, 1966.

Chapter 11

230 *They catch up with Mayer and his wingman*: *Air Force Magazine*, "Know Your Enemy," June 1944.

234 Motion Picture Daily *dutifully runs a story*: Motion Picture Daily 55, No. 72, "Radio Men will Aid Belle Promotion," April 12, 1944, accessed via the National Archives, https://archive.org/stream/motionpicturedai 55unse_0#page/n55/mode/2up.

239 *Smith frequently listening to morning briefings*: Russel Strong notes his presence in correspondence that the association keeps in its publicly available archives, http://www.306bg.us/CORRESPONDENCE/s/smith _maynard.pdf.

244 *Miller is delighted to see the hangar packed with people*: There's a description of the show on the web page for Pat DiGeorge's book, whose parents lived in Bedford: Pat DiGeorge, "Liberty Lady: Glenn Miller and the Bedford Corn Exchange," posted April 28, 2013, https://

libertyladybook.com/2013/04/28/glenn-miller-and-the-bedford-corn
-exchange/.

245 *"We didn't come here to set any fashions in music"*: Leonard Feather, "In
the Mood for All of Glenn Miller?," *Los Angeles Times*, November 17,
1990.

250 *report from July 1944 describes the camp*: Greg Hatton, "American Prisoners of War in Germany, Prepared by Military Intelligence Service War
Department," July 15, 1944, http://www.stalagluft4.org/luft%204%20
reports.html.

Chapter 12

254 *"reduced to the grade of private for inefficiency"*: There are several
examples in his file of an effort by the 306th historical association
to seemingly ensure that Smith's controversies are known, including unflattering letters about him and collections of negative news
clippings. The letter from Witt is also included in the file. It is available online at http://www.306bg.us/CORRESPONDENCE/s/smith
_maynard.pdf.

254 *"decision to adopt deliberate terror bombing"*: Howard Cowan, "Terror
Bombing Gets Allied Approval as Step to Speed Victory," *Washington
Star*, February 18, 1945.

255 *"restraint shown by the USAAF in these early months"*: Robert Morgan
and Ron Powers, *The Man Who Flew the Memphis Belle* (New York: Penguin Random House, 2011).

258 *"About 100,000 prisoners are moving"*: United Kingdom, Released British
Prisoners of War (Repatriation), UK House of Commons debate, vol. 408
cc960-1, February 22, 1945, https://api.parliament.uk/historic-hansard
/commons/1945/feb/22/released-british-prisoners-of-war.

259 *"Morgan sees the island of Iwo Jima"*: Robert Morgan and Ron Powers,
The Man Who Flew the Memphis Belle (New York: Penguin Random
House, 2011).

262 *"The reporters and photographers came rushing from all directions."*: "Caro
Gives Smith Great Homecoming," *Tuscola County Advertiser,* March 23,
1945, accessed via Caro Area District Library online portal.

267 *"it was, after all, my hometown"*: Bill Porterfield, "From B-17 to Old Pink
Buick: The War-Lorn Years of Snuffy Smith," *Detroit Free Press*, June 12,
1966.

Chapter 14

281 *his flair for the dramatic proves useful*: Uncredited, "Attorney John W. Rae Dies," *Ann Arbor News*, August 10, 1971.

282 *"Rae will leave today for Washington D.C."*: Uncredited, "Rae to Leave for Washington," *Michigan Daily*, July 31, 1946, archives accessed via University of Michigan, https://digital.bentley.umich.edu/midaily.

283 *"My father told me you should either be so rich"*: The "official publication of the Air Force Sergeants Association" ran a hugely useful Q&A interview with Smith. Edwin Kosier, "Q&A Interview with Smith," *Sergeants Magazine* 17, no. 2 (February 1979).

284 *"I know human nature"*: Bill Porterfield, "From B-17 to Old Pink Buick: The War-Lorn Years of Snuffy Smith," *Detroit Free Press*, June 12, 1966.

284 *Smith creates a narrative around Firmo*: United States Food and Drug Administration, Notices of Judgment Under the Federal Food, Drug, And Cosmetic Act, issues 1-2670 (Washington: U.S. G. P.O., 1940).

285 *"Federal agents raided Smith's apartment"*: Washington Bureau, "Salve Puts War Hero in 'Jam,'" *Detroit Free Press*, April 28, 1948.

290 *"Snuffy is a daring type of fellow"*: Associated Press, "Smith Denies Hoax Involved in Preventing Suicide Attempt," August 5, 1952. See also United Press, "War Hero Accused of Phony Rescue," August 5, 1952.

291 *"It isn't a penalty to be the mother of a hero"*: Gordon Friesen, "Citizens Recall Boyish Pranks of Hokey Smith," *Detroit Times*, July 17, 1943.

297 *"The losses were appalling"*: Ed Rasimus, *When Thunder Rolled: An F-105 Pilot Over North Vietnam* (New York: Presidio Press, 2004).

Chapter 15

298 *The* Detroit Free Press *publishes its update*: Bill Porterfield, "From B-17 to Old Pink Buick: The War-Lorn Years of Snuffy Smith," *Detroit Free Press*, June 12, 1966.

302 *His name is Charles M. Huckins*: New York Lottery, "History of the New York State Lottery," https://www.nylottery.org/ information/history.

305 *the Department of Justice weighed in*: Charles Cooper, "Congressional Authority to Adopt Legislation Establishing a National Lottery," Memorandum Opinion for the Assistant Attorney General, April 4, 1986, accessed via the Department of Justice, https://www.justice.gov/file/23816 /download.

305 *Messett is assigned to the 433rd*: Wayne Thompson, *To Hanoi and Back:*

the United States Air Force and North Vietnam 1966–1973 (Washington D.C.: Smithsonian Books, 2000).

309 *"Smith has contacted many prominent men"*: Edward Kulik, "Can a Lottery Fix NYS $ Woes?," *Long Island Press*, October 5, 1975.

311 *no independent confirmation of Smith's story*: Michael Skinner, "Maynard Smith Remembers the Big One," *Orlando Sentinel*, November 16, 1980.

312 *"Snuffy elevated his ultimate participation"*: Neal Shine, "Snuffy Was a Certified War Hero, but He Wasn't Always on the Mark," *Detroit Free Press*, September 2, 1984.

Chapter 16

318 *seems to speak about his troubled boys obliquely*: Edwin Kosier, "Q&A Interview with Smith," *Sergeants Magazine* 17, no. 2 (February 1979).

320 *"Maynard belonged to a vanishing breed"*: Davis Miller, "Empty Chair Will Honor a Hero," *St. Petersburg Times*, May 26, 1984.

323 *Recruitment and retention is a constant struggle*: Stephen Losey, "The Military's Stunning Fighter Pilot Shortage," *Military Times*, April 11, 2018. See also Government Accountability Office, "DOD Needs to Reevaluate Fighter Pilot Workforce Requirements," Report 18-133, April 11, 2018.

323 *Members of Barksdale Air Force Base*: Stuart Bright, "Sgt. Smith Honored," United States Air Force news release, February 1, 2018. There are several photos, including a close-up of the plaque itself.

INDEX

Courtesy of the author

JOE PAPPALARDO is the author of the critically acclaimed books *Sunflowers: The Secret History* (2008) and *Spaceport Earth: The Reinvention of Spaceflight* (2017). Pappalardo is a writer and former associate editor of *Air & Space Smithsonian* magazine, a writing contributor to *National Geographic* magazine, and a former senior editor and current contributor to *Popular Mechanics*. He has also appeared on the television shows *What on Earth?* and *Strange Evidence* on the Science Channel and *Roswell: The First Witness* and *Chuck Norris's Epic Guide to Military Vehicles* on History.